THE FUTURE OF BIBLICAL STUDIES

THE SOCIETY OF BIBLICAL LITERATURE
SEMEIA STUDIES
Lou H. Silberman, Editor

THE FUTURE OF BIBLICAL STUDIES

THE HEBREW SCRIPTURES

Richard Elliott Friedman and H.G.M. Williamson

Editors

SCHOLARS PRESS
Atlanta, Georgia

The Conversation in Biblical Studies was held in April, 1984, at the University of California, San Diego, and was supported by a grant from the Bruner Foundation

Preparation of this volume for publication
was supported by
the Jerome and Miriam Katzin Publication Fund
of the Judaic Studies Endowment
at the University of California, San Diego

Library of Congress Cataloging in Publication Data

The Future of Biblical studies.

(Semeia studies)
1. Bible. O.T.--Criticism, interpretation, etc.--History
--20th century. 2. Bible. O.T.--Study. I. Friedman,
Richard Elliott. II. Williamson, H. G. M. (Hugh Godfrey
Maturin), 1947- . III. Series.
BS1160.F87   1987   220'.07   86-27963
ISBN 1-55540-097-3 (alk. paper)
ISBN 1-55540-098-1 (pbk. : alk. paper)

Printed in the United States of America
on acid-free paper

TABLE OF CONTENTS

INTRODUCTION

The methods, one must say it ten times, *are* what is essential,
also what is most difficult, also what is for the longest time
opposed by habits and laziness.

Nietzsche

In April, 1984, a group of biblical scholars from various parts of
the United States, Canada, England, Japan, and Israel came to San
Diego, California, to meet and to exchange ideas about the future of
their field. They were invited as members of a younger generation of
scholars who had already made significant contributions to biblical
study and who were likely to be in the field for years to come. Eight
of them were asked to present papers on where they thought their
area of special interest was likely to go—or where it *should* go—in
the coming years. It was an opportunity to make their respective
statements about method to an audience of individuals who were
likely to be their colleagues and friends over the course of their
professional careers. Among the results of their conversations is this
book. It is not like a conference volume. It is certainly not an
assemblage of papers that were once read in quick succession and
then collated. Rather, the San Diego meeting was titled a "Conversation" and was constructed to be just that. There was only one
paper read at each hour-and-a-half session. The sessions were ap-
proximately half paper and half discussion. Every session was followed by free time for continued informal discussion of the issues
that the respective papers raised. And the discussions continued
through individual meetings and exchanges of correspondence for
months afterwards. And so the eight chapters of this book are the
original eight statements presented at the conference refined
through the reactions, advice, and challenges of an outstanding,
thoughtful gathering of scholars.

The biblical field has had an unusual history, being one of the
oldest and one of the most modern fields of learning. The book was
studied for two millennia primarily in a religious spirit, not in the
manner in which most other works were studied. When recent

centuries opened this book to a new spirit and mode of inquiry, there were already two millennia of knowledge collected and two millennia of emotions attached to it, and this had an impact even on the critical study of the book. Here were opportunities to look into a mass of revered compositions in new ways. Matters of method were often, perhaps too often, not so much addressed as assumed. What are sufficient grounds to identify a text as historically accurate, as development from legend, or as "pious fraud"? What is sufficient evidence to date a text as having been written in one period or another? How can we uncover the relationship between biblical writers and their sources? What can we learn about the society that produced the Hebrew Bible, and by what methods can we study it? What can we know of authorial and editorial intention in the artistry of biblical writing? The present generation of biblical scholars appears to be giving more conscious, articulated attention to questions of method than the founding parents did. This is not to suggest any lack of respect for our predecessors on these grounds. On the contrary, it may be a natural development in any field of the humanities to produce a certain critical mass of research before taking on methodology. In any case, each of the chapters of this book deals both with specific cases (the *what*) and with critical method (the *how*).

The book is not organized around biblical sections (prophecy, wisdom, law, etc.) or around associated fields (cognate languages and literatures, archeology, etc.) but rather speaks of the field as a whole, its roots, its methods, and, particularly, its future. In fact, it has proved to be a stimulating task for us just to decide in which order to present the chapters which follow. Our solution has been to move from discussions of how we are to relate the future of biblical studies to the *past* of biblical studies (chapters 1–2) to discussions of issues in approach and method (chapters 3–6) to treatment of methodological issues arising out of a consideration of particular texts (chapters 7–8).

Because the contributors were allowed a free hand in the choice of the topics they would address, there are some notable gaps in the coverage of our field as a whole. In particular, no direct attention is paid to the prophetic books, whilst other poetical books are dealt with only in broad terms. Similarly, the cognate disciplines of textual criticism, archeology and comparative studies are not given separate treatment, but are touched on only where they bear directly on the subjects of the various chapters. These gaps are not intended in any

way to imply that some subjects are of less importance than others.
If much in this volume is of most relevance to the study of narrative
and historical texts, that is merely the result of a coincidental con-
vergence of interests on the part of those who were invited to
contribute to the Conversation. We dare to believe, nevertheless,
that beyond the individual topics addressed there is an atmosphere
of inquiry reflected in these chapters which will find a ready echo
from our colleagues engaged in these other fields. We hope, therefore, that all readers will be stimulated to reflect more self-con-
sciously on what methods and approaches are more suitable to their
own areas of specialization.

The authors do not agree about everything, as the chapters by
Alan Cooper and Richard Elliott Friedman will readily show. They
come from different backgrounds and traditions. If there is something that is a common denominator among them, it is precisely a
consciousness of method—and a spirit of cooperation by persons of
different training and perspectives. This is a time of interest in new
tools and approaches in biblical studies, notably sociological and
literary analyses, and the participants in the San Diego Conversation showed considerable openness to such new approaches.
The important and difficult thing is to fit these approaches in, to use
them in association with the other tools of the trade in order to
enrich our study of the text—not to treat them (as their more
aggressive proponents do) as a revelation like that of Sinai, come to
pull the carpet out from under those who came before.

There was one more common element that was apparent among
the participants in the Conversation, and that was respect for their
teachers. As these chapters will show at numerous points, the
writers are keenly aware of the intellectual traditions from which
they come. The spirit of pluralism and good fellowship that persisted
through the Conversation made for fruitful meeting of those traditions. Even at their most independent, the participants were conscious of their debt to their mentors. There was no sense that the
future of biblical studies requires some break with the past. On the
contrary, as the chapters by Robert Oden and Jon Levenson particularly show, there is a striving—and sometimes a struggling—on
the part of this generation to find its place in continuing traditions of
scholarship. It is worthwhile for us to keep in mind that even when
we think that we may see farther than our predecessors did, it is
only because we are sitting on their shoulders. We respectfully
dedicate this book to our teachers.

Chapter 1

INTELLECTUAL HISTORY
AND THE STUDY OF THE BIBLE

Robert A. Oden, Jr.

Department of Religion, Dartmouth College

Thoughts about the future of biblical studies can arise, as they do in part today, from some sense that the study of the Hebrew Bible and of the religion of Israel exists in a context quite different from that in which our immediate and more distant ancestors worked. Just what the setting of this study is today, or will be in the future, is an issue to which all the contributions to the present collection are devoted and for which I want to provide some background. Primarily, I want here to assert and then to demonstrate the following: if any or all of us have some sense that a new setting obtains today for the study of the Bible, then this sense demonstrates our conventional, not our exceptional, place within the intellectual tradition of our discipline. To put this somewhat differently: the history of the study of the Hebrew Bible falls into discernible periods, each of which has defined itself in response to the perception of a new setting. I want to describe here three such periods—three surprisingly distinct eras within the past century when those who were to become, or who were already, the leaders in the discipline of biblical studies established their agendum in response to a perceived change in their own intellectual or institutional setting.

I.   Wellhausen

The first of these three moments I label simply "Wellhausen." It is the only moment I will designate by the name of a single scholar. In this case, such designation is, I think, just. It is just because Wellhausen, even if many have cautioned us to regard his work as largely the systematic presentation of work initiated by others, was a uniquely great and influential systematizer and because Wellhausen steadfastly refused to establish any sort of school.[1] Among the many reasons for his influence, it is worth saying if only in passing, is his prose style. Wellhausen may well be the one great prose stylist among biblical scholars; and certainly his writing is far freer from lapses into the easy conventions which characterize the works of some (e.g., Gunkel) whose styles are standardly lauded.

What was the new setting in which Wellhausen saw biblical study and hence his own task? Chiefly this: the German historiographic tradition which had achieved a confident maturity by the third quarter of the nineteenth century. This tradition made such great claims for itself, and these claims were so favorably received, that scholars in many fields—not just Wellhausen and not just biblical study—perceived a necessity to re-establish the foundations of their own disciplines.

To give a full account of the origin and shape of the German tradition of historical understanding is both impossible and unnecessary here—impossible because of the complexity of this tradition and unnecessary because several such accounts exist (Engel-Janosi, 1944; Gooch, 1952; Meinecke, 1959; Iggers, 1969; Ringer, 1969; Rüsen, 1969; Mandelbaum, 1971; Hanns Reill, 1975; Oden, 1980). Though many might lay claim to the title of the founder of this tradition, the scholar on whose behalf one can make the strongest case for this title is probably the same man who helped to found the University of Berlin, Wilhelm von Humboldt. Many of what were to become the chief emphases of the German tradition in historiography are to be found in early form in von Humboldt's works, especially the essays *"Über der Gesetze der Entwicklung der menschlichen Kräfte"* (1791) and *"Über die Aufgabe des Geschichtschreibers"* (1822).[2] If von Humboldt inaugurated this tradition in important ways, the tradition's chief theoretical spokesman was J.G. Droysen, whose *Grundriss der Historik* (1858) comes closest to presenting a systematic portrait of the German historical tradition in the nineteenth century.[3] However, neither von Hum-

---

[1] Indeed, Wellhausen apparently avoided even attending academic conferences. On this and Wellhausen's distaste for establishing a "school" of like-minded scholars, see Smend (1982).

[2] These essays can be conveniently found in Albert Leitzmann (1905, vol. 1 [1785–1795] 86–96 and vol. 4 [1820–1822], 35–56). On von Humboldt, see Paul R. Sweet (1978) and Joachim Wach (1926–1933: 1.227–266).

[3] See J. G. Droysen, *"Grundriss der Historik,"* in Rudolf Hubner, ed., (1967: 317–366). I was first alerted to the signal importance of Droysen's work by the essay of Arnaldo Momigliano (1975: 1.109–126).

boldt nor Droysen is the historian whose name comes first to mind in connection with the tradition. This honor belongs rather to Leopold von Ranke, later to be labelled *"die Inkarnation des historischen Sinnes."*[4]

So completely are we in this century the grateful recipients of the gifts of the German historiographic tradition that an outline of the tradition's key theses appears initially to coincide with the methods of what any right-minded student of the religion of Israel (or any other such phenomenon) would do almost intuitively. However, as Maurice Mandelbaum has reminded us, "because it is now deeply entrenched in our thoughts, it is easy to forget that the tendency to view all matters in terms of their histories may itself have had a history"(51). That is to say, there is something beyond intuition behind this intellectual tradition. Thus, an outline of the tradition's central concerns is not out of place in the present context.[5]

The first of these concerns is that which distinguishes sharply between the investigation of human phenomena and all other phenomena. The claim is made within the German historiographic tradition that only historical inquiry can approach an understanding of matters human because only such matters change in non-repetitive fashion. Thus, the methods to be utilized in the human science of history ought to be very different from the methods utilized in the natural sciences. The natural sciences can safely and profitably utilize abstractions; history cannot. Georg Iggers characterizes this aspect of the tradition with the unwieldy but accurate adjective anti-*Begrifflichkeit* (Iggers: 10)

A second emphasis of the same historiographic tradition is the tendency to apply, almost without reflection, organic analogies in the study of social phenomena. Behind such application lies the belief that both entire societies and separate eras within these societies have distinct "lives" and "deaths," that societies are truly analogous to living organisms. Nations, that is to say, are persons. Just as one speaks of the birth, growth, maturity, and old-age of a person, one can speak in the same terms of a nation. The most important implication of this belief is probably the constituent claim that different cultures, different nations and different epochs within the overall "life" of a nation each demand different categories of

---

[4] Wach (3.89). On Ranke generally, see Wach (3.89–133); Gooch (1952:72–97); Meinecke (1959: 585–602); Theodore Von Laue (1950); and Leonard Krieger (1977).

[5] See my "Hermeneutics and Historiography" for an elaboration upon and further documentation of this tradition.

understanding. This aspect of the tradition is something we, as the inheritors of the tradition, follow quite naturally and unreflectively. But it is important to remember that the wide utilization of the organic analogy is hardly necessary, in any absolute sense, and is a key element in the particular tradition of historical understanding summarized here.

Thirdly, it was this German historiographic tradition which argued that historical understanding demanded the emphasis upon *Entstehung* and *Entwicklung*. To understand any human phenomenon historically, asserted von Humboldt, Droysen, von Ranke, and many others, is to investigate above all that phenomenon's origin and development. Each of the three concerns in this necessarily artifical schematization of the German historiographic tradition is, of course, closely related to the others; but this is particularly clear of the relationship between the second and third concern noted here. That is, the concentration upon origins and developments makes best sense when the subject investigated is defined as in some sense an organic entity.

A summary of the nineteenth-century German tradition of historical understanding, even one so brief as this, is revealing. It is so initially, and again, because it makes clear that history has a history. But more than this, such a summary reveals that the German historiographic tradition is not uniformly empirical, despite the assertions of those within the tradition that they were proceeding purely empirically. There is, of course, an empirical element in the tradition, an element which resulted in the vast and extremely valuable research agenda which this tradition generated. But there is also a fair amount of real metaphysical idealism. This becomes clear above all in the statements by Droysen, von Ranke and others that the "life" of a nation can reveal the larger designs of divine purpose or providence (Southard, 1979: 378–396). What Jorn Rüsen says of Droysen's *Historik* can be said of the entire tradition: it is a combination of "*kritische Geschichtswissenschaft*" and "*idealistische Geschichtsphilosophie*." (Rüsen: 11).

This tradition, then, is partly, perhaps even primarily, responsible for defining the setting for research into the history of Israel's religion in which Wellhausen and others of his generation saw themselves. So clear is it that Wellhausen's historical constructions are founded squarely upon the foundation provided by the recently mature German historiographic tradition that sustained demonstration of the correspondence between the dictates of that tradition and

Wellhausen's own methods and conclusions is unnecessary. This correspondence will be clear from a few examples drawn from Wellhausen's *Prolegomena zur Geschichte Israels* (Wellhausen, 1883). That the *Prolegomena* obeys the first law of the historiographic tradition—to heed concrete data as the human sciences should, not abstract laws—is in a sense demonstrated by the very length and comprehensiveness of the volume, which documents a fairly simple thesis with massive evidence. That this empirical demonstration is at the same time founded upon a basic, idealistic abstraction has, of course, long been noted. Interestingly, Wellhausen's adherence to the first dictate of the historiographic tradition is also betrayed internally through the judgments he passes on material in the Hebrew Bible. Wellhausen admires and praises the Books of Samuel, and other materials he judges early, because these materials are concrete and fully human. He condemns later materials because they are abstract. Again, as the historiographical tradition we have traced asserted that authentic history must be based more in the concrete date of life than upon the eternal laws which operate in the natural sciences, so Wellhausen approves of the religion of Israel when it seems similarly based in life and disapproves when it is divorced from everyday activity. Thus, a sentence like the following is revealing more of Wellhausen's stance in this particular tradition than it is of the issue of centralization of worship: "*Man lebte in Hebron, man opferte in Jerusalem, Leben and Gottesdienst fielen auseinander.*" (Wellhausen: 80)

Secondly, Wellhausen's response to what he and others in the era defined as their new setting shares equally clearly in the German historiographical tradition's habit of employing the organic analogy to social phenomena. For Wellhausen, as for this tradition, one can meaningfully speak of "*dem Einfluss des Zeitgeistes,*" (Wellhausen: 177) a statement which makes sense only within the boundary of an assumed correspondence between the lives of nations and the lives of organisms. The same point is made well by an attention to the adjectives with which Wellhausen labels materials he thinks he has proved are early or late. Early materials are thus: fresh, clear, spontaneous, vivid, heroic, generous, authentic, or confident. Late material, chiefly that found in Chronicles or the stratum Q or P, is: static, abstract, narrow, perverse, anxious. Both sets of adjectives are drawn from the basic organic analogy. An extended example of Wellhausen's sensitivity to the epochs within the life of a nation is his summary of the later portrait of David:

Was hat die Chronik aus David gemacht! Der Gründer des
Reichs ist zum Gründer des Tempels and des Gottes-
dienstes geworden, der König und Held an der Spitze
seiner Waffengenossen zum Kantor und Liturgen an der
Spitze eines Schwarmes von Priestern und Leviten, seine so
scharf gezeichnete Figur zu einem matten Heiligenbilde,
umnebelt von einer Wolke von Weihrauch (Wellhausen:
189)

The entire portrait of David is colored, Wellhausen goes on to say,
according to *"dem Geschmack der nachexilischen Zeit"* (Well-
hausen:189).

Finally, a single sentence may serve to document the extent to
which Wellhausen also obeys the third dictate of the tradition of
historical research which reached its peak in Germany in just this
era. This dictate is that which demands attention above all to the
origin and to the unfolding development of a nation's life. The single
sentence comes near the end of the introduction *("Das Thema")* of
the *Prolegomena,* where Wellhausen most directly addresses issues
of method. With reference to the problem of dating the three
streams he will follow in the volume (the Jehovist, the Deuteronomist, and the Priestly Code), Wellhausen says that it is necessary to test his chronological scheme against "an independent criterion" *("eines unabhängigen Masses"), "nämlich mittelst des inneren
Ganges der israelitischen Geschichte"* (Wellhausen: 13). Following
the internal development of a nation's history is just what the German historiographical tradition most keenly recommended; it is also
the central achievement of Wellhausen's *Prolegomena.*

II.   The History-of-Religions School and the "Crisis in Historical Understanding"

Wellhausen, then, and his response to what he and others saw as
a newly formulated method for reconstructing the life and religion of
a nation, is one example of a turn taken in biblical scholarship in
response to the perception of a new intellectual setting. A second
example is the *religionsgeschichtliche Schule* and its response to
what came to be called "the crisis in historical understanding."[6] A
list of the participants in this *Schule* or *Kreise* is also a list of the

[6]On this "crisis," see H. Stuart Hughes (rev. ed.; 1977), and Michael Ermarth
(1978). Many scholars (both in this period and in later periods when reflecting back
upon the turn-of-the-century era) use some such phrase as "the crisis of historical
understanding."

founders of several sub-disciplines within the study of religion in the present century. The school's acknowledged leader was Albert Eichhorn, the only one whose name will not be found to dominate a tray in the card catalog of any good research library (Gressmann, 1914; Klatt, 1969; Kraus, 1969: 327–367; Rogerson, 1974: 57–65). Other members included Wrede, Bousset, Troeltsch, Heitmüller, and of course Gressmann and Gunkel.

A standard answer to the question of what was new in the setting in which this group of scholars saw themselves is the availability of extra-biblical, comparative material for the analysis of the religions of Israel and early Christianity. For example, Albright's introduction to an English edition of Gunkel's *The Legends of Genesis* contrasts Wellhausen with Gunkel on just this point: Wellhausen, Albright argues, "was essentially isolationist" and for him "the ancient Orient . . . exerted no serious influence on early Israel," while Gunkel made early and extensive use of extra-biblical evidence from the ancient Near East (vii).

Certainly, this argument carries some force and does explain an important difference between Wellhausen on the one hand and the members of the History-of-Religions movement on the other. However, I do not think that the use or neglect of extrabiblical material is either the key to the new setting in which this movement saw itself or goes to the heart of the dispute between Wellhausen and this circle. The new setting and the heart of the controversy are rather to be found in the description of the decades immediately preceding and following the turn of the century as a period which witnessed a "crisis" in the ability to understand phenomena historically. The use of a term like "crisis" may seem hyperbolic. That it was not for some in this era is clear from the statements of those like Wilhelm Dilthey, the period's chief theoretical spokesman on hermeneutical issues. As Michael Ermath notes, "In 1900 . . . Dilthey reflected that the present age was more helpless in the face of the basic question of life than any previous period" (Ermath: 16).

What was the crisis and what was the proposed remedy? Initially, the sense of crisis in these years was prompted by the strength, indeed the vehemence, with which those in this era criticized the historical methods and conclusions of their immediate predecessors. According to this criticism, the historical works produced in the years from about 1850 through the 1880s were insufficiently "spiritual." Rather, these works were too "positivistic," "specialized," "fragmented," and "mechanical" (Ringer: 260–265). That which was needed to correct the portraits produced by the mid-century historians, thus stigmatized by those in the decades around the turn of the century, was a return to the fuller spirit of the German historiographic tradition. What was required was a stress once more upon the scholar's personal and spiritual relationship with the material and with the era under investigation. Such diagnoses and remedies belong, of course, to an entire Neo-Romantic movement, a movement which also found distasteful many elements in urban and technological life and longed for what was seen as the simpler and more authentic rural life. (Oden: 141–142).

In addition, those associated with the "crisis" at the turn of the century also called for more attention to the individual and group, human setting of historical texts. This too is little different from what von Humboldt, Droysen, and von Ranke had earlier suggested; but the sense was that this suggestion had been insufficiently followed. Those in the era around 1900 argued that what history was really after was the concrete, experiential, fully human sources of texts and of their transmission. The route to this goal was a route which paid much greater heed to the human worlds apparent behind the texts.

Thus described, the decades of the "crisis in historical understanding" provided the seemingly inevitable setting for the directions taken by those in the *religionsgeschichtliche Schule*. Statements from the leaders of this movement could hardly express more clearly than they do just this sense of a new setting. Thus, writing about the century's turn, Gressmann could assert, *"wir am Anfang einer neuen Epoche in der Auffassung der alttestamentlichen Religions- und Literaturgeschichte stehen."*[7] Or, Gunkel could describe in 1914 the entire foundation of the History-of-Religions movement as follows: *"In Wirklichkeit ist sie nichts anderes als eine neue Welle des gewaltigen geschichtlichen Stromes, der sich von unseren grossen idealistischen Denkern und Dichtern herüber unser gesamtes Geistesleben und auch seit lange in unsere Theologie ergossen hat"* (Klatt: 26)

In general, then, the various emphases of Gressmann, Gunkel, and others are to be accounted for partially as the direct responses to the laments of those associated with the "crisis in historical understanding." This is true of their emphasis upon levels behind that of the written text, of their stress upon the necessity for the historian

---

[7] The assertion comes from unpublished material cited by Klatt, *Hermann Gunkel*, 26.

to have an empathy with the texts under investigation, and of their concern that the historian appreciate the *"Eigentümlichkeit"* of the culture described.[8] Three additional statements, all from Gunkel again, will make this yet clearer. First, for him "the cardinal principle of historical study is this: That we are unable to comprehend a person, a period, or a thought dissociated form its antecedents, but that we can speak of a real living understanding only when we have the antecedent history" (Gunkel, 1902–1903: 404). Secondly, it is Gunkel who uttered the famous claim that *"Exegese im höchsten Sinne ist mehr eine Kunst als eine Wissenschaft"* (Gunkel, 1913: 14). Finally, and equally predictably, is Gunkel's advice *"Wer also eine antike Gattung verstehen will hat zunächst zu fragen, wo sie ihren Sitz im Volksleben habe"* (Gunkel, 1906: 53).

As this last exhortation from Gunkel makes especially clear, it is more than the general agendum set by the History-of-Religions circle which is correctly to be seen as a response to the criticisms made by those writing at the turn of the century of their immediate predecessors. It is more particularly the basic enterprise of form-criticism which is to be so seen. Hence, the issue of whether Gunkel, for example, inherited form criticism from Germanists or rather from classicists (Klatt: 106–116) is less revealing than is the perception that form criticism responds directly to the claim that true historical understanding involves a prior comprehension of the human roots and settings for the composition and transmission of traditional material. This is, of course, the same claim made by many and in many disciplines at the turn of the century.

So too the same background accounts for the fact and the strength of the History-of-Religion's movement's participants' criticisms of Wellhausen. The genesis of these criticisms is not centrally the extent to which Wellhausen did or did not utilize non-Israelite materials. The criticisms rather begin with this question: is Wellhausen truly a historian? So formulated, this question cannot but sound radically unfair: surely, Wellhausen merits the title historian as much as does any biblical scholar. This Gunkel and others had at times to admit. But in the context of the rarefied sense accorded to the term historian at the turn of the century, Wellhausen was not fully a historian. He was too mechanical, too interested in institutions rather than their deeper origins, too concerned with the

---

[8] For example, though Gunkel argues that the scholar must begin with an examination of comparative material, in the end such material will reveal *"die Eigentümliche des israelitischen Geistes"* (1913: 37).

surface of the text. It was this issue which prompted Gressmann to assert that *die religionsgeschichtliche Schule* was born out of dis-agreement with Wellhausen (Gressman: 30); it is this issue which shows how clearly this circle was responding to the intellectual currents of the era.

III.   Israelite Origins, Israelite Institutions and the Objective Reality of the Social

The title for the third and final moment in biblical study which I want to summarize here is one which is not easy to formulate—least of all to formulate elegantly. An alternative title might be: "Sociology and the Emphasis upon Yahweh as God of the Covenant in the Years after the Great War." It is equally difficult to list briefly the partici-pants in this third moment. This is the case simply because the force of this moment's response to its perception of a new setting was so powerful that it came to engulf most students of the religion of Israel in the first half (at least) of the twentieth century.

The initial two moments described above were generated, in the case of the first, by the fully developed German historiographic tradition, and, in the case of the second, by a sense articulated a generation later that historical understanding had lost touch with its deepest task. What is the setting for the third and final moment? It is this: the perceived explanatory power of several new disciplines whose titles were still neologisms in the era before the First World War—disciplines like psychology, anthropology, and especially so-ciology.

The origins of the growing tendency to appeal to the social formation in the explanation of religious phenomena are to be sought, at least with regard to their impact upon biblical study, in the works of William Robertson Smith, Emil Durkheim, and Max Weber. The first of these did much of his work in the years before and during the period in which Gunkel, Gressmann, and others of their circle were active, so that there is some chronological overlap here. Robertson Smith begins his *The Religion of the Semites* with the extraordinarily optimistic assertion, with which of course Gunkel and Gressmann would come to disagree, that the work of Kuenen and Wellhausen has meant that "nothing of vital importance for the historical study of the Old Testament religion still remains uncertain" (Smith, 1972: vii). Robertson Smith elsewhere describes Wellhausen's work in a fashion which lends surprising credence to the above analysis of this work against the background of the German historiographical tradition. The *Prolegomena*, Robertson Smith writes, "must be full of interest to everyone who has tasted the intense pleasure of following institutions and ideas in their growth, and who has faith enough to see the hand of God as clearly in a long providential development as in a sudden miracle" (Smith, 1973: ix).

Given that for Robertson Smith the work of Wellhausen and others means that the historical issues are solved, what remains to be done? What remains to be done is the investigation of the meaning and function of religious and social phenomena whose significance in the Hebrew Bible is assumed—phenomena like sacrifice, which, as Robertson Smith notes, is "nowhere fully explained" and is rather "taken for granted" as "an essential part of religion" (1972: 3).

The true meaning of sacrifice is then discovered by Robertson Smith to lie in society, the same setting in which Durkheim and Weber were later to find the meaning and function of most religious phenomena. For Robertson Smith, as is well known, sacrifice is "an act of social fellowship between the deity and his worshippers" (1972: 224). Thus, "the leading idea in the animal sacrifices of the Semites . . . was not that of a gift made over to the god, but of an act of communion, in which the god and his worshippers unite" (1972: 226–27). What is true of sacrifice becomes for Robertson Smith true of religion more generally. As he argues, "the fundamental conception of ancient religion is the solidarity of the gods and their worshippers as part of one organic society" (1972: 32). Moreover, the same conception accounts for the very origin of religion:

> There is then a great variety of evidence to show that the type of religion which is founded on kinship, and in which the diety and his worshippers make up a society united by bonds of blood, was widely prevalent, and that at an early date, among all the Semitic peoples. But the force of the evidence goes further, and leaves no reasonable doubt that among the Semites this was the original type of religion, out of which all other types grew (1972: 50–51).

Hence, the essential meaning and role of religions everywhere: "Religion did not exist for the saving of souls but for the preservation and welfare of society" (1972: 29).

This same line of reasoning is then taken up and greatly extended by Durkheim, who often gives to Robertson Smith the credit for discovering the place of the social formation in the explanation of religion (Durkheim, 1925: 63, n. 1; 126-127; 480-500). Durkheim, one of the acknowledged founders of sociology, begins his *Les formes élémentaires de la vie religieuse* by masterfully disposing of first animism and then naturism as the original forms of religious expression. His criticisms of the views of Tylor on behalf of animism and of Müller on behalf of naturism are too well known to require repetition here. But it is important to note that the fundamental basis of Durkheim's critique here is the argument that both animism and naturism attribute to religion a hallucinatory subject (1925: 67–122). That is, both deny to religion any real, objective subject. Since one cannot deny that religions have persisted, Durkheim regards it as self-evident that the subject of religion must be something real and non-hallucinatory. This something, of course, is society itself. "*La société,*" Durkheim concludes, is "*la cause objective, universelle et éternelle de ces sensations sui generis dont est faite l'expérience religieuse*" (1925: 597). Or, more plainly still, "*l'idée de la société est l'âme de la religion*" (1925: 599).

If the sociological explanation of religion begins in some important ways with Robertson Smith and is then extended greatly by Durkheim, Max Weber gives to such explanation its widest application. In the context of the present discussion, Weber is in something of an odd position. This is because he is the first and only scholar here discussed who is at once part of the new setting to which biblical scholarship will try to respond and also and at the same time a part of that response. Unlike either Robertson Smith or Durkheim, Weber wrote a major volume devoted to explaining the origins and development of Israelite religion as a response to various social formations. This is the third volume of his *Gesammelte Aufsätze zur Religionssoziologie,* a volume sub-titled *Das antike Judentum* (Weber, 1921).

Despite the open modesty with which Weber begins this work, many areas of biblical study in the present century are expansions upon single paragraphs, sometimes even brief sentences, in the volume. Any list of these areas is extraordinary testimony to Weber's brilliance and industry. For example, here one finds the first emphasis upon charismatic leadership, especially in explanation of the period of the judges. It is here that emphasis is first placed upon that nation which produced the Hebrew Bible as "*die israelitische Eidgenossenschaft*", as "*ein Kriegsbund*" one of whose fundamental institutions was holy war (1921: 90). It is here that the prophets are first accounted for in terms of their social location (1921: 118–120), and here too that the Joseph narrative is seen as having its origins in the wisdom tradition.[9]

For our purposes, none of these individual insights is as vital as is the presupposition which prompts them all—the view that the religion of Israel mirrors the entire social formation and that changes in Israelite society will effect corresponding changes in Israelite religion. Of central importance for Weber, and hence for the future of biblical study, was his elevation, on the basis of this presupposition, of the notion of *berit* to its position as the chief model to be used in explaining the religion of Israel. Where, asks Weber, lies the distinctiveness of Israelite religion? This distinctiveness is to be found in the *"weite Erstreckung der religiösen 'berith' als der wirklichen (oder konstruierten) Grundlage der verschiedensten rechtlichen und sittlichen Beziehungen"* (1921: 82). In Israel, Weber continues, *"die 'Bundes'-Vorstellung wurde so, in einer Art wie bei keinem anderen Volk, die spezifische Dynamik der ethischen Konzeptionen der Priesterlehre und Prophetie"* (1921: 129). This observation about the uniqueness and centrality of the covenant for Israel carried with it a host of implications, including that which saw Yahweh as above all a god of history: *"Jahwe blieb ein Gott der Geschichte"* (1921: 239).

The history of the study of the Hebrew Bible in the twentieth century is in so many ways the history of the development and modification of several of Weber's arguments that I am confident no elaboration upon this history is necessary here. This is true above all in the central instance of the organizing and generating significance granted by Weber to the notion of the covenant between Yahweh and Israel. The issue of whether or not the covenant is as ancient and important a metaphor as Weber and those who followed him wished to assert[10] is less important for our purposes here than is the

[9] See Weber (1921:209). Though any brief list of the contributions Weber's study made for later biblical scholarship is impressive, that he should have seen in 1917–1919 the role of wisdom in the novella of Genesis 37–50 is especially so.

[10] It is an over-simplification but still basically accurate to say that the covenant notion continued to play a key role in biblical scholarship through the 1950's. Since then, questions about the date and significance of the covenant relationship have been raised once again; and there is a general tendency to return to a position much closer to that of Wellhausen. This tendency is most evident in the volumes of Lothar Perlitt (1969) and Ernst Kutsch (1973) but it is already discernible in the earlier work of F. Nötscher, C. F. Whitley, Alfred Jepsen, Georg Fohrer and others, for a summary of which see Georg Fohrer (1966: 801–816 and (esp.) 893–904), and my "The Role of Covenant in the Religion of Israel" (forthcoming, 1987).

demonstrable fact that Weber's stress upon covenant departed widely from the quite minor role given to the covenant by Wellhausen.[11] Weber stressed covenant as he did because it seemed to provide him with clear proof that Yahweh was a social god, that the religion of Israel served a preeminently social function. That is to say, his stress upon covenant is a direct response to the last of the three moments in biblical study here summarized, that which found in society the origin and truest subject of religion generally.

IV. Conclusion: The Past and Present of Biblical Study

A voice which is heard again today with some frequency is that which urges biblical scholarship to turn to other disciplines in order to broaden its focus and to raise fresh questions. Though the particular discipline to which biblical scholars are advised to turn varies (anthropology, sociology, linguistics, literary criticism, and others), the advice is fairly constant. The clearest single conclusion from the historical inquiry offered above is that this is precisely what biblical scholars have been doing, and doing very successfully, for well over a century. Wellhausen turned to the mature German historiographic tradition, the tradition of von Humboldt, Droysen, van Ranke, and others. Gunkel and Gressmann turned to the philosophers and historians of the end-of-the-century period, to those who assured them that a new stage was prepared for the correct comprehension of historical phenomena. And many in this century have turned, though not always consciously, to sociologists like Robertson Smith and Weber for the formulation of new categories of potential use in understanding the religion of Israel.

I do not think that biblical scholarship, thus described, is unhappily or uniquely parasitic. The same pattern of help from without obtains in many academic disciplines, perhaps in all of them. If there is a single, broadly useful conclusion from a study as powerfully influential as T. S. Kuhn's *The Structure of Scientific Revolutions*,[12] it is that the avenue to making a lasting contribution in any academic field is to approach that field from a quite different disci-

---

[11] Wellhausen's treatment of *"berit"* in the *Prolegomena* is essentially limited to the three-page section entitled *"Die Theokratie als Idee und als Anstalt"* (1883: 442–444).

[12] See Thomas S. Kuhn (1970). Kuhn's central thesis has hardly gone unchallenged; for a collection of critical articles devoted to such challenges, see Imre Lakatos and Alan Musgrave, eds., (1970).

pline. Let me close with a final piece of documentation which proves that this conclusion is emphatically born out in the study of the religion of Israel. This documentation is the initial sentence in Weber's *Das antike Judentum*, a sentence which suggests that the greatness and creative power of this volume is due in part to just such willingness to seek questions from without: *"Das eigentümliche religions-geschichtlich-soziologische Problem des Judentums lässt sich weitaus am besten aus der Vergleichung mit der indischen Kastenordnung verstehen"* (1921: 1–2).

WORKS CONSULTED

Albright, William F.
 1964   "Introduction," in Hermann Gunkel, *The Legends of Genesis*. New York: Schocken.

Droysen, J. G.
 1967   *"Grundriss der Historik"*, in *Historik: Vorlesungen über Enzyklopädie und Methodologie der Geschichte*. Ed. Rudolf Hübner, 5th ed.; München: Oldenbourg.

Durkheim, Emile
 1925   *Les formes élémentaires de la vie religieuse*. Travaux de l'Année Sociologique; 2d ed.; Paris: Librairie Félix Alcan.

Engel-Janosi, Friedrich
 1944   *The Growth of German Historicism*. Johns Hopkins Studies in Historical and Political Science, Series 62, no. 2; Baltimore: Johns Hopkins.

Ermarth, Michael
 1978   *Wilhelm Dilthey: The Critique of Historical Reason*. Chicago and London: University of Chicago.

Fohrer, Georg
 1966   "Altes Testament— 'Amphiktyonie' und 'Bund'?", *TLZ* 91, 801–816, 893– 904.

Gooch, G. P.
 1952   *History and Historians in the Nineteenth Century*. 2d ed.; London: Longmans.

Gressmann, Hugo
 1914   *Albert Eichhorn und die religionsgeschichtliche Schule*. Göttingen: Vandenhoeck & Ruprecht.

Gunkel, Hermann
    1902–1903　"The Religio-Historical Interpretation of the New
            Testament," *The Monist* 13.
    1906　　"*Die israelitische Literatur,*" in Paul Hinneberg, ed.,
            *Die Kultur der Gegenwart: Die orientalischen Liter-
            aturen.* Berlin und Leipzig: B. G. Teubner.
    1913　　"*Die Grundprobleme der israelitischen Liter-
            aturgeschichte,*" in *Reden und Aufsätze.* Göttingen:
            Vandenhoeck & Ruprecht.

Hughes, H. Stuart
    1977　　*Consciousness and Society: The Reorientation of Euro-
            pean Social Thought 1890–1930.* Rev. ed.; New York:
            Vintage.

Iggers, Georg G.,
    1969　　*The German Conception of History.* Middletown:
            Wesleyan University Press.
    1973　　"Historicism," in *The Dictionary of the History of
            Ideas* (New York) 2:457–464.

Klatt, Werner
    1969　　*Hermann Gunkel: Zu seiner Theologie der Re-
            ligionsgeschichte und zur Entstehung der form-
            geschichtlichen Methode.* FRLANT 100; Göttingen.
            Vandenhoeck & Ruprecht.

Krieger, Leonard
    1977　　*Ranke: The Meaning of History.* Chicago and London:
            University of Chicago.

Kraus, Hans-Joachin
    1969　　*Geschichte der historisch-kritischen Erforschung des
            Alten Testaments.* 2d ed.; Neukirchen-Vluyn: Neu-
            kirchener Verlag.

Kuhn, Thomas
    1970　　*The Structure of Scientific Revolutions.* 2d ed.; Chicago
            and London: University of Chicago.

Kutsch, Ernst
    1973　　*Verheissung und Gesetz: Untersuchungen zum
            sogenannten 'Bund' im Alten Testament.* BZAW 131;
            Berlin and New York: Walter de Gruyter.

Lakatos Imre & Musgrave Alan eds.,
    1970　　*Criticism and the Growth of Knowledge.* Proceedings
            of the International Colloquium in the Philosophy of
            Science 4; Cambridge: Cambridge University.

Leitzmann, Albert, ed.,

1905   *Wilhelm von Humboldts Gesammelte Schriften.* Berlin:
            B. Behrs, vol. 1 (1785–1795) and vol. 4 (1820–1822).

Mandelbaum, Maurice
1971   *History, Man & Reason: A Study in Nineteenth Cen-
            tury Thought.* Baltimore and London: Johns
            Hopkins.

Meinecke, Friedrich
1959   *Die Entstehung des Historismus.* Ed. Carl Hinrichs;
            München: Oldenbourg.

Momigliano, Arnaldo
1975   "J. G. Droysen Between Greeks and Jews," *Quinto
            Contributo alla storia degli studi classici e del
            mondo antico* Roma: Edizioni di storia e letteratura,
            1.109–126.

Oden, Robert.
1980   "Hermeneutics and Historiography: Germany and
            America," *SBL Seminar Papers,* 135–157.
forthcoming "The Role of Covenant in the Religion of Israel."

Perlitt, Lothar
1969   *Bundestheologie im Alten Testament.* WMANT 36;
            Neukirchen-Vluyn: Neukirchener

Reill, Peter Hanns
1975   *The German Enlightenment and the Rise of Histor-
            icism.* Berkeley, Los Angeles, and London: Univer-
            sity of California.

Ringer, Fritz K.
1969   *The Decline of the German Mandarins.* Cambridge,
            Mass.: Harvard University, 1969.

Rogerson, J. W.
1974   *Myth in Old Testament Interpretation.* BZAW 134;
            Berlin and New York: Walter de Gruyter.

Rüsen, Jörn
1969   *Begriffene Geschichte: Genesis und Begründung der
            Geschichtstheorie J. G. Droysens.* Paderborn:
            Schöningh.

Smend, Rudolf
1982   "Julius Wellhausen and His *Prolegomena to the History
            of Israel,*" Semeia 25: 1–20.

Smith, William Roberstson
1972   *The Religion of the Semites.* New York: Schocken [orig.
            pub. 1889].
1973   "Preface" to Julius Wellhausen, *Prolegomena to the*

History of Ancient Israel. Edinburgh: A. & C. Black, 1885; reprinted Gloucester, Mass.: Peter Smith.

Southard, Robert
1979   "Theology in Droysen's Early Political Histography: Will, Necessity, and the Historian," *History and Theory* 18: 378–396.

Sweet, Paul R.
1978   *Wilhelm von Humboldt: A Biography: Volume One: 1767–1808*. Columbus: Ohio State University.

Von Laue, Theodore
1950   *Leopold Ranke: The Formative Years*. Princeton Studies in History 4; Princeton: Princeton University.

Wach, Joachim
1926–1933 *Das Verstehen: Grundzüge einer Geschichte der hermeneutischen Theorie im 19 Jahrhundert*. 3 vols. Tübingen: J. C. B. Mohr.

Weber, Max
1921   *Gesammelte Aufsätze zur Religionssoziologie, III: Das Antike Judentum*. Tübingen: J. C. B. Mohr (Paul Siebeck).

Wellhausen, Julius
1883   *Prolegomena zur Geschichte Israels: Zweite Ausgabe der Geschichte Israels, Band I*. Berlin: Georg Reimer.

Chapter 2

THE HEBREW BIBLE, THE OLD TESTAMENT, AND HISTORICAL CRITICISM

Jon D. Levenson
The University of Chicago

> "What could be more glorious than to brace one's self up to discover New South Wales and then realize, with a gush of happy tears, that it was really Old South Wales."
> G. K. Chesterton,
> *Orthodoxy*

If there has ever been a book which has thriven in a plurality of contexts, it is surely the Hebrew Bible. In the Jewish tradition this book, known as the *Tanakh* or the *Miqra'*, is properly placed alongside the Talmud, Midrash, and medieval rabbinic commentaries. These books, highly diverse and delightfully argumentative, establish a pluriform yet bounded context of interpretation for the Tanakh. In the Church, the Hebrew Bible, known as the "Old Testament," appears as the first of the two volumes of sacred scripture, the "Bible," and interpretation is not complete until Volume I is related to Volume II, the Old Testament to the New, so as to proclaim together Jesus Christ. In both the Jewish and the Christian traditions even as they were constituted before the Enlightenment, there is substantial precedent for searching out the meaning of a passage in the Hebrew Bible apart from the meanings directly suggested for it by the books that mark out its traditional contexts of interpretation. At least from the eleventh century C.E., the "plain sense" (Hebrew, *pĕšāṭ*) was much prized. It is important to remember that this "plain sense" was itself culturally conditioned and a matter of communal consensus and that among rabbinic Jews and Christians, it was not pursued with the intention of undermining the normativity of the larger context. A *paštān* like Rabbi Samuel ben Meir (Northern France, 1080–1160) could be uncompromising both in his pursuit of the plain sense and in his allegiance to *hălākâ* (rabbinic law), which often bases itself on the biblical text in a way that contradicts the *pĕšāṭ*. He is paralleled by those Christian exegetes who recognized an "historical sense" to the Old Testament without relinquishing a Christocentric interpretation of it. In both the Jewish and the Christian cases, the unity of the religion was maintained, even though it was not seen as operative in all forms of exegesis. There could be concentric circles of context, but the smaller circle, the plain sense, finally yielded to the larger one of tradition, however constituted. The unique religious value of the plain sense remained an open question.

In the last three centuries, there has arisen another context of interpretation of the Hebrew Bible, the *historical* context: No part of the book is to be read against literature, either internal or external, which cannot be reasonably presumed to have existed at the time. To be sure, historical criticism has affinities with the pursuit of the plain sense. They differ, however, in that historical critics place all the emphasis on development and historical change and fearlessly challenge the historicity of the foundational events (e.g., Sinaitic revelation, the resurrection of Jesus) and traditional ideas of authorship, for example, that Moses wrote the Pentateuch or that the gospels were written by the evangelists to whom they are ascribed. Historical critics take the text apart more ruthlessly than traditional *paštānîm*, and, *qua* historical critics, they lack a method of putting it back together again. They reconstruct history by concentrating on contradictions, which they then allow to stand. The traditions, of course, often recognized the same contradictions. The difference is that traditionalists had a method that could harmonize the contradictions and, in the process, preserve the unity of the text and its religious utility. Consider, for example, the contradiction between Exod 12:15, which mandates the eating of unleavened bread during Passover for a full seven days, and Deut 16:8, which specifies six days of observance for the same commandment. Below, we see how the rabbis handled the contradiction:

> How can both these passages be maintained? The seventh day had been included in the more inclusive statement and then was taken out of it. Now, that which is singled out from a more inclusive statement means to teach us something about the whole statement. Hence, just as on the seventh day it is optional, so on all the other days it is optional. May it not be that just as on the seventh day it is optional, so on

all the rest, including the first night, it is optional? The
scriptural passage: "In the first month, at evening ye shall
eat unleavened bread" [Exod 12:18] fixes it as an obligation
to eat unleavened bread on the first night.[1]

The assumption of the rabbis is that the Deuteronomic law is not
independent of that given in Exodus. On the contrary, the operative
law is to be discovered by taking *both* passages into account. The
unity of the Mosaic Torah requires that *all* its data be considered.
The two laws do not compete; together, they enable the ingenious
exegete to discover the truth. The law which emerges, and which is
hălākâ to this day, reflects neither the seven days of Exod 12:15 nor
the six of Deut 16:8, but only one day.[2] In short, rabbinic exegesis of
the Torah here yields a norm for which, *prima facie*, the Torah
provides no evidence at all. If this seems absurd, consider that the
alternative is simply to choose arbitrarily and subjectively one Torah
verse over the other, as if they were not of equal sanctity. If one
assumes, with the rabbis, that they are of equal sanctity and that
they exist in the same mind (the mind of God) at the same moment
(eternally), then one is required to undertake just the sort of exegetical operation in which the rabbis are here engaged, one that is,
in fact, in continuity with the redactional process that helped produce the Hebrew Bible itself (Kaufmann: 4.327–328). In the minds
of historical critics, this operation is an historically indefensible
homogenization of the past. By harmonizing inconcinnities, the
tradition presents itself with a timeless document, one that appears
to speak to the present only because the historical setting of the
speaking voice or the writing hand has been suppressed, and all
voices and all hands are absorbed into an eternal simultaneity.

The historical critics have a different way of handling the contradiction between Exod 12:15 and Deut 16:8. They feel no compulsion
to see the two verses as derived from one synchronic reality, but
readily consign them to different historical periods or to different
locales or to different social sectors. Whereas the traditionalist begins with the assumption that the tradition (and certainly its most
sacred texts) has a stable core and that there is a unified, if varie-
gated, religion that can be derived from it—"Judaism" or "Chris-

---

[1] *Mek.*, *Pisḥa'* 8. The translation is from Lauterbach (1.62).
[2] This law refers only to the positive commandment, the commandment to eat
unleavened bread. The negative commandment, the prohibition on leavening, applies, of course, throughout Passover.

tianity"—the historical critic begins with no such assumptions of stability and continuity, but with a commitment to restore the texts to their historical contexts. Passages are to be read against their age, not against the book into which they eventually came (not, that is, until they have at long last arrived there). Knowledge of that age is to be gained by excavating within the text, but also by means of archaeology and the extra-biblical texts and forgotten biblical manuscripts it unearths, without the traditionalist's concern that the resultant picture will depend upon an illicit mixture of sacred and profane sources.

In a sense, historical criticism of the Bible is like its contemporary, psychoanalysis. It brings to light what has been repressed and even forgotten, the childhood, as it were, of the tradition. But if Wordsworth was right that "the Child is the Father of the Man," it is wrong to think that the man will be happy to meet the child within him whom he thinks he has outgrown. Like psychoanalysis, historical criticism uncovers old conflicts and dissolves the impression that they have been resolved rather than repressed. It is only reasonable to expect both to encounter "resistance" in those to whom they are applied. Although most historical critics of the Bible consider themselves still somehow adherents of the Jewish or the Christian traditions, it must be conceded that the position of the majority of traditionalists who fear historical criticism is not groundless. Later, we shall examine ways in which some eminent Christian critics have dealt with the dissonance between two contexts, that of the Hebrew Bible of historical criticism and that of the Old Testament of Christian faith.

I have argued that the price of recovering the historical context of sacred books has been the loss of the literary contexts that undergird the traditions that claim to be based upon them. In modern times, the multi-contextuality of the Hebrew Bible has been the source of acute dissension. Much of the polemics between religious traditionalists and historians over the past two centuries can be reduced to the issue of which context shall be normative. When historical critics assert, as they are wont to do, that the Hebrew Bible must not be taken "out of context," what they really mean is that the *only* context worthy of respect is the ancient Near Eastern world as it was at the time of composition of whatever text is under discussion.[3] Religious traditionalists, however, are committed

---

[3] Volumes are spoken by the title of the collection of essays, *Scripture in Context* (ed. Hallo et al.). Which context? The historical, of course!

to another set of contexts, minimally the rest of Scripture, however delimited, and maximally, the entire tradition, including their own religious experience. Their goal is not to push the Book back into a vanished past, but to insure its vitality in the present and the future: "The word of our God endures forever" (Isa 40:8). Their interest in the past is usually confined to an optimistic examination of how the vitality of yesteryear can energize the present. The discontinuities that absorb the historical critic are of little or no use to the traditionalist.

In recent years, increasing numbers of scholars have been asserting the validity of both the historical and the literary (or canonical) contexts. Some have sought to develop a hermeneutic that respects the integrity of the received text for purposes of literary analysis or theological affirmation, without in the process slipping into a fundamentalistic denial of historical change.[4] In this, the "second naiveté" of the historical critic is to be distinguished from the innocence of the orthodox believer who has never become aware of the historical context and who does not feel the claim of historical investigation. In truth, the literary interests of these scholars of the "second naiveté" have little in common with the search for prooftexts so important to the growth of both Judaism and Christianity.

Underlying the literary context affirmed by religious traditionalists is the conviction that the text is somehow the expression of a reliable God. Harmonization is the exegetical counterpart to belief in the coherence of the divine will. The uniformity of Scripture reflects the uniformity of truth. The alternative to this traditional religious position has never been stated more boldly than it was by a great pioneer of the historical criticism of the Christian Bible, Baruch (Benedict) de Spinoza (1632–1677) when he wrote that ". . . great caution is necessary not to confuse the mind of a prophet or historian with the mind of the Holy Spirit and the truth of the matter" (Spinoza: 106). For Spinoza, the excommunicated Jew who never became a Christian, the idea of inspiration was simply another shackle constricting the exegete. No longer need exegesis take place within the believing community. Scripture must be followed wherever it leads, come what may. The author of a biblical text will be the person who wrote it; its meaning will be what *he meant*, not what *God means*, and no intellectually responsible exposition of it can take place without locating the text unshakeably within the histor-

---

[4] An example, motivated by theological concerns, is Childs.

ical circumstances of its composition. Jews and Christians can participate equally in the Spinozan agenda only because its naturalistic presuppositions negate the theological foundations of both Judaism and Christianity. Ever since Spinoza, those Jews and Christians who wish both to retain historical consciousness *and* to make a contemporary use of Scripture have been on the intellectual defensive.

II

The concept that the Bible has many authors rather than one Author has been as brutal to the New Testament as it has been to the Hebrew Bible. It was not long before scholars noticed that the four canonical gospels contradict each other not only in details (Did Jesus say "Blessed are the poor" or "Blessed are the poor in spirit"?), but even in theology. In fact, the New Testament, too, ceased to be a single book in the minds of critical scholars. For example, they noted that for Paul, Christ is "the end of the law" (Rom 10:4), whereas the Sermon on the Mount in Matthew denounces those who set aside "even the least of the law's commandments" for "not a jot or a tittle will disappear from the law until all has been fulfilled" (Matt 5:17–20). No wonder Matthew's Jesus commends obedience to the Pharisees, who "sit in the chair of Moses" (Matt 23:2–3).[5] Now if "the law" in the Sermon on the Mount means the Mosaic Torah, then St. Matthew's gospel, or at least this document in it, is guilty of the heresy of "Judaizing," for the Pauline position that redemption in Christ means exemption from the Torah (Galatians) became normative. And so the possibility emerges that the Church has canonized a heretic—and his gospel! If, on the other hand, the position of Matthew 5 is valid, then what is to be said to all those gentiles who believe, with Paul, that Christ allows them to come into the bosom of Abraham while bypassing the Mosaic Torah? And even if Matthew 5 refers not to the Mosaic Torah but to Jesus' own Torah or to his particular exposition of Moses', then the Pauline doctrine of justification through faith by grace alone, so central to Protestantism, still stands indicted *sola scriptura,* "through scripture alone." In short, the reason these various theological positions, including the heresy of "Judaizing," have kept turning up throughout the history of the Church is that they are all biblical.

---

[5] See Betz (1985: 44). I find it difficult to accept that "commandments" in v. 19 refers to something different from "law" in v. 18, however.

Martin Luther at the Diet of Worms could still express a commitment to "Scripture and plain reason" rather than "the authority of
popes and councils, for they have contradicted each other." Historical criticism has shown that Scripture, too, is contradictory, a
potpourri drawn from what are, in fact, different religions. In the
process, historical criticism of the Christian Bible has shattered the
Protestant dream of an orthodox church founded on biblical authority alone (Bainton: 185; Gerrish: 51–68).[6]

The relationship between theological heterodoxy and the critical study of history is reciprocal. The historian soon discovers that
orthodoxy hangs from a thread that is very thin, if it exists at all.
Some of the traditionalist's heroes were heterodox; alive today, they
might be accused of heresy. On the other hand, the person of
heterodox leanings is driven to the study of history, in part because
he or she can use history and historical documents, even the Bible,
in support of his or her "heresy." The suppressed or forgotten past
provides precedents helpful in dissolving the current consensus:
historical criticism is invaluable to the classic liberal (and, in my
view, illogical) argument that the inevitability of unwilled change
legitimates willed change, that the fact that the tradition was, *de
facto*, always changing validates, *de jure*, contemporary efforts to
alter it. In this way, just as fundamentalists suspect, historical criticism of the Bible can aid in the rehabilitation of heresies, for the
dismantling of the (orthodox) canon (a *sine qua non* of historical biblical
criticism) and the normalization of heterodoxy imply each other. The
frankest admission of this of which I know is the last paragraph of
James M. Robinson's presidential address to the Society of Biblical
Literature in 1981:

> For Jesus to rise in disembodied radiance, for the initiate to
> reenact this kind of resurrection in ecstasy, and for this
> religiosity to mystify the sayings of Jesus by means of her-
> meneutically loaded dialogues of the resurrected Christ
> with his gnostic disciples is as consistent a position as is the
> orthodox insistence upon the physical bodiliness of the res-
> urrected Christ, the futurity of the believer's resurrection
> back into the same physical body, and the incarnation of
> Jesus' sayings within the pre-Easter biography of Jesus in
> the canonical Gospels. Neither is the original Christian

---

[6] For an argument that biblical criticism is, in fact, a triumph of Catholic over
Protestant ideas, see Miles (esp. pp. 28–30).

> position; both are serious efforts to interpret it. Neither can
> be literally espoused by serious critical thinkers of today;
> both should be hearkened to as worthy segments of the
> heritage of transmission and interpretation through which
> Jesus is mediated to the world today.[7]

In reconstructing these various christologies, Professor Robinson
uses not only the canonical literature, but also documents such as
the Gospel of Thomas and Q. The last-named source is especially
germane to a discussion of his method. Q (for German *Quelle*,
"source") is the material that is common to Matthew and Luke but
not to Mark. The theory of most scholars is that Mark and Q served
as two sources for Matthew and Luke. Of course, Q, a collection of
Jesus' sayings (or sayings attributed to him) without narrative, is
hypothetical. It is found only in Matthew and Luke. But the probability that it existed independently has increased in light of the
discovery of the Gospel of Thomas, which is a very similar collection. Robinson does not ignore the fact that the surviving tradition
does not recognize Thomas and subordinates Q to a different genre.
On the contrary, these moves he views as simply stations on the way
to orthodoxy. His claim, however, is that historical excavation of a
literary kind (to recover Q) and of an archaeological kind (to recover
Thomas, which was found in a jar in the ground in Egypt) enables us
to recover the alternative as it stood before it was branded with the
stigma of heterodoxy. Historical study cuts the Gordian knot that
holds together the canon and even individual books within it. As a
result, the long-suppressed and forgotten gnostic position becomes a
"worthy segment [ ] of the heritage of transmission."! The assumption is that one of the traditional obstacles that Christians must
overcome in their effort to hear the gospel is the proto-orthodoxy of
the gospel redactors themselves. If the redactors are orthodox, Jesus
is a heretic.

One of the Gordian knots that some gnostics tried to untie was
the one that binds the Hebrew Bible and the Christian documents
together as one (Christian) Bible. The idea that the two are linked is,
of course, internal to the books that came to be called the "New
Testament." Chief among the devices that connect the two is the
idea that what the Hebrew Bible, soon to become only an "Old

---

[7]Robinson (37). For a fine example of the startling results of literary-critical
decomposition of the text in the pursuit of historical reconstruction, see the chapter
by R.E. Friedman in this volume (pp. 81).

Testament," predict is fulfilled in the New Testament. Thus, for example, Matthew interprets the "voice crying in the wilderness" of Isa 40:3 as John the Baptist (Matt 3:1–3), and taking the poetry of Zech 9:9 ("humble and mounted on an ass/on a foal, the young of a she-ass") literally, he has Jesus ride into Jerusalem on two animals (Matt 21:1–7). A related technique can be found in Gal 4:21–27, in which Paul understands the slave girl Hagar's son Ishmael to be Israel according to the flesh, that is, the Jews, and Sarah's son Isaac, who is born of the promise (Genesis 21), as the Church. Here, Hagar stands for Mount Sinai and the slavery that Paul thought to be its legacy. Sarah suggests the heavenly Jerusalem and the freedom from the Torah that Paul considered characteristic of it. One son, the Jews, is a slave; the other, the Church, is free. Hence, a Christian who observes Toraitic law trades freedom for slavery. Although Paul's technique is based not on the idea of prediction, but on allegory, he, like Matthew (and the apocalyptic Jewish sects of the time), sees the real meaning of scripture as something in his own time. In and of itself, the Hebrew Bible is incomplete. As the Pauline theology became increasingly normative in the post-canonical era, such allegorical or typological interpretation of the Old Testament became all the more necessary. The Church father Origen (died 254 C.E.) put it nicely: on a plain-sense reading, without allegory, the Old Testament commands the sacrifice of calves and lambs! (Gunneweg: 40).

Christian exegesis requires that the Hebrew Bible be read in a literary context that includes the New Testament. To read it on its own would be like reading the first three acts of *Hamlet* as if the last two had never been written. It is a *sine qua non* of Christian exegesis to relate the two testaments, lest either the Marcionite gnostics or the Jews win the ancient debate. But the two anthologies cannot be collapsed into one, lest the newness of the New Testament be lost. It is not simply the continuation of the old, but its fulfillment, not simply another volume in the same series, but the climax and consummation of them all, the one that tells what the others mean. For by New Testament times, almost all the books of the Hebrew Bible were already considered canonical. The thrust of Christian exegesis, thus, is to present the "Old Testament" as somehow anticipating the New, but only anticipating it. The "Old Testament" must be made to appear essential but inadequate. In modern times, the question of how to bring about such a treatment, how to relate the Old and the New, has once again become a crisis, for the old techniques seem discredited. Critical scholars rule out clairvoyance as an explanation axiomatically (not empirically). Instead of holding that the Old Testament predicts events in the life of Jesus, critical scholars of the New Testament say that the gospel writer sought to exploit Old Testament passages in order to bolster his case for the messianic and dominical claims of Jesus or of the Church on behalf of Jesus. Today, only fundamentalists interpret Old Testament passages in terms of New Testament narratives. Allegory has fared no better. To most biblicists, it seems woefully arbitrary. It is difficult to imagine Paul's interpretation of Genesis 21 persuading anyone who needed persuading. Although most Christians continue to accept the theology of Gal 4:21–27, its exegetical basis in the Torah has lost all credibility among historical critics.

The question arises to whether a practitioner of historical criticism can speak of an "Old Testament" at all, whether the concept, like the term (the issue is not merely taxonomic), is not anachronistic. Whereas in the Middle Ages Homer and Virgil were regularly given an *interpretatio Christiana*, today the Hebrew Bible is the only non-Christian book still commonly given a Christian reading. What is at stake is the very existence of the Christian Bible in non-fundamentalistic minds. The challenge to the historical critic of the Old Testament who wishes to be Christian and his work to be Christian has been to find a way to read the Old Testament which is historically sound and which also lends credibility to its literary context, its juxtaposition to the New Testament to form a coherent book. The following pages are devoted to an examination and critique of the ways Christian critics have sought to meet the challenge.

III

Perhaps the most important synthesis of the experience of Ancient Israel is that devised by Julius Wellhausen (1844–1918), the son of a German Lutheran pastor, who became the great pioneer of the historico-critical study of both testaments of his Bible. In his classic work, *Prolegomena to the History of Ancient Israel* (1878), Wellhausen divided the history of Israel's religion into three stages, each marked by a document or set of documents, which, woven together, eventually came to constitute the Pentateuch now in our hands. In the first stage, to be inferred from the Yahwistic history (J) and the closely related Elohistic source (E), religion is natural, free from law and the compulsiveness that Wellhausen associates with it.

The sacred feasts are natural in character, tied unobtrusively to the cycle of the agricultural year, without any precise mathematical dates. The priesthood is universal, and one may sacrifice anywhere. In the next phase, known from the Deuteronomic strand (D), the festivals have begun to be detached from nature. Mathematical calculations begin to determine the dates of their celebration (e.g., Deut 16:9; cf. Exod 23:16). The priesthood becomes exclusively Levitical (Deuteronomy 18), and tithing begins (Deut 14:23). Most importantly, whereas in the earlier centuries any place could serve as the locus of a legitimate sanctuary (Exod 20:24), now only one shrine is permitted (Deut 12:1–7); the connection with the soil and the rhythm of natural life has been dealt a severe blow. In the third and final stage of the religion of Israel, represented in the Pentateuch by the Priestly source (P), the festivals are fixed on precise days of a calendar (Leviticus 23), and a new festival, unattested in the earlier calendars of JE (Exod 23:14–17 and 34:18, 22–24) and D (Deuteronomy 16), the Day of Atonement, intrudes (Leviticus 16 and 23:26–32). "Just as the special purposes and occasions of sacrifice fall out of sight, there comes into increasing prominence the one uniform and universal occasion—that of sin; and one uniform and universal purpose—that of propitiation."[8] The priesthood becomes limited to the clan of Aaron, all non-Aaronite priests have been demoted to the status of minor clergy (Ezek 44:9–16), and tithing becomes a matter of great concern (Numbers 18). Finally, in the fiction of the Tabernacle (*ʾōhel môʿēd*) of Moses' age, the cultic centralization and unity for which D had fought is simply assumed. With the triumph of P, insisted Wellhausen, the last trace of connection to the soil, the last trace of naturalness, has disappeared. The period of the wilderness becomes normative, as one should expect for a people uprooted in the exile of the sixth century B.C.E. "With the Babylonian captivity, the Jews lost their fixed seats, and so became a trading people."[9] The term "trading people," of some

---

[8] Wellhausen (1973: 80). The original (1878) version of the *Prolegomena* was entitled simply *Geschichte Israels* (vol. 1). The first edition of which I have been able to find full bibliographic information is *Prolegomena zur Geschichte Israels* (Berlin: G. Reimer, 1883). On the origins and affinities of Wellhausen's historiography, see R.A. Oden's chapter in this volume (pp. 1).

[9] Wellhausen (1973:108). The negative judgment upon post-biblical Judaism through its association with landlessness and trade is something Wellhausen shared with the early Zionists. It has affinities with Marx as well. On the general question of the attitude of liberal Christians toward Jews in the Second Reich, see Tal (160–222). On the pervasiveness of anti-Jewish tendencies in German biblical scholarship, see Klein; Rendtorff (1981 and 1983); and Blenkinsopp.

utility for medieval and modern Jewish history but of none for the biblical and the rabbinic periods, shows Wellhausen's estimation of the outcome of this long process of development. "Judaism" is Israelite religion after it has died:

> When it is recognized that *the canon* is what distinguishes Judaism from ancient Israel, it is recognized at the same time that what distinguishes Judaism from ancient Israel is *the written Torah*. The water which in old times rose from a spring, the Epigoni stored up in cisterns (1973: 410).

In short, the Torah defines Judaism, and Judaism is the ghost of ancient Israel. "Yet it is a thing which is likely to occur, that a body of traditional practice should only be written down when it is threatening to die out," wrote Wellhausen in one of his most striking observations, "and that a book should be, as it were, the ghost of a life which is closed."[10] The ultimate apparition of this ghost, according to Wellhausen, was the Pharisees of Jesus' day, who were "nothing more than the Jews in the superlative" (Wellhausen, 1874: 17)—narrow, legalistic, exclusivistic, obsessive, compulsive, and hypocritical.

Wellhausen's three-stage evolutionary schema has often suggested that the major influence upon his reconstruction was G. W. F. Hegel, who had interpreted world-history in terms of a dialectic of thesis, antithesis, and synthesis (e.g., Cross, 1973: 82). To be sure, there is an analogy to be drawn between the two. It was after all, Hegel who wrote of Jesus' reception by the Jews that

> His effort to give them the consciousness of something divine was bound to founder on the Jewish masses. For faith in something divine, in something great, cannot make its home in excrement. The lion has no room in a nest; the infinite spirit, none in the prison of a Jewish soul; the whole of life, none in a withering leaf (Hegel: 63).[11]

---

[10] Wellhausen, (1973:405, n.1). The use of death language to describe Judaism was hardly unique to Wellhausen among Christians in Germany in the last century. Schleiermacher (176), for example, described Judaism as "a dead religion" (*eine tote Religion*) whose practitioners sit lamenting in the presence of their "imperishable mummy" (*unverweslichen Mumie*).

[11] My translation—JDL. The essay was written in 1798–99.

These German theologians' use of death language (see n. 10 above) and excrement-language to describe Judaism suggests a connection to the Holocaust. The inmates of the deathcamps were forced to live in their own feces. See the chapter on

Wellhausen simply sought to document the stages of the historical process by which so spiritual a thing as the religion of Israel came to be the ghost he calls "Judaism." On the other hand, there are remarkable differences between Hegel and Wellhausen.[12] The latter's evolutionary model was degenerative, whereas the former's was one of increasing manifestation of the spirit. Thus, Wellhausen's P (Judaism, Pharisaism) is in no sense an Hegelian synthesis of JE and D. Furthermore, the state plays no great role in Wellhausen's schema, whereas it is the manifestation of the Absolute for Hegel. But most significantly of all, Wellhausen, in point of fact, reconstructed more than the three stages that dominate the *Prolegomena*. In his *Israelitische und jüdische Geschichte*, Wellhausen treats a fourth stage, the Gospel. His conclusion is, "[The Gospel] preaches the most noble individualism, the freedom of the children of God" (Wellhausen, 1895: 356).[13] For Wellhausen, of course, that freedom was the Pauline freedom from the Law, every jot and tittle of it. No wonder he described Paul as "the great pathologist of Judaism" (Smend: 263) and made Rom 2:14 ("Not having the Law, they do the works of the Law by nature") the motto of Part I of his *Prolegomena*, and Rom 5:20 ("The Law came in between") the motto of Part III, "Israel and Judaism."

The personal motivation for Wellhausen's reconstruction of Israelite history can be discerned in an uncharacteristically revealing passage in the introduction of his *Prolegomena:*

> In my student days I was attracted by the stories of Saul and David, Ahab and Elijah; the discourse of Amos and Isaiah laid strong hold on me, and I read myself well into the prophetic and historical books of the Old Testament. Thanks to such aids as were accessible to me, I even considered that I understood them tolerably, but at the same time was troubled by a bad conscience, as if I were beginning with the roof instead of the foundation; for I had no thorough acquaintance with the Law, of which I was accustomed to be told that it was the basis and postulate of the whole liter-

---

"Excremental Assault" in Des Pres (51–71). One inmate reported "They had condemned us to die in our own filth, to drown in mud, in our own excrement" (p. 62). See also Rubenstein (1966: 34).

The Holocaust was many different and contradictory things. Enacted theology is one of them.

[12] The interpretation of Wellhausen as a Hegelian has been effectively attacked by Perlitt (206–243).

[13] My translation—JDL.

> ature. At last I took courage and made my way through
> Exodus, Leviticus, Numbers. . . But it was in vain that I
> looked for the light which was to be shed from this source
> on the historical and prophetic books. On the contrary, my
> enjoyment of the latter was marred by the Law; it did not
> bring them any nearer me, but intruded itself uneasily, like
> a ghost that makes a noise indeed, but is not visible and
> really effects nothing. . . At last, in the course of a casual
> visit in Göttingen in the summer of 1867, I learned through
> Ritschl that Karl Heinrich Graf placed the Law later than
> the Prophets, and almost without knowing his reasons for
> the hypothesis, I was prepared to accept it; I readily ac-
> knowledged to myself the possibility of understanding
> Hebrew antiquity without the book of the Torah. [14]

In essence, Wellhausen tells us, the Law provoked a bad conscience
in him, which ever more attentive involvement in the Law could not
assuage. The Law "makes a noise" but "effects nothing." Only the
possibility that the Law is later than the rest of the Old Testament
saved the book for him. Discovery of this point of chronology thus
proved to be the great liberating experience of his intellectual life. It
is fair to say that all his conceptual works on Israelite religion and
Judaism are merely a footnote to that experience in the summer of
1867.

To any student of the Christian Bible, Wellhausen's autobiographical story has a familiar ring:

> What follows? Is the Law identical with sin? Of course not.
> But except through the Law I should never have become
> acquainted with sin. For example, I should never have
> known what it was to covet, if the Law had not said, 'Thou
> shalt not covet.' Through that commandment sin found its
> opportunity, and produced in me all kinds of wrong desires.
> In the absence of the Law, sin is a dead thing. There was a
> time, when in the absence of the Law, I was fully alive; but
> when the commandments came, sin sprang to life and I
> died. The commandment which should have led to life
> proved in my experience to lead to death, because sin found
> its opportunity in the commandment, seduced me, and
> through the commandment killed me (Rom 7:7–11). [15]

[14] Wellhausen (1973: 3–4). Note the "ghost" language again.

[15] The translation here essentially follows the New English Bible, except that I
have put in the definite article and capitalized "Law" throughout, since the context
indicates that Paul is speaking of the Mosaic Torah. It is essential to note, however,
that Paul does not always distinguish between the Mosaic Torah and other forms of
"law."

In this text Paul, Wellhausen's great "pathologist of Judaism," offered a pathologist's analysis of himself as Jew, or at least as Paul the Christian would like to reconstruct Paul the Jew, his dead self. It is not that the Torah is bad; on the contrary, Paul asserted that it is "holy" (Rom 7:12). But the injunctive dimension of the Torah, the commandments, produces death. They define what is bad, the negative side of the Torah. If the holiness and value of the Torah are to be associated with life, then a means must be found to suspend the obligations that its commandments announce. In many places, Paul developed an exegesis of the Torah that he hoped would persuade his correspondents that its commandments are dispensable. One such passage, the allegory of Gal 4:21–27, we have already examined. In Romans 4, Paul gave a kind of chronology of Torah "history" in support of the same point: Since Abraham could be reckoned righteous through faith without the Mosaic Torah, which had not yet been given (Gen 15:6), then the possibility exists for others also to be so reckoned without the Sinaitic commandments. Paul saw the Christ event as the mechanism by which this theoretical possibility becomes real. In short, there are essentially three stages to the sacred history of Pauline Christianity: righteousness without the Torah (Abraham), sin and death through the Torah (Moses, Sinai), and the restoration of righteousness without the Torah (participation in Christ). These correspond to the three stages of Julius Wellhausen's personal experience of the Old Testament: enjoyment of the nonlegal sections, the intrusion of the Torah or at least its most legal books (Exodus, Leviticus, Numbers), and enjoyment of the Old Testament again, with a clean conscience now that the Torah has been shown to be later. In his intellectual life, Wellhausen reenacted Paul's experience, which Lutheran tradition had long taken to be autobiographical and normative.[16] Göttingen was his Damascus. For all his problems with the Church over his use of the historico-critical method, Wellhausen's deepest instincts remained profoundly Lutheran.

In light of the influence of this Pauline archetype on him, Wellhausen's reconstruction of Israelite and Jewish religion becomes more readily understandable. JE was his Abraham, righteous and secure without the Torah. P was his era of the Mosaic Torah, dead and death-dealing, "pharisaical" (D is only intermediate between JE and P). Finally, the Gospel was for him, as for Paul, that which

---

[16] This is not to deny that the Lutheran-Romantic reading of Paul may be a misinterpretation. See Stendahl.

liberates from Toraitic tyranny, restoring the innocence of the distant past, Adam before the Fall or Abraham for Paul, and JE for Wellhausen. But note what Wellhausen did: He historicized Paul's exegesis. Instead of individuals within one book of unitary authorship, Wellhausen wrote of historical periods. JE and P both write on Abraham. It is not Abraham who was the ideal for Wellhausen, but the historical period of JE. Not being a fundamentalist, Wellhausen did not accept the Pauline exegesis as it stood. Instead, he converted it into historical categories, to produce critical history that witnesses to the truth of salvation-history. The Torah in its entirety is no longer the norm; *it has been replaced by the historical process that produced it.* Scrutiny of that historical process discloses what is essential to the Torah and what is dispensable. What is dispensable is law, "Judaism." In short, Wellhausen de-composed the Torah into its constituent documents, reconstructed history from those components, and then endowed history with the normativity and canonicity that more traditional Protestants reserve for Scripture. Biblical history replaces the Bible, but biblical history demonstrates the validity of the biblical (i.e., Pauline) economy of salvation and thus serves to preserve the literary context of the Hebrew Bible. Its conjunction to the New Testament as Volume I of the Christian Bible is logical after all. The logic is no longer the logic of faith, but the logic of history. The historical context replaces the literary context, but without casting into doubt the anti-Judaic and anti-Toraitic thrust of Pauline-Lutheran theology. The Hebrew Bible remains only an "Old Testament."

IV

Wellhausen's *Prolegomena* appeared at the last moment at which its method and its conclusions could have seemed sound. To be sure, the Documentary Hypothesis, upon which so much of it is based, retains the support of the overwhelming majority of critical scholars, whatever the religious communities from which they hail. And many of the details of his reconstruction, such as those involving the centralization of the cult and the evolution of the calendar, remain for the most part, a matter of consensus. But already in the decades following the publication of the *Prolegomena* in 1878, archaeological excavations produced an exponential growth in our knowledge of the biblical world, much of it as lethal to Wellhausen's reconstructed evolution as it is to the traditionalist's cherished belief in the uniqueness of Israel (Weinfeld, 1979; 1981: 423–434). In our century, any critical scholar who wishes to address the religion of biblical Israel must treat the cultures of her neighbors as well. There are now far more materials available for a description of the ancient Near Eastern world than was the case when the *Prolegomena* appeared in 1878. For Wellhausen, no choice between historical description and normative theology was necessary, since he thought history shows a development toward the theological affirmation that claimed his allegiance, the anomian individualism that he considered to be the essence of Christianity. In this century, however, the relationship between historical description ("was") and normative theology ("ought to be") has become a pressing problem. Only fundamentalists, who do not think historically, and those critical scholars who lack religious commitment will fail to feel its claim.

In 1933, Walther Eichrodt, Professor of Old Testament and History of Religion at the University of Basel, Switzerland, published his *Theologie des Alten Testaments* with the announced determination to break "the tyranny of historicism in OT studies." The only way to "succeed in winning back for OT studies in general and for OT theology in particular," wrote Eichrodt, "that place in Christian theology which at present has been surrendered to the comparative study of religions" is *"by examining on the one hand its religious environment and on the other its essential coherence with the NT. . . The only way to do this is to have the historical principle operating side by side with the systematic in a complementary role"* (Eichrodt: 1.31–32). Herein lay an admirable intention to navigate between the Scylla of fundamentalism and the Charybdis of positivism in the hope of producing a religious affirmation that is historically accurate and intellectually honest. Eichrodt's goal was to combine the historical context of the Hebrew Bible ("its religious environment") and its literary context in Christianity ("its essential coherence with the NT"). What he did not contemplate, however, is the possibility that the two contexts may not be complementary, but unrelated or even antithetical. What if the Hebraic indictment of the polytheistic cults applies also to certain central aspects of New Testament Christianity? There is, for example, the issue of child-sacrifice. Substantial evidence exists for a cult of the Canaanite god El that centered upon the sacrifice of children. A Phoenician source tells us of El's own sacrifice of two of his sons, Yadid and Mot, and in Ugaritic myth, the divine father El hands over the younger god Baal for bondage, but also rejoices in the latter's resurrection (Cross, 1977: 1.248; Coogan: 87, 113). Although hints of such a practice on the part of good YHWHists exist (Gen 22:1–19; Exod 22:28; Mic 6:1–8), biblical law explicitly prohibits it (Exod 13:13; Lev 20:2–5), and the prophets vehemently condemn it as incompatible with the worship of YHWH, the true God, and emblematic of idolatry (Jer 7:31; Ezek 20:25–26). In contrast to El (and to most of the gods of polytheism), the biblical YHWH has no children at all (except metaphorically, as in Deut 14:1), no parents, and no wife (except, again, metaphorically, as in Hosea 1–3). If these elements are to be seen as characteristic of Israelite religion when one examines it, in Eichrodt's words, against *"its religious environment,"* then how could he assert *"its essential coherence with the NT, . . .,"* which announces that "God so loved the world that he gave his only son so that everyone who has faith in him may not die, but have eternal life" (John 3:16)? To be sure, there are trajectories with the Hebrew Bible which can be construed to lead to the assertion that a man was literally God's son. One thinks of royal formulae such as that of Ps 2:7—"You are my son; this day I have begotten you." But these are exceedingly few and in tension with a demythologized, utilitarian concept of monarchy (evident, for example, in Deuteronomic tradition) and with the pointed assertion of the unbridgeable difference between human beings and God (Hos 11:9; 1 Sam 15:29; Gen 6:1–4). In short, it is simplistic to hold that the Hebrew Bible prepares the way for the high Christologies of the early Church. It both prepares the way and blocks the way. Eichrodt does not reckon with the fact that the concept of an individual in biological descent from the creator god would have had a much clearer way among Canaanites and Egyptians, for example, than among Jews (Jacobson: 188–190; Saggs; 188; Assmann: 13–61). The possibility that some aspects of Christianity resulted from a syncretism of the religion of the Hebrew Bible and the cults many of its sources strove unsuccessfully to eradicate is simply inconceivable within Eichrodt's method. Whatever is good in the "Old Testament" must have continued, uncompromised, in the New. The rich and diverse texture of the Hebrew Bible, its plurality of religious stances, has been flattened into a monolithic *praeparatio evangelica*. For all Eichrodt's intentions to do justice to the historical and comparative contexts, he allowed theology to emasculate the history of religions. It is consistently the literary context of the Christian Bible which took precedence in Eichrodt's presentation. That preference is what keeps his book Christian (Gunneweg: 87–88) and the Hebrew Bible an "Old Testament."

The thematic continuity that Eichrodt developed was "covenant." Whatever other weaknesses this idea has, it immediately raises the possibility that not the Church, but the Jews are the real heirs of the Old Testament, for whereas Christianity sees the stipulations of covenant made void through Christ, Judaism retains those stipulations *(miṣwôt)* and rests more structural weight upon covenant than does Christianity (Urbach, 1975a: 1.525–541; 1975b: 466–480). Or, to put it differently, to the extent that "covenant" survives as a meaningful term in Christianity, it does so without the specificity and concreteness of the *miṣwôt*, upon whose observance almost every book of the Hebrew Bible insists. To avoid conceding defeat to the Jews, Christian covenant theologians must do one of two things: Either they must reassert the classic New Testament claim that covenant does not require observance (i.e., that, in good Pauline fashion, the Mosaic/Sinaitic dimension is dispensable), or they must show that the Jews have perverted the covenant faith of their ancestors, so that Judaism is *more* discontinuous with the religion of Israel than Christianity (another New Testament theme, found especially in Hebrews). In fact, Eichrodt chose both paths, although it is the second that is the more revealing. Judaism, he said, has only "a torso-like appearance . . . in separation from Christianity" (1.26). "It was not," he wrote, "until in later Judaism a religion of harsh observances had replaced the religion of the Old Testament that the Sabbath changed from a blessing to a burdensome duty" (1.133). It is in the Mishnah (promulgated ca. 200 C.E.) that "real worship of God [was] stifled under the heaping up of detailed commands from which the spirit has fled" (2.348, n.1). In Judaism, he informed his readers, "the living fellowship between God and man . . . shrivelled up into a mere correct observance of the legal regulations" (1.168). In short, in Judaism "the affirmation of the law as the revelation of God's personal will was lost" (1.218).

In making these statements, Eichrodt capitulated *in toto* to the pole of his method defined by the New Testament; critical historiography did not inform him here at all. He accepted New Testament caricatures, stereotypes, and outright perversions of Judaism in the same manner as would the most unlettered fundamentalist. For example, what literary source in "later Judaism" (by which curious locution is meant early Judaism) ever saw the Sabbath as "a burdensome duty" rather than a blessing? Volumes are spoken by

Eichrodt's silence about the numerous passages in the Talmud and Midrash that describe the Sabbath as a pearl, as Israel's bride, or the like (e.g., *Šôḥēr Ṭôb* 92:1; *Ber. Rab.* 11:8). The likelihood is that he did not know they existed and had no interest in learning what spiritual treasure, what wealth of love, joy, camaraderie, and thought, the observant Jew found (and finds) in the Sabbath.[17] Christian anti-Jewish polemics were so much more readily at hand and, especially in the Germanophone world of 1933, so much more readily accepted. Eichrodt's idea that the personal will of a gracious God fell out beneath rabbinic legalism fares no better. It cannot survive a confrontation with the numerous rabbinic sayings that present observance of *miṣwôt* as a response to God's grace (e.g., *Mek. Baḥōdeš* 5.).

In one instance, however, Eichrodt did try to cite a rabbinic text in support of his anti-rabbinic theology:

> This means that for the heathen, being sinners without the Law, the only real possibility is God's punitive righteousness; and this state of affairs is not altered by Aqiba's fine saying: 'The world is judged by the measure of God's mercy' (1.249).

Eichrodt's footnote to this quotation from the Mishnah reads:

> Pirqe Aboth 3.16. The continuation, "and everything is done according to the multitude of works" proves conclusively that here, as in Wisd. 12.15, the only idea is one of resignation in the face of resistless and overwhelming Omnipotence.[18]

An examination of the complete dictum shows that Eichrodt simply did not understand Rabbi Aqiba's point:

---

[17] One wonders how Eichrodt would have reacted had he read Heschel.

[18] Eichrodt, 1.249, n. 3. I have here corrected the English translation, which mistakenly inserts "his" before "works." Unable to procure the sixth edition of the *Theologie* (from which the translation was made), I have checked the fifth (Stuttgart: Ehrenfried Klotz, 1957) 1.161, n. 96. On the other hand, Eichrodt's concluding comment in the note probably suggested the innocent change to the translator.

On the text of the logion, see now Safrai. Safrai chooses a textual variant that reads "but *not* according to the majority of deeds." This variant destroys the exquisitely paradoxical structure of Aqiba's statement. But if accepted, it would be another example of the rabbinic theology of grace—the very theology whose existence Christian theologians tend to deny.

> All is foreseen, but freedom of choice is given. In goodness
> the world is judged, but all is according to the amount of
> work.

So far as I can determine, the Jewish tradition has always understood the last word of Rabbi Aqiba's dictum as a reference to human
efforts, not God's action. In other words, Rabbi Aqiba (d. early 2nd
century C.E.) here states two paradoxes—the coexistence of divine
providence and human free will, and the importance of both divine
grace and human effort in God's judgment of the world. Works are
neither sufficient nor dispensable; they are essential but ultimately
inadequate. The point is one that one would have expected a Calvinist theologian to understand immediately. But for Eichrodt, to
have understood it and to have rendered it accurately would have
been to forfeit his argument that the Jews lost sight of the nature of
the divine-human relationship, substituting a legalistic works-
righteousness for the more paradoxical and nuanced biblical stance.
And to forfeit that argument would have been to forfeit the claim that
historico-critical scholarship is compatible with the Christian tenet
that the Hebrew Bible is *best* approached when it is within the same
covers as the New Testament.

Our examination of the theology of Walter Eichrodt shows that
his anti-Judaic remarks were not incidental to his theological
method. They were owing not simply to social prejudice, but to his
intention to show that the covenantal religion of ancient Israel is of a
piece with Christianity. His willingness to accept traditional Christian slurs at face value both contributed to and was influenced by his
apparent inability to read the rabbinic sources. In this, he re-
sembled Wellhausen, who confessed his lack of knowledge of Jewish
literature, especially the Talmud, and his consequent dependence
on Greek sources,[19] but did not allow this handicap to prevent him
from presenting a very negative picture of Judaism throughout his
career. The disastrous effects on both Wellhausen and Eichrodt of
ignorance of literature in post-biblical Hebrew underscore a truism
that the scholarly world still evades: One cannot be a competent
scholar of the Christian Bible without a solid command of rabbinic

---

[19] See Smend (256–257). On the pernicious effects of the ignorance of rabbinic
literature on New Testament scholars, see Sanders (33–59). On the underlying
sociopsychological dynamics, see Levenson (1985).

literature and rabbinic Hebrew (and Aramaic). Hebrew did not die on the cross.[20]

V

If Eichrodt's assertion that the same theme dominates each half of the Christian Bible is unlikely, even the lesser claim of thematic unity throughout the Old Testament has proven problematic. This search for the unity (or the center) of biblical theology is, in a sense, reactionary: it aims to diminish the impact of historical criticism, which leaves one with the impression that, at least with respect to the Bible, Heraclitus' dictum is correct—"everything flows." Biblical theology seems to be like his river: One cannot step into the same one twice. A less reactionary response is to be found in the work of Gerhard von Rad, especially in his *Theologie des Alten Testaments*, first published in 1957. Making a virtue of necessity, von Rad saw the reappropriation and reinterpretation of the legacy of tradition as a precious theological asset. Behind that reinterpretation lay a continuing history of salvation *(Heilsgeschichte)*, at the onset of which was a promise for which "there was, oddly enough,

[20] A frequent assumption is that not only Hebrew, but Israel disappeared about the time of the rise of the Church. This is simply a secularization of the Christian doctrine that the Church is the real Israel (but cf. Romans 9–11). One can often see the influence of this doctrine in books entitled *History of Israel* (or the like) which ignore or slight rabbinic and all subsequent Jewish history. A particularly ugly example is Noth, *Geschichte Israels* (1954), which concludes with this sentence: "Thus ended the ghastly epilogue of Israel's history" (ET, p. 454). The fact that Noth could write these words (about the Hadrianic period) in Germany less than one decade after the Holocaust is chilling. No sooner had the smoke cleared from above the charnel houses of Europe than a German biblical historian dared write that Israel came to an end eighteen centuries earlier. It will avail little to argue that Noth meant by "Israel" only a nation in the conventional sense, for, in fact, he conceded at the outset of his *History* that Israel "did lack certain elements which are usually considered essential to the concept of a 'nation'" and that "it may even be better to discard [the concept of a nation] altogether and speak simply of 'Israel'" (ET, pp. 4–5). But if so, why end the study in 135 C.E.? For Jewry (to use the outsiders' term in place of the native term "Israel"), on the one hand, had known dispersion for many centuries already and, on the other, would continue to dwell in Palestine in large numbers for several more centuries and to experience considerable autonomy there until the emperor Theodosius II abolished the patriarchate in 425. John Bright seems to have concluded his own *History of Israel* with the commendable aim of correcting Noth's biased and insensitive conclusion. He seems to be going out of his way when he insists that "It is a legitimate answer and, from a historical point of view, a correct one [to hold that] Israel's history does continue in Judaism [and not in the Church alone]" (p. 464). Note also the more accurate title of a work like Siegfried Herrmann's *Geschichte Israels in alttestamentlicher Zeit* (1973). In accordance with his title, Herrmann wisely ends his study with the Hellenistic era.

never any satisfactory historical fulfillment and consummation."
Therefore, "the Old Testament can only be read as a book of ever
increasing anticipation" (Von Rad, 1965: 2.319). The fluctuation of
tradition is to be seen theologically as Israel's effort to keep that
promise and the hope for its fulfillment alive. For example, the
YHWHist (J) has reinterpreted the promise of land to the Patriarchs
as a reference to the conquest under Joshua generations later (Gen
15:13–15; von Rad, 1965: 2.322). And the great anonymous prophet
of the Exile, writing when the promise of grace to the House of
David seemed to have been voided, reinterpreted "the sure grace to
David" as applying to the entire people Israel (Isa 55:1–7; von Rad,
1965: 2.325). Thus could the Davidic Covenant be saved at a time
when the messiah was seen not in a scion of David, but in the
Iranian liberator, Cyrus (Isa 44:24–45:3). If Old Testament theology
recognized this process of recontextualization and reinterpretation of
the promise, which, despite the changes, remains valid, then, in
von Rad's words, "the material itself would bear it from one actu-
alisation to another, and in the end would pose the question of the
final fulfillment." (von Rad, 1965: 2.428). For him, of course, this
was Jesus as the Christ of the New Testament. Hence, the difference, for example, between Israelite messianism and New Testament christology need not be denied or minimized. The New Testament simply continues the traditionary process of the Old, which
was itself always in flux. Thus could von Rad, on grounds very
different from Eichrodt's, oppose, like him, those who take "the Old
Testament in abstraction as an object which can be adequately
interpreted without reference to the New Testament . . ."(von Rad,
1965: 2.321).

Von Rad's method allowed the texts of the Hebrew Bible to
speak more in their own voice than did the historicism of Wellhausen or the monolithic dogmatism of Eichrodt. His ear was more
finely attuned to the plurality of notes sounded in the Hebrew
Bible, and his mind was, relative to theirs, less inclined to force
external schemes onto the texts themselves. The fact remains, however, that von Rad's effort to preserve the bifurcated Bible of Christianity without deviation from historical criticism was deeply flawed.
Brevard Childs is surely right that

> . . . a major problem with von Rad's *Old Testament The-*
> *ology* is that he has failed to deal with the canonical forces at
> work in the formation of the traditions into a collection of

> scripture during the post-exilic period, but rather set up the
> New Testament's relation to the Old in an analogy to his
> description of the pre-exilic growth of Hebrew tradition
> (Childs: 669).[21]

In other words, already by the time of the New Testament documents, Israelite tradition had crystallized into sacred scripture. The
claim of the primitive Church was not that its gospel was yet another
link in an ongoing chain of tradition, but that it was *the* fulfillment of
canonical writ. Von Rad thus preserved the bifurcated Bible by
destroying the bifurcation. The New Testament is only the continuation of the Old. But if tradition in the sense of recontextualization is what legitimates the more recent past and binds it to distant
antiquity, then why did von Rad not consider rabbinic tradition,
which, especially in the form of midrash, also recontextualized the
Hebrew Bible, often strikingly? Why is the Israelite past to be seen
only in light of the early Church, the Hebrew Bible only as an "Old
Testament"? At times von Rad seemed to answer this in the same
way Wellhausen and Eichrodt did, through the disparagement of
Judaism, as when he wrote that

> The end was reached at the point where the law became an
> absolute quantity, that is, when it ceased to be understood
> as the saving ordinance of a special racial group (the cultic
> community of Israel) linked to it by the facts of history, and
> when it stepped out of this function of service and became a
> dictate which imperiously called into being its own com-
> munity (1965: 1.201).

But, in general, he seems to have been oblivious to the question,
perhaps because as a Christian theologian in the *judenrein* Germany
of the post-Holocaust era, he had no one to raise it with him. Like
Hegel, Wellhausen, and Eichrodt, he simply assumed the spiritual
necrosis of Judaism after Jesus: After "the end was reached," why
consider the Jews?

[21] Childs correctly notes that the same criticisms apply to Hartmut Gese. Gese
sees the elucidation of continuities, in this case the continuities of the Old Testament
and the New Testament, as a central task of the theologian. But neither he nor von
Rad reckons with the fact that the "heresies" (e.g., gnosticism) are also in continuity
with the past and can be, as Robinson points out (see n. 7), as ancient as the
"normative" position. Since heresy and orthodoxy can be part of the same culture,
cultural affinities cannot be an adequate criterion for determining the validity of a
theology. Thus, Gese's great efforts to establish the Hebraic character of the New
Testament, even if valid, fail to achieve his larger theological goal.

The finality that von Rad attributed to the New Testament is in contradiction to his emphasis on the ongoing nature of tradition. Apparently, he expected us to respect the continuousness of history up to and perhaps including the experience of the Apostolic Church, but then to make a leap of faith that would deny the continuousness and ongoing nature of all subsequent history. All fulfillments before Jesus are to be seen as provisional. Jesus is to be seen as final and unsurpassable. But must not historical critics point out that history also passed up Jesus? His prediction that the kingdom would come within the generation (Mark 9:1) proved false, forcing his later followers to devise extenuations and explanations, which are themselves recontextualizations (Achtemeier: 231–248). In fact, the entire history of Christian theology can be seen as testimony to the provisional character of the New Testament and its putative "fulfillments." History continues, and for the Christian who reads his tradition in light of Nicea, Aquinas, Luther, Trent, or Vatican I and II, the New Testament has long been an "Old Testament," in need of reinterpretation and supplementation. *No* statement is final because, whatever apocalypticists may say, history continues. And if we are to assume the validity of recontextualization, why stop with Judaism and Christianity? Islam, after all, claims to have superseded the Church in a way not altogether different from the way the Church claims to have superseded the Jews: Jesus is a link in the chain of prophets that culminates in Muhammad (the supersessionists superseded). Von Rad would probably claim, in rebuttal, that the ultimate fulfillment in Christ is known only through faith; the critical historian can never see it. But in that case, he would have conceded that an historico-critical examination of the religion of the Hebrew Bible does not point to Jesus Christ at all. In short, von Rad seems to have wanted to move from the Hebrew Bible to the New Testament by means of certain methods that, whether accurately applied or not, are in accord with historical criticism. Having done so, he then wished to suspend those methods and to introduce an act of faith in the consummative finality of Jesus. It is this anti-critical act of faith that distinguishes the "biblical theologian," in von Rad's terminology, from the "historian of the religion of Israel." (von Rad, 1965: 2.428–429).[22] When the radical implications of historical criticism got close to home and began threatening the unity and

---

[22] The resort to fideism is hardly surprising. Von Rad's inordinate emphasis on soteriology suggests a Christian set of priorities from the beginning.

sufficiency of the Christian Bible, von Rad reverted to a position formally indistinct from fundamentalism. He expected faith to stop Heraclitus' river.

At first glance, von Rad's emphasis upon tradition at the expense of canonical scripture seems strange in a Lutheran theologian. Was it not the Reformers who asserted that all Church tradition must be scrutinized according to the norm *sola Scriptura,* "by scripture alone"? At the point when scripture is shown to be the product of tradition, it surely becomes more difficult to assert the sovereignty of the scripture over the tradition, as the Reformation sought to do (Miles). On the other hand, von Rad's assumption that traditions, as recovered by form-criticism, are the fundamental units to be interpreted, does serve one traditional Lutheran goal, the polarization of grace and law. In an early programmatic essay (von Rad, 1966a), von Rad argued that beneath the earliest documents of the Hexateuch (Genesis–Joshua) lay two sets of traditions. One, connected with the Festival of Booths, centered on the experience at Sinai and the proclamation of cultic law. The other, connected with Pentecost, was the tradition of the settlement in the land, a tradition in which the exodus was of prime import. Thus, originally, one could narrate the story of descent into Egypt, enslavement, liberation, and the assumption of the Land without any mention of the revelation at Sinai. Von Rad thought that texts such as Deut 26:5b–9, Josh 24:2–13, and 1 Sam 12:8, which omit reference to the Sinaitic experience, bore out his claim. Of course, many texts witness to the merger of the two sets of traditions (e.g., Nehemiah 9 and Psalm 106). In von Rad's mind, that merger, that "incorporation of the Sinai tradition into the Settlement tradition should be attributed to the [YHWHist]" (J). "The blending of the two traditions," he concluded, "gives definition to the two fundamental propositions of the whole message of the Bible: Law and Gospel" (Von Rad, 1966a: 53–54). Thus, through a very different method from Wellhausen's, von Rad, like him, was able to reverse the canonical merger of "Law and Gospel" (assuming he was right that they were once separate) and thus to cast doubt upon the theology of those tradents in whose mind they were not to be so distinguished. On the basis of this, von Rad could then replicate the classic Pauline subordination of norm to soteriology. Once again, an historical method—this time, form-criticism—has been employed to decompose the received text and to reorder it according to the needs of a Christian theology. This use of historical criticism has proven to be the most important in Old Testament theology, for it enables the theologian to find meanings in the book which the *textus receptus* does not suggest. The retrieved past (the Hebrew Bible) can thus be rapidly assimilated to the familiar present (the Old Testament). The man can repress the child within and go about his business as if nothing has changed.

The same *Tendenz* can be seen in von Rad's teacher, Albrecht Alt, a form-critic for whom the problematics of contemporary theological affirmation were not a central concern. Alt found that biblical law separates into two broad categories, "casuistic" and "apodeictic." Casuistic law is case-law, characteristically phrased in the form "if a man . . . then"; it specifies crimes and punishments. Apodeictic law tends to be phrased in the imperative; it takes the form of a personal command and omits any mention of sanctions. Alt's discovery was that the distinction is not simply formal, but substantive as well. Casuistic law tends to be secular, whereas apodeictic law (e.g., the Decalogue) is sacral. Casuistic law is general in the ancient Near East (Alt thought it a borrowing from the Canaanites), whereas apodeictic law is native to Israel and reflects the unique character of YHWH. Ultimately, according to Alt, the apodeictic law expanded at the expense of the casuistic. It "pursues the Israelite out of the sanctuary of [YHWH] into his daily life, and inevitably clashed with the carefully itemized instances and exceptions of the casuistic law" (Alt: 170–171). Essentially the same dichotomy appeared in America in the work of George E. Mendenhall, only under the rubrics of "law" and "covenant." A decade ago, Mendenhall published an essay in which he argued that these two stand in a contrastive relationship. Law, for example, "presupposes a social order," whereas covenant is based on "gratitude." Law is "binding upon each individual by virtue of his status . . . usually by birth," but covenant comes "by voluntary act in which each individual willingly accepts the obligations presented," etc. (Mendenhall: 174–175).

A full critique of these theories of von Rad, Alt, and Mendenhall lies outside the purview of our discussion.[23] Each has been challenged or severely qualified. What is of interest here is that each comes to a position that is in profound harmony with the Pauline-Lutheran understanding of the Torah, which holds that one can inherit the promise to Abraham and the status of his lineage without "the Law." Von Rad is the most explicit and probably the most self-

---

[23] See the discussion and bibliography in Childs (109–127, esp. pp. 124–129). See also Weinfeld (1973) and Levenson (1980).

conscious: He openly uses the terms "Law and Gospel" and defines them as "the two most fundamental propositions of the whole . . . Bible." Obviously, the last word refers to the two-fold Bible of Christianity. What von Rad has done is to show that this Christian dichotomy, ostensibly so alien to the thought-world of the Hebrew Bible, is, in point of fact, basic to the evolution of that set of documents.[24] Alt, despite his lesser involvement in theological tradition, makes essentially the same point. Is it coincidence that Jesus (so far as we know) spoke only apodeicticly and bequeathed no case-law? To one who stands in the Christian tradition, it is surely of use to argue that case-law was always foreign and secular—that is, religiously inessential: What Paul abolished was always dispensable, so much cultural baggage from the environment. Mendenhall's dichotomy of law and covenant makes the same point. "Law" here sounds very much like the same term in Paul, for whom it is an unpleasant entity, now happily superseded. Unlike covenant, for example, it is for Mendenhall usually a matter of birth (cf. Rom 9:6–8). Christians, however, sought to retain the term "covenant," applying to themselves the prophecy of a "new covenant" (Jer 31:31), which they interpreted as anomian, a covenant without law (Heb 8:6–13). Thus, it is no surprise to find most Old Testament theologians in favor of covenant and against Torah or "law." This is credible only when law and covenant can be made into contrasts.[25]

The claim that there was a time, before the composition of the canonical Pentateuch (or Hexateuch), when Israel could tell her story without the intrusion of law is simply a form-critical analogue to Paul's argument in Galatians 3 that Abraham was justified through faith without the Law, which came fully 430 years later, in the generation of Moses (v. 17). The theory is older than Paul. The

---

[24] See also von Rad's attempt to offer a historico-critical argument for Paul's interpretation of Gen 15:6 in Gal 3:6 (1966b). Von Rad did not seem to recognize that if one approaches Gen 15:6 with respect for its context inside the Hebrew Bible, then the state of righteousness through faith alone is to be seen as inadequate or only an anticipation of the fuller righteousness made possible through Sinaitic revelation. It is, of course, highly unlikely that *heʾĕmīn* ("trust," "have faith," "believe") in Gen 15:6 implies any kind of dichotomy between faith and works. In general, the portrait of Abraham in Genesis is one of a man in whom promise and obedience to commandments were held together in the tightest way (e.g., Gen 22:16–18; 26:5). Contrary to von Rad's assumption, nothing in Gen 15:6 implies righteousness by faith *alone*. See my essay on "Why Jews are Not Interested in Biblical Theology" (1987:301–304).

[25] Mendenhall's christological concerns are patent: "The permanent symbol of the necessity as well as the reality of that rule of God is the crucifixion of Jesus . . ." (178). Is this the view in the Hebrew Bible? On the contemporary political context of Mendenhall's position, see Rubenstein (1983: 457–458).

Hellenistic writer Posidonius (ca. 135–50 B.C.E.) claimed "that the good and simple legislation of Moses had been falsified at a later period by superstitious and forceful priests who by separatist regulations had changed the simple and truthful worship of God intended by the founder into something quite different" (Hengel: 300). It has been plausibly suggested that this theory influenced the Jewish Hellenizers of Seleucid times and that Paul may have been their heir (Betz, 1979: 139). If so, then this Hellenizing trend, with its eagerness to suspend the *miṣwôt*, has been preserved for two millennia through the triumph of Pauline Christianity, and the process of its intellectual self-justification continues in the step-child of the Church, biblical criticism. The great vulnerability, however, of those who wish to pursue this line of self-justification through the study of the Hebrew Bible is that the hypothetical two themes—law and gospel, casuistic and apodeictic law, law and covenant—have been woven together so thoroughly that their separation must be effected through the dismantling of the canonical literature. Nothing is more characteristic of the biblical law codes than the meshing of casuistic and apodeictic law. In fact, the Pentateuch endows all its laws with the status of personal commandments from God by reading them into the revelation through Moses on Mount Sinai: Law and covenant are one. It is here that the techniques of von Rad, Alt, and Mendenhall become useful for Christian apologetics, for these techniques allow the scholar to penetrate back to a putative era that supports the Christian dichotomy, whereas the canonical shape of the literature only casts doubt upon it. Like Wellhausen, those scholars are really engaging in reconstructive surgery, whose purpose is to produce an "Old Testament" in place of the Hebrew Bible, to use *historico-critical methods* to validate the *literary context* that is the Christian Bible. Such surgery becomes all the more essential to the Christian historical critics when they discover that this characteristic interlacing of norm and narrative continues in the Talmud, where *hǎlākâ and ʾaggādâ* alternate uneventfully, a fact that raises the alarming possibility that not the Church, but the Jews are the rightful heirs to the Hebrew Bible. It is no coincidence that the dispossession of the Jews has been a motive force behind much of the study of "biblical theology."

VI

I have argued that the essential challenge of historical criticism to book-religions lies in its development of a context of interpretation, the historical context, which is different from the literary (or canonical) contexts that underlie Judaism and Christianity in their different ways. In one way or another, the religions presuppose the coherence and self-referentiality of their foundational books. These things are what makes it possible to derive a coherent religion, *one* religion (one's own), from the Book. The historical critic who is uncompromisingly honest, on the other hand, exploits the inconcinnities and the discontinuities as part of his or her effort to decompose the Book into its several strata in order to reconstruct the history that redaction has repressed. It is not surprising, to resume our psychoanalytic metaphor, that the recovery of repressed material should meet with "resistance," in this case, the angry salvoes of fundamentalists. What is surprising, however, is that so many religious traditionalists who pledge their troth to historical criticism insist that their work only *enriches* and never *undermines* their religious identity, as if the fundamentalists, who are far more numerous, are simply silly. What makes this optimism possible is the use of historical method only in defense of the traditional canon and its underlying theology. In the case of the five scholars discussed— Wellhausen, Eichrodt, von Rad, Alt, and Mendenhall—the Hebrew Bible is analyzed in ways that support its relegation to the status of an "Old Testament" (itself an a-historical, or anachronistic term) and that defuse the threat that historical criticism poses to Christian supersessionism. If this is the case, then it is evident in what genre these studies ultimately belong: They are midrash. Like the *midrāšîm* that we examined in Section I, they seek to harmonize discordant texts. This time the texts are not, as there, the differing Passover laws of Exodus 12 and Deuteronomy 16, but Leviticus and Galatians, for example, or Deuteronomy and Romans. For the Christian Old Testament scholar who wishes his or her work to be *Christian* and not simply historically accurate, the urge to harmonize arises, as it did for the rabbis, from the conviction that the sacred text is a unity, that all those seemingly diverse passages belong in the same book. The differences must be shown to be complementary or in dialectical tension; no outright contradictions may be allowed to stand. For if they are, then it will be apparent that Christianity attempts to keep the scriptures of at least two different religions in its bifurcated Bible, and the Christian Bible will cease to give a univocal endorsement to Christianity. The endurance and vigor of Judaism should always have cast doubt upon the claim of univocality, but, as we have seen, the dominant Christian theologi-

cal tradition, practiced by ostensible historical critics no less than by
fundamentalists, has blindfolded itself to that vigor and clung religiously to the old defamations. The defamations of Judaism in the
"Old Testament theologies" and related works are not incidental.
They are indispensable to the larger hermeneutical purpose of
neutralizing historical criticism from within.

Most Christians involved in the historical criticism of the
Hebrew Bible today seem to have ceased to want their work to be
considered distinctively Christian. They do the essential philological, historical, and archeological work without concern for the larger
constructive issues or for the theological implications of their labors.
They are Christians everywhere except in the classroom and at the
writing-table, where they are simply honest historians striving for
an unbiased view of the past. Even in the world of "Old Testament
theology," however, there has grown over the last twenty years or so
some awareness that the historico-critical enterprise may not be in
harmony with the demands of Christian proclamation. One thinks of
Friedrich Baumgärtel's argument that ". . . we cannot eliminate the
fact, derived from the history of religion, that the Old Testament is a
witness out of a non-Christian religion" (Baumgärtel: 135). A. H. J
Gunneweg has drawn the hermeneutical implication:

> But it is impossible to give a Christian interpretation of
> something that is not Christian; Christian interpretation of
> something that is not Christian is pseudo-interpretation.[26]

With these two sentences, Gunneweg has pronounced judgment on
two millennia of biblical studies in a distinctively Christian mode.
He has sent a torpedo into the prediction-fulfillment schema of the
Gospels, into Paul's allegories and all their patristic, medieval, and
Reformation kin, into Wellhausen's historicism, Eichrodt's and Mendenhall's anomian covenantalism, von Rad's salvation-history, and
much else. For all these efforts to make a Christian use of the
Hebrew Bible commit the greatest sin known to the historico-
critical method, the sin of anachronism.

[26] Gunneweg (222). It is not adequate to argue, as does Westermann (135), that
this denies the Church its Old Testament. Literary units are not discrete individuals
without relations to each other or to the mind in which they are perceived. A passage
from the Hebrew Bible, presented historically, changes when it is injected into a
Christian universe of discourse. The Christian *qua* Christian may indeed have access
to the Old Testament—but not to the Hebrew Bible of the historical critics or to the
Tanakh of the rabbis.

The Jew who may be inclined to enjoy the thought that historical criticism may at long last be about to liberate the Hebrew Bible from the New Testament had best observe the admonition of Prov 24:17–18, for the wrath of historical criticism has already fallen upon Judaism and not only upon the Church. No critical scholar of the Hebrew Bible believes in its *historical* unity or even in the *historical* unity of the Pentateuch. If Leviticus and Galatians cannot be accommodated in one religion, then neither, perhaps, can Exodus and Deuteronomy, and certainly Isaiah and Qohelet cannot. Jews need their harmonistic midrash no less than Christians need theirs, for it is midrash that knits the tangled skein of passages into a religiously usable "text" (Latin, *texo*, "to weave"). Midrash continues the redactional process beyond the point of finalization of the text. The pulverizing effects of the historico-critical method do not respect the boundaries of religions; the method dismembers all midrashic systems, reversing tradition. Rigorous historical critics are not likely to accept a rabbinic interpretation of literature that is not rabbinic, a Deuteronomic interpretation of literature that is not Deuteronomic, or a monotheistic interpretation of literature that is not monotheistic. All religious use of past literature is, to some extent, at cross-purposes with historical criticism, if only because the world of the contemporary religious person is not the world of the author. It is a world into which the author's work comes recontextualized through redaction, canonization, and other forms of tradition.[27] The matrix in which the ancient text speaks to the contemporary community is this larger, anachronizing context. To be sure, historico-critical and traditional religious study are not always mutually exclusive. They may occasionally cross-fertilize or check each other. But it is naive to expect the historico-critical study of the Book only to serve and never to undermine traditional religious purposes, whether the *miṣwâ* of *talmûd tôrâ* (the central Jewish obligation of Torah study) or Christian kerygmatic proclamation. Both sacred and profane modes of study may have value and meaning, but they must not be collapsed one into the other.

Two factors account for the remarkable endurance of the tendency to collapse or muddle contexts of interpretation. First, the

---

[27] One sometimes meets in unsophisticated Protestants the idea that in Protestantism the biblical text speaks directly, without mediation. This ignores the fact that the operations performed on the text even in communities that think they adhere to a doctrine of *sola scriptura* are matters of post-biblical convention. On this, see Kelsey.

motivation of most historical critics of the Hebrew Bible continues to be religious in character. It is a rare scholar in the field whose past does not include an intense Christian or Jewish commitment. That commitment brings scholars to the subject, but they then pursue it with methods whose origins lie not in the religious traditions, but in the Enlightenment critique of them. The incongruity of the motivation and the methods is painful to acknowledge. It is more convenient to maintain a private expectation that somehow the historico-critical method will, in the last analysis, *only* vindicate, purify, and enrich the original religious motivation. The second factor is simply the institutional correlative of the first. It is that most of the critical scholarship in Hebrew Bible is still placed in Christian theological schools. Indeed, were it not for the religious connection, the field would be no more prominent in Christendom than are most other forms of orientalism. But the religiousness of this location sets up a continuing expectation that, in principle, this antitraditional, atheistic method will serve traditional theistic goals, such as Christian ministry. The dissonance caused by the placement of Hebrew Bible in Christian contexts is a profound inducement for the creation of a mediating myth that will mask the contradiction. Each of the five scholars whose work we have examined aided profoundly in this myth-making enterprise. Indeed, as I argue elsewhere (Levenson, 1987), the field known as "Old Testament theology," in which Eichrodt and von Rad remain leading lights, is marked by a profound ambivalence as to whether the endeavor is a branch of Christian theology or not. The nearly universal tendency is to have it both ways: Old Testament theology is to be both historical and Christian. Acknowledgement of the survival and vibrancy of Judaism would be difficult to harmonize with this belief in a *historically* responsible *Christian* exegesis of a non-Christian set of books, for, if nothing else, the Jewish presence would serve to relativize the Christian reading and to suggest that it is particularistic and confessional and not simply some self-evident "plain sense." The anxiety that this possibility produces accounts, in part, for the eagerness of most Old Testament theologians to ignore or negate post-biblical Judaism: out of sight, out of mind.[28] The relativistic implications of the multi-contextuality of its sacred book are difficult, and perhaps impossible,

[28] Another mediating myth, found mostly among North American Christians but rare otherwise, is the idea of a "Judeo-Christian tradition." It masks the opposition between the Tanakh and the Old Testament. On this, see Cohen, van Buren (65–67); and Halpern (185–195). Halpern puts the issue most succinctly:

for any religion to accept.[29] In the case of Christianity, however, the tendency to conceive of itself as universal makes the evidence for its own particularism more painful to embrace. The path of least resistance is to assume that the Christian context subsumes all others.

The principal threat to muddling the contexts arises from the recent emergence of scholars and academic departments that are not beholden to any religious perspective. The explosion in knowledge of the ancient Near East has shifted the focus of most advanced programs in Hebrew Bible from theology to philology and archaeology. As we saw in our discussion of Eichrodt, the hope that the new focus would only complement the old one (New Testament) bore little or no good fruit. In North America, the emergence of Religion departments and Jewish Studies programs and departments has further contributed to the dethronement of Christian theology, indeed any theology, as the ruling paradigm for the study of the Hebrew Bible. As a consequence, in the elite academic world, those for whom the term "Old Testament" is more than vestigial are

---

> While we speak about our "Judeo-Christian civilization," the coupling of the two terms "Judaic" and "Christian" does not suffice to eliminate the underlying tension between them. Judaism is one of a family of *rival* religions, and the scriptures of Jewish antiquity are texts employed by each scriptural religion in a sense contrary to the readings of the others. The classic literature of the Hellenic culture, on the other hand, may be subject to varying scholarly and aesthetic readings, but it has not set the Greeks against the English, French, German, or any other national traditions of classical study (p. 186, his italics).

The notion of a "Judeo-Christian tradition" implies the existence of a common conceptuality to Judaism and Christianity, so that the divergences are limited to minor isses (e.g., the name of the messiah). This position does not reckon with the inner character of rabbinic thought, a character to which justice cannot be done by elucidation of some putative "rabbinic theology." The tools that will enable a Hellenico-Christian culture to grasp the inner dynamics of rabbinic thinking have not yet been forged, although there are some hopeful signs on the horizon. In the meantime, see the works of Kadushin and Handelman (esp. pp. 51–82).

[29] Relativism is also problematic for philosophy and probably indefensible. On the contemporary debate, see Bernstein. If, indeed, as Bernstein says, a position beyond these antinomies is emerging, it should help those wishing to live in both the religious and the historico-critical worlds without imposing one paradigm upon the other. In the terms of his dichotomy, both the traditionalist and the historical critic are objectivist. They believe that religious faith and historical reconstruction, respectively, provide us secure knowledge of what the text really means (although not all religions are equally universalistic/imperialistic). The desegregation of programs in biblical studies in recent decades promotes a contrasting relativism. Whether the desegregation can endure without producing interpretive anarchy remains to be seen.

being put into the unenviable position of an ex-emperor who has to learn to be a good neighbor. As of yet, no new emperor has assumed the throne. Given the social mix increasingly characteristic of the field, the throne is likely to be vacant for a long time. In this, the future of biblical studies will surely be different from the past.[30]

WORKS CONSULTED

Achtemeier, P. J.
1983   "An Apocalyptic Shift in Early Christian Tradition,"
          CBQ 45: 231–248.

Alt, A.
1968   "The Origins of Israelite Law," In *Essays on Old Testa-
          ment History and Religion.* Garden City: Double-
          day. Pp. 101–171. ["Die Ursprünge des is-
          raelitischen Rechts". Berichte über die Verhand-
          lungen der Sächsischen Akademie der Wissenschaft
          zu Leipzig, Philologischhistorisch Klass 86:1;
          Leipzig: S. Hirzel, 1934].

Assmann, J.
1982   "Die Zeugung des Sohnes," in *Funktionen und
          Leistungen des Mythos: Drei Altorientalische
          Beispiele.* Eds. J. Assmann et al.; OBO 48; Göt-
          tingen: Vandenhoeck and Ruprecht; Freiburg: Uni-
          versitätsverlag. Pp. 13–61.

Bainton, R.
1950   *Here I Stand: A Life of Martin Luther.* Nashville and
          New York: Abingdon-Cokesbury.

Baumgärtel, F.
1963   "The Hermeneutical Problem of the Old Testament,"
          in *Essays on Old Testament Hermeneutics.* Ed. C.
          Westermann. Richmond: John Knox. Pp. 134–159.
          ["Das hermeneutische Problem des Alten Testa-
          ments," *TLZ* 79 (1954): 199–212.

[30]Thanks are due to Professors J. Coert Rylaarsdam, Robert Cohn, John J. Collins, Lynn Poland, and Tsvi Abusch, Rabbi Joel Poupko, Mr. Jeffrey Gresser, and Mr. John Burgess for their comments about earlier drafts of this paper. Any errors that remain are my responsibility. Early forms of this essay were given at a meeting of the Old Testament professors group of the Chicago Cluster of Theological Schools in November, 1983, and at the faculty retreat of the University of Chicago Divinity School, November, 1984.

Bernstein, R. J.
1983   *Beyond Objectivism and Relativism: Science, Hermeneutics, and Praxis.* Philadelphia: University of Pennsylvania.

Betz, H. D.
1985   "The Hermeneutical Principles of the Sermon on the Mount (Matt 5:17–20)," in *Essays on the Sermon on the Mount.* Philadelphia: Fortress. Pp. 37–53. ["Die hermeneutischen Prinzipien in der Bergpredigt Mt 5, 17–20," in *Verifikationen.* Ed. E. Jüngel et al.; Tübingen: Mohr/Siebeck, 1982. Pp. 27–41].
1979   *Galatians.* Hermeneia; Philadelphia: Fortress.

Blenkinsopp, J.
1984   "Old Testament Theology and the Jewish-Christian Connection," *JSOT* 28: 3–15.

Bright, J.
1981   *History of Israel.* 3rd ed.; Philadelphia: Westminister.

van Buren, P. M.
1976   *The Burden of Freedom: Americans and the God of Israel.* New York: Seabury.

Childs, B. S.
1979   *Introduction to the Old Testament as Scripture.* Philadelphia: Fortress/London: SCM.

Cohen, A. A.
1969   "The Myth of the Judeo-Christian Tradition." *Commentary* 48:5, (November): 73–77.

Coogan, M. D.
1978   *Stories from Ancient Canaan.* Philadelphia: Westminster.

Cross, F. M.
1973   *Canaanite Myth and Hebrew Epic,* Cambridge: Harvard University.
1977   "'el'', in *Theological Dictionary of the Old Testament* (Eds. G. J. Botterweck and H. Ringgren); rev. ed.; Grand Rapids: Eerdmans 1.242–261. [*Theologische Wörterbuch zum Alten Testament,* fascicle 1–4; Stuttgart: W. Kohlhammer, 1970–1972].

Eichrodt, W.
1961   *Theology of the Old Testament,* Philadelphia: Westminster. [*Theologie des Alten Testaments* [Leipzig: J. C. Hinrichs, 1933–39 (3 vols.)].

Gerrish, B. A.
1982   "The Word of God and the Words of Scripture: Luther
          and Calvin on Biblical Authority," in *The Old Protes-
          tantism and the New: Essays on the Reformation
          Heritage*. Chicago: University of Chicago. Pp. 51–
          68.

Gese, H.
1981   *Essays on Biblical Theology*. Minneapolis: Augsburg.
          [*Zur biblischen Theologie: Alttestamentliche
          Vorträge*. Munich: Chr. Kaiser, 1977].

Gunneweg, A. H. J.
1978   *Understanding the Old Testament*. OTL; Philadelphia:
          Westminster [*Vom Verstehen des Alten Testaments*.
          ATD Sup 5; Göttingen: Vandenhoeck and Ruprecht,
          1977].

Hallo, W. W. et al. (Eds.).
1980   *Scripture in Context*. Pittsburgh: Pickwick.

Halpern, B(en)
1983   "History and Religion: The Ambiguous Uses of Jewish
          History," in *Take Judaism, for Example: Studies To-
          ward the Comparison of Religions*. Ed. J. Neusner;
          Chicago: University of Chicago. Pp. 185–195.

Handelman, S. A.
1983   *The Slayers of Moses: The Emergence of Rabbinic In-
          terpretation in Modern Literary Theory*. Albany:
          State University of New York.

Hegel, G. F. W.
1970   *Der Geist des Christentums und sein Schicksal*. Texte
          zur Kirchen—und Theologiegeschichte 12; Güter-
          sloh: Gütersloher Verlagshaus.

Hengel, M.
1974   *Judaism and Hellenism, vol. 1*. Philadelphia: Fortress/
          London: SCM. [*Judentum und Hellenismus* (2nd
          ed.; WUNT 10; Tübingen: J. C. B. Mohr/Paul Sie-
          beck, 1973].

Herrmann, S.
1975   *A History of Israel in Old Testament Times*. Phila-
          delphia: Fortress/London: SCM. [*Geschichte Israels
          in alttestamentlicher Zeit*. Munich: Chr. Kaiser,
          1973].

Heschel, A. J.
1951   *The Sabbath*. New York: Farrar, Straus, and Giroux.

Jacobson, D.
1982   *The Story of the Stories*. New York: Harper and Row.
Kadushin, M.
1938   *Organic Thinking: A Study in Rabbinic Thought*. New
          York: Jewish Theological Seminary of America.
Kaufmann, Y.
1937–1956 *Tôlĕdôt Hāʾĕmûnâ Hayyiśrāʾēlît*. Jerusalem: Bialik;
          Tel-Aviv: Debir, 5736 [seventh printing]) (The
          book appeared in segments between 1937–1956.).
Kelsey, D. H.
1975   *The Uses of Scripture in Recent Theology*. Philadelphia:
          Fortress.
Klein, C.
1978   *Anti-Judaism in Christian Theology*. London: SPCK.
Lauterbach, J. Z. (Ed.)
1933   *Mekilta de-Rabbi Ishmael*, 3 vols. Philadelphia: Jewish
          Publication Society.
Levenson, J. D.
1987   "Why Jews are Not Interested in Biblical Theology," in
          Judaic Perspectives on Ancient Israel. Ed. J. Neus-
          ner et al. Philadelphia: Fortress. Pp. 281–307.
1985   "Is There a Counterpart in the Hebrew Bible to New
          Testament Anti-Semitism?", *JES* 22: 242–260.
1980   "The Theologies of Commandment in Biblical Israel,"
          HTR 73: 17–33.
Miles, J. A.
1981   "Radical Editing: Redaktionsgeschichte and the Aes-
          thetic of Willed Confusion," in *Traditions in Trans-
          formation*. Eds. B(aruch) Halpern and J. D.
          Levenson. Winona Lake, IN: Eisenbrauns. Pp. 9–
          31.
Mendenhall, G. E.
1975   "The Conflict Between Value Systems and Social Con-
          trol," in *Unity and Diversity*. Eds. H. Goedicke and
          J. J. M. Roberts; Johns Hopkins Near Eastern Stud-
          ies; Baltimore and London: Johns Hopkins Univer-
          sity. Pp. 169–180.
Noth, Martin.
1954   *Geschichte Israels*. 2nd ed., Göttingen: Vandenhoeck
          and Ruprecht. [*The History of Israel*. New York and
          Evanston: Harper and Row, 1958].

Perlitt, L.
1965   *Vatke und Wellhausen*. BZAW 94; Berlin: Töpelmann.

Des Pres, T.
1976   *The Survivor: An Anatomy of Life in the Death Camps*.
            New York: Oxford University.

Von Rad, G.
1965   *Old Testament Theology*. New York and Evanston:
            Harper and Row. [*Theologie des Alten Testaments*.
            Munich: Chr. Kaiser, 2 vols., 1957–1960].
1966a   "The Form-Critical Problem of the Hexateuch," in *The
            Problem of the Hexateuch and Other Essays*. New
            York: McGraw-Hill.
1966b   "Faith Reckoned as Righteousness," in *The Problem*
            (1966a). Pp. 125–130. ["Die Anrechung des
            Glaubens zur Gerechtigkeit," *TLZ* 76 (1951): 129–
            132.]

Rendtorff, R.
1981   "Die Hebräische Bibel als Grundlage christlich-the-
            ologischer Aussagen über das Judentum," in *Jüdi-
            sche Existenz und die Erneuerung der christlichen
            Theologie*. Ed. M. Stöhr; Abhandlungen zum
            christlich-jüdischen Dialog 11; Munich: Chr. Kaiser.
            Pp. 32–47.
1983   "The Jewish Bible and its Anti-Jewish Interpretation,"
            Christian Jewish Relations 16 (1983): 3–20.

Robinson, J. M.
1982   "Jesus: From Easter to Valentinus (or to the Apostles'
            Creed)," *JBL* 101: 5–37.

Rubenstein, R. L.
1966   "Religion and the Origins of the Death Camps, A Psy-
            choanalytic Interpretation," in *After Auschwitz*. In-
            dianapolis: Bobbs-Merrill, Pp. 1–44.
1983   "The Besieged Community in Ancient and Modern
            Times," *Michigan Quarterly Review* 22: 447–463.

Safrai, S.
1983   "And All is According to the Majority of Deeds," *Tarbiz*
            53: 33–40 (in Hebrew).

Saggs, H. W. F.
1978   *The Encounter With the Divine in Mesopotamia and
            Israel*. London: Athlone.

Sanders, E. P.
1977   *Paul and Palestinian Judaism*. Philadelphia: Fortress.

Schleiermacher, F.
1926   *Über die Religion: Reden an die Gebildeten unter ihren Verächtern* (Göttingen: Vandenhoeck and Ruprecht. [Original publication: Berlin: J. F. Unger, 1799].

Smend, R.
1982   "Wellhausen und das Judentum," *ZTK* 79: 249–282.

de Spinoza, B.
1951   *A Theologico-Political Treatise and a Political Treatise.* New York: Dover. [*Tractatus theologico-politicus.* Hamburg: Henricus Künraht, 1670].

Stendahl, K.
1963   "The Apostle Paul and the Introspective Conscience of the West," *HTR* 56: 199–215. rpt. in *Paul Among Jews and Gentiles.* Philadelphia: Fortress, 1976. Pp. 78–96.

Tal, U.
1975   *Christians and Jews in Germany.* Ithaca and London: Cornell University.

Urbach, E. E.
1975a   *The Sages.* Jerusalem: Magnes.
1975b   [Hebrew version: *Ḥazal.* Jerusalem: Magnes.

Weinfeld, M.
1981   "Old Testament—the Discipline and its Goals," *VT Sup* 32, Congress Volume, Vienna, 1980.
1979   "Getting at the Roots of Wellhausen's Understanding of the Law of Israel on the 100th Anniversary of the *Prolegomena*", Institute for Advanced Studies, The Hebrew University, report no. 14/79; Jerusalem: Hebrew University.
1973   "The Origin of the Apodictic Law," *VT* 13: 63–75.

Wellhausen, J.
1973   *Prolegomena to the History of Ancient Israel.* Edinburgh: A. and C. Black, 1885; rpt. Gloucester: Peter Smith. [*Prolegomena zur Geschichte Israels.* Berlin: G. Reimer, 1883].
1895   *Israelitische und jüdische Geschichte,* 2nd ed.; Berlin: Georg Reimer.
1874   *Die Pharisäer und die Sadducäer.* Greifswald: Bamberg, 1874.

Westermann, C.
1963   "Remarks on the Theses of Bultmann and Baumgärtel,"
            in *Essays on Old Testament*. Ed. Westermann; Rich-
            mond: John Knox. Pp. 123–133. [*Probleme alttesta-
            mentlicher Hermeneutik* TB 11; Munich: Chr. Kai-
            ser, 1960. Pp. 102–113].

Chapter 3

ON READING THE BIBLE CRITICALLY
AND OTHERWISE

Alan Cooper
Hebrew Union College
Jewish Institute of Religion

A colleague who knew of my predilection for literary theory and holistic biblical interpretation once asked me if I "accepted" Wellhausen. The question, as I learned later on, was prompted by two fears: that I might be a closet fundamentalist (that is, using literary criticism to make fundamentalism respectable); or that I might not be able to "do" higher criticism (that is, using literary criticism to mask incompetence). The underlying assumption, of course, is that the historical-critical study of the Bible represents "real" scholarship, while other approaches are at best ancillary, or at worst meretricious. There is, I think, a lingering feeling among biblical scholars that historical criticism represents the field at its scientific, value-free best. That feeling, in my view, is rooted in two hermeneutical errors: first, that *any* way of reading a text can be value-free; second, even granting the possibility of such a method, that it would be worth reading texts that way.

I do not deny the validity of historical-critical claims; I know that I am not a fundamentalist, and I hope I am no charlatan. But I am troubled by virtually all the historical-critical presuppositions about what the Bible is and about how and why it ought to be read. At the very least, I do not find them interesting. I also object to the historical-critical distancing of scholarly reading from so-called "precritical" interpretation, and from the general Bible-reading public which is rightly baffled by most biblical scholarship. The burgeoning "literary-critical" reaction against historical criticism provides a good opportunity for hermeneutical reflection, and for some speculation about the future of biblical studies.

The founder of modern biblical science, Benedict de Spinoza was, as Leo Strauss observes, "devoid of any sense of need for Scripture." (Strauss, 1965: 258). Spinoza's denigration of the Bible—his claim that it is (merely) a "human book" (Strauss, 1965: 263)—presupposes his hostility towards religion in general and religious authority in particular. As Richard H. Popkin notes, Spinoza "transformed Scripture from a source of knowledge, to an object of knowledge . . . . Scripture is . . . reduced to some odd writing of the Hebrews over two thousand years earlier, and is to be understood in this context." (Popkin, 1979:234).

"The whole knowledge of the Bible," according to Spinoza (1951: 1.101-103), "must be sought solely from itself"—which means three things: knowledge of "the nature and properties" of Hebrew; interpretation "in relation to the context . . . solely by means of the signification of the words . . . ."; and acquaintance with the author of each biblical book, "who he was, what was the occasion, and the epoch of his writing, whom did he write for, and in what language."

Spinoza illustrates his revolutionary "method of interpreting Scripture from its own history" with an illuminating anecdote (1951: 1.111-112). "It often happens," he writes, "that in different books we read stories in themselves similar, but which we judge differently, according to the opinions we have formed of the authors." Spinoza then mentions some stories, from Ariosto, Ovid, and the Bible respectively, about heroes who fly through the air and do other things "which from the point of view of reason are obviously absurd." Despite the likeness of the three stories, however, "we judge them very differently": Ariosto "only sought to amuse," Ovid "had a political object," and the Bible "a religious object." Spinoza does not explain the specific effects produced by those presumed different intentions. He simply reasserts his initial claim: the distinction is based on the different "opinions we had previously formed of the authors." "Thus," he concludes, "it is evidently necessary to know something of the authors of writings which are obscure or unintelligible, if we would interpret their meaning."

Now every one of Spinoza's methods of interpretation can be paralleled in the earlier writings of those pious commentators whom he despises (1951: 1.98-99). Here, for example, are some excerpts from Augustine's *De doctrina christiana* which may be considered in relation to Spinoza's three exegetical principles. First, on knowledge of languages:

Against unknown literal signs the sovereign remedy is a
knowledge of languages. And Latin-speaking men, whom
we have here undertaken to instruct, need two others for a
knowledge of Divine Scriptures, Hebrew and Greek . . . .
(2.11.16)

Second, on contextual interpretation:

. . . when a meaning is elicited whose uncertainty cannot
be resolved by the evidence of places in the Scriptures
whose meaning is certain, it remains to make it more clear
by recourse to reason, even if he whose words we seek to
understand did not perhaps intend that meaning. But this is
a dangerous pursuit; we shall walk much more safely with
the aid of the Scriptures themselves. When we wish to
examine passages obscured by figurative words, we should
either begin with a passage which is not controversial, or, if
it is controversial, we should conclude with testimonies
applied from places where they are found in the same
Scriptures.[1] (3.28.39)

And third, on history and authorial intention:

. . . whatever evidence we have of past times in that which
is called history helps us a great deal in the understanding of
the sacred books, even if we learn it outside of the Church
as a part of our childhood education. (2.28.42)

. . . he who examines the divine eloquence, desiring to
discover the intention of the author through whom the Holy
Spirit created the Scripture, whether he attains this end or
finds another meaning in the words not contrary to the right
faith, is free from blame if he has evidence from some other
place in the divine books. For the author himself may have
seen the same meaning in the words we seek to understand.
(3.27.38)

For Augustine, then, as for Spinoza, the first goal of the interpreter
is to use philological and historical knowledge, and sound exegetical
method, in order to recover the intended meaning of the biblical
author(s).

Spinoza's statement that the Bible sometimes appears "absurd,

---

[1] This is precisely the procedure Spinoza advocates for distinguishing between
"literal" and "metaphorical" meanings (1951: 1.101–103).

. . . obscure, or unintelligible" is also unoriginal. Biblical anthropomorphism, for example, posed exegetical problems for the earliest intepreters (Kadushin, 1973: 273-340). According to Origen (1966: 288), anyone who believes that the events related in Genesis 1–3 actually took place is "silly": "I do not think anyone will doubt that these are figurative expressions which indicate certain mysteries through a semblance of history and not through actual events."[2] All exegetical traditions of late antiquity took it for granted that the Bible abounded in obscurity and esoterica; the question was what to do about it.

The principal difference between Augustine and Spinoza lies not in the details of their exegetical methods, but in what they expected to find when they applied them. Augustine sought "knowledge" (e.g., 2.42.63), and Spinoza was after "meaning." Augustine would have agreed with Spinoza that we judge books "according to the opinions we have formed of their authors," but his Bible was a divinely authored or inspired repository of truth, while Spinoza's was a record of "the prejudices of an ancient people" (Strauss, 1965: 254–255; 1983: 150–151).

For earlier exegetes, obscurity was a goad to painstaking interpretation.[3] For Spinoza, it was mere defect—either in the author's ability to convey meaning, the process of transmission, or the historical knowledge of the interpreter. There was no "mystery" to discover, no precious knowledge or truth to be refined out of the ore of the text. The meaning of difficult passages may be worked out, but we must not "confound the meaning of a passage with its truth."(1951:1.101).

It is no surprise, then, that the first post-Spinozan historical critics sought to disengage Spinoza's exegetical method from the anti-religious and anti-biblical prejudices that produced it. Richard Simon, for example, advocated Spinoza's methods of Bible study while asserting that they need not lead to Spinoza's harsh conclusions about the Bible (Popkin, 1979: 236–237). Simon was perhaps first in the long line of historical critics to make this error about

[2] Cf. Philo, De opif. 54 (154); Leg. all. 1. 14 (43) (Loeb Philo, vol. 1, 122–123, 174–175). But contrast Augustine, De genesi ad litteram 8. 1. 1–4 (English translation: The Literal Meaning of Genesis, Vol. 2 [Ancient Christian Writers, No. 42; New York: Newman Press] 32–35, with the parallels cited on p. 253, n. 2).

[3] See, e.g., Augustine's commentary on Gen 3:9, in De genesi ad litteram 11. 34. 45 (ET, p. 167). Cf. Saadia's rationale for scriptural obscurity in the introduction to his Torah commentary, in Moshe Zucker (1984:4 [Arabic], 167 [Hebrew]).

Spinoza, for the historical method presupposes the anti-biblical attitude (*not* the reverse, as Simon would have it) (Strauss, 1965: 258–59; Combs, 1983: 7–28), and is inseparable from it. The method trivializes the Bible by design, and its application inevitably produces results which confirm the biases that engendered it.[4]

I refer to my interests and procedures as "literary-critical" because they are derived from writings on literary theory and studies of non-biblical literatures. Advocacy of literary-critical method does not, however, entail the ontological claim that the Bible *is* literature, only the assertion that it is interesting and enjoyable to read it that way.[5] The literary study of the Bible (as I understand it and practice it, anyway) seeks to redress imbalances in the perception of the Bible fostered by historical criticism.

Most fundamentally, it rejects the relegation of the book to the status of historical artifact—a work with documentary value but little else (Weiss, 1984: 28–46). The literary critic does not confuse understanding with archeology:

> When interpreting a text from a past age, the interpreter does not empty his mind or leave the present absolutely; he takes it with him and uses it to understand the dialectical encounter of his horizon with that of the literary work (Palmer, 1969: 251).

Authorial intention, even if it were recoverable—which it is not[6]—would be trivial for literary interpretation. And the historicity of the

---

[4]Spinoza's offspring often proved to be worse than the parent. For relevant discussion, see e.g., Jon Levenson's essay in this volume. Also Lou Silberman (1983: 75–82); Bernard Levinson (1979).

[5]On the difference between ontological and hermeneutical claims about the Bible, see my article, "On Reading Biblical Poetry," *Maarav* (in press).

[6]See especially David Hoy (1978: 11–40). For an alternative (with which I disagree) see Geoffrey Strickland (1981: 120–122). In general, literary theorists have followed Wayne Booth (1961: 71–77) in emphasizing an "implied author" who emerges from the text, as opposed to the "real author" who lies outside the bounds of the communication between text and reader. Readers create the intentionality of the text by their interpretations, and thus create an "author" in their own image. Spinoza's claim that we interpret texts in the light of the opinions we form about their authors is valid in a certain sense. He is, however, talking about the putative "real author" whose intentions can supposedly be determined from some a priori knowledge about "him." Contrast the remarks of Robert Crosman (1980: 161): "[W]e arrive at the 'author's meaning' precisely when we decide we have arrived there: we *make* the author's meaning! This is not to deny that readers generally believe, whatever interpretation they make of a text, that they have discovered the author's intended meaning. Their belief is perhaps the single most successful instance of what Stanley

events described in the Bible is irrelevant; indeed, the idea that either the meaning of the Bible or its truth depends on its historical accuracy is probably the silliest manifestation of historical criticism.[7]

The literary critic redefines history and historical knowledge in terms of *literary* history—as distinct from the events supposedly narrated by the text and the extrinsic factors that purportedly led to its creation. History thus defined is nothing but *our* relation to the work through time or, more concretely, the work mediated through the history of its interpretation (Jauss, 1982: 62–64; Holub, 1984: 159). We do not understand a text by placing it in *its* "historical context," but in *ours*. And we do that by assessing our response to the text in the light of the history of response to it, just as Spinoza did (for example in his critique of Maimonides, 1951: 1.114–119)— and just as I am doing in this paper. The great illusion that we must disavow is the idea that some "objective" meaning inheres in the text, a meaning which, as Hans Robert Jauss writes,

> . . . is revealed once and for all in the original work, and which an interpreter can restore at any time, provided he sets aside his own historical position and places himself, without any prejudices, into the original intention of the work. But the form and meaning of a work formative of tradition [and what work is more formative of tradition than the Bible?—AMC] are not the unchangeable dimensions or appearances of an aesthetic object, independent of perception in time and history: its potential of meaning only becomes progressively visible and definable in the subsequent changes of aesthetic experience, and dialogically so in the interaction between the literary work and the literary public (1982: 64).

The meaning of the work is not *in* the work, but in its actualization or concretization by interpreting communities (Fish, 1980: 170–173, 338–355; Cooper, in press).

Method, then—and this is true for *any* method—does not recover meaning but, instead, creates it. And the task of biblical scholarship, as I understand it, is not to invent increasingly arcane

---

Fish [1980] calls an 'interpretive strategy'—that is, a convention of reading." In a similar vein, see Northrop Frye (1982: 50), "A reader recreates everything he reads, more or less in his own image. . . ."—including, I would add, the author.

[7] See Morton Smith (1969:19–35), although I dispute his basically positive assessment of historical criticism.

methods in pursuit of exegetical novellae or chimerical histories, but to grapple with the process of interpretation itself. I make three assertions: that the Bible we possess is interpretable;[8] that it is worth interpreting; and that every moment in the history of interpretation—which is, as I have said, the Bible's true history—has its own claim to validity. And the goal of my reading is not to state what the text *does* mean, but what it *can* mean in the light of what it has meant.[9] In the rest of this paper, I will give two examples of how I strive towards that goal. The first illustrates how traditional exegesis (in this case both uncritical and unliteral) can get to the heart of a difficult text; the second points up the affinity between traditional and modern ideas about the openness or ambiguity of the text.

> *wayyiqrā' 'abrāhām šēm hammaqôm hahû' YHWH yir'eh*
> *'ăšer yē'āmēr hayyôm běhar YHWH yērā'eh*
>
> And Abraham named that site Adonai-yireh, whence the present saying, "on the Mount of the Lord there is vision."
> (NJPSV)

Genesis 22:14 has defeated modern critical commentators. The general consensus is that the verse contains a garbled etiology—"an explanation for a now lost name," in Burke Long's words (1968: 28–29). Verse 14a, according to John Skinner (1932: 330–331; also Proksch, 1924: 318–319), has been altered so that it no longer expresses its author's intention. Skinner praises Gunkel's "brilliant ingenuity" in reconstructing the lost original (missing place name and all). And verse 14b, Skinner avers, yields "no sense appropriate to the context."

For Martin Noth (1972: 115), it is clear that the whole story of the Akedah originally had nothing to do with Abraham: "The question as to why and when Abraham came to be the center of the story remains unanswerable." If, however, verse 14 did not obfuscate the name of the story's locale, it might, according to Noth, be possible to explain how the tradition was connected with Abraham.

The peculiar gist of such commentary on this verse is its penchant for seeking what is not in the text at the expense of what *is*

---

[8]This statement, of course, does not rule out text criticism. See Weiss (1984: 68–73) on this point.

[9]See the eloquent (and generally unheeded) remarks of Moshe Greenberg (1982–83: 10–12; 1981: 88–91).

there. After all, as Skinner argues [on what basis?], "the naming of the place is an essential feature of the legend." The historical critic is not required to interpret the defective received text, only to explain how it got corrupted and what it should have said. Traditional interpretations can safely be ignored; they are doomed from the outset by their uncritical response to the defective text (Greenberg, 1982–83: 10).

A few modern critics recognize that Genesis 22:14 is not incomprehensible as it stands. S.R. Driver, for example, offers a perfectly respectable interpretation, even allowing that the verse might contain ambiguous multiple entendres (1904: 219–220). Driver, naturally, does not pre-empt interpretation with the self-defeating assumption that the text has become something that it was not intended to be. Gerhard von Rad does believe that the text is a transformed etiology, but he offers, nonetheless, a brilliant interpretation—evidently because he takes the transformation to be artful rather than corrupting:

> . . . the name of the place has disappeared from the narrative; only the pun is left, and it now lends itself all the more to a subtle playful change of the supposedly basic word "see" from active to passive . . . The reader is here summoned to give free reign to his thoughts (1972: 242).

Von Rad's concluding sentence should, in my view, apply to the entire Bible. Engagement with the opaque (even esoteric) biblical text enables the willing reader to participate in the creation of a remarkable world of imagination (Cooper, 1983: 61–68)—a world in which, for example, a divine voice can order a father to sacrifice his son and thus his destiny.

Traditional exegesis of Genesis 22:14 contains many interesting efforts to understand the verse in its biblical context, and to determine its significance for the religious community. Shalom Spiegel, drawing on several Midrashic interpretations, notes that the verse is part of a "deliberate conjunction of . . . wordplays" about the root r-ʾ-h, "to see." (1967: 52, 67–70). Only in light of that stylistic play can the exegete hope to make sense of verse 14. As Martin Buber had already observed, r-ʾ-h is the "theme-word" of the entire Abraham story (1968: 41–42). The significance of Abraham's special "seeing" emerges in Genesis 22 "in all its depth and meaningfulness." In verse 14, Abraham "makes known the imperishable essence of this place. . .[T]he reciprocity of seeing between God and man is directly revealed to us."

Rashi's interpretation of Genesis 22:14 provides an object lesson in creative actualization of a difficult text. Here is his commentary in full:[10]

> *YHWH yir²eh.* Its literal meaning is in accordance with the Targum: "May the Lord choose this place as the dwelling of his Presence so that sacrifices may be offered here."
>
> *²ăšer yē²āmēr hayyôm.* That they might say of it throughout the generations, "In this mountain the Holy One, Blessed be He, reveals Himself to his people."
>
> *hayyôm.* [That is,] in future days, comparable to the expression *ʿad hayyôm hazzeh* ("until this day") which occurs throughout Scripture; for all future generations who read this verse will say *ʿad hayyôm hazzeh* in reference to their own time.
>
> Midrash Aggadah: May the Lord look upon this Akedah in order to forgive Israel each year and save them from retribution, so that it might be said on this day by all generations who come to the Mount of the Lord, "May Isaac's ashes be heaped up as an offering of atonement."

Rashi begins by asserting that Targum Onkelos has captured the "literal meaning" of the verse *(pĕšûtô kĕtargûmô).* What makes the assertion extraordinary is that this particular Onkelos is notoriously periphrastic:[11]

> And Abraham worshipped and prayed there in that place, saying, "Here before the Lord shall (future) generations worship." Therefore it is said, "On this day on this mountain did Abraham worship before the Lord."

As Mordechai Loewenstein correctly observes in his commentary on Onkelos, in the Targum's rendering the verse does not describe Abraham's naming of a place, but his praying, and the words *YHWH*

[10] The text can be found in any Rabbinic Bible *(Miqrā²ôt Gĕdôlôt)*, or in Abraham Berliner's edition (Frankfurt: Kauffmann, 1905) 44–45; the translation is mine.

[11] Even Skinner calls the Targum "interesting" (1930: 330). My translation of Onkelos is adapted from Moses Aberbach and Bernard Grossfeld (1982: 130). I depart from them in the last sentence, where I believe they have misconstrued the Targum's exegesis (see below). Note the discussion of the problems in the Targum in their notes (pp. 130–131). Other Targumic traditions are consistent with Onkelos, but are more expansive.

yirʾeh comprise the prayer.[12] There is nothing outlandish about translating Hebrew *q-r-ʾ* as "pray"; in this case, it cements the obvious literary relationship of Genesis 22 with Genesis 12 (especially 12:8; cf. also 13:4, 21:33). A modern Jewish commentator, Moshe Emanueli (1978: 307–308), has expanded this point nicely, suggesting that Abraham's words *YHWH yirʾeh* in verse 8 are an optative prayer ("May the Lord 'see' . . ."), which in verse 14 Abraham transforms into thanks in the durative ("The Lord always 'sees'.").[13]

The Targum reads the beginning of the verse as if it were *wayyiqrāʾ ʾabrāhām šām (!) ba(!)mmāqôm hahûʾ;*[14] the "alterations" are almost certainly exegetical, not evidence for a variant Hebrew text, since the translation is free in other respects. The Targum's elaboration of *YHWH yirʾeh*, which follows, contains no vestige of the underlying Hebrew. Rashi rectifies this problem by, in effect, rewriting the Targum—retaining its sense while drawing nearer to the Hebrew text:

> Targum: Here before the Lord shall future generations worship.
> Rashi: May the Lord choose [*yihḥar wĕyirʾeh lô*] this place
> . . . so that sacrifices may be offered here.

Rashi's *pĕšûtô kĕtargûmô* evidently applies only to the first half of the verse (Lowenstein, 1972: 75), since he goes his own way in the continuation. The crux of the matter is the interpretation of *hayyôm*, which the Targum takes retrospectively. Onkelos avoids the problem of the referent of *hayyôm* by making it adverbial to the following clause,[15] as if the Hebrew were *bayyôm hazzeh/hahûʾ*. There is no

---

[12] Mordechai Loewenstein, *Nepeš Haggēr* (1972: 75). Isaac Abravanel, among others, notes that there is no such place as "Adonai Yireh" anyway. He agrees that the words constitute a prayer (*Commentary on the Torah*, Warsaw ed., Vol. 1, 276a). Other commentators, including many of the Tosaphists, follow the tortured efforts of *Gen. Rab.* 56:10 (Albeck/Theodor ed., pp. 607–608) to turn *yirʾeh* into the *yĕrû*-element in "Jerusalem." See conveniently Jacob Gellis (1983: 2.216–218, §§ 1, 2, 4, 12).

[13] Note especially Abravanel's remarks on the verbal tenses (*Commentary on the Torah*, Warsaw ed., Vol. 1, 276a).

[14] Alternatively, with Nathan Adler (1973: 6a), *wayyiqrāʾ bĕšēm* (!) [YHWH] *ba(!)yyôm hahû*. Note also Adler's suggestion that Onkelos has conflated two originally distinct interpretations. In one, Abraham performed some ritual or offered a sacrifice; in the other, he prayed.

[15] Against the translation of Aberbach and Grossfeld (1982).

question, then, of *hayyôm* reflecting the point of view of a later author or editor, which would implicitly cast doubt on the Mosaic authorship of the verse.[16]

Rashi avoids that problem as well, but in a different way than the Targum. For him, the word *hayyôm* is to be understood from the historical standpoint of the reader rather than the author. The word occurs in the biblical text to stimulate all future readers of the text to make it meaningful for themselves. Thus, hermeneutically, Rashi anticipates von Rad's suggestion that "the reader is here summoned to give free reign to his thoughts." (Von Rad, 1972: 242). Rashi's suggestion, though, is not offered for lack of anything better, but as *the whole point* of the verse's problematic character. The text is purposefully and significantly difficult, and not defective for that.

The rest of Rashi's interpretation supplies two suggestions for how later readers might understand the verse. The first interpretation of *běhar YHWH yērā'eh* continues to find favor with many commentators:[17] "On this mountain the Holy One, Blessed be He, reveals Himself to His people"—obviously connecting this mountain with Jerusalem (so already 2 Chron 3:1). But this interpretation cannot apply for the *hayyôm* of the Jewish communities in the Diaspora, living long after the destruction of the Temple.

For his community, then, Rashi offers the "Midrash Aggadah," which is a homiletical gloss on Genesis 22:14 freely adapted from Genesis Rabbah 56:9 (Albeck/Theodor, pp. 605–607). Following the same method he used with the Targum, Rashi rewrites his midrashic source in order to make the nexus between the homily and the biblical text explicit. "In reference to their own time," then, Jews will incorporate the Akedah into their prayers:

> May the Lord look upon [*YHWH yir'eh*] this Akedah in order to forgive Israel each year. . .[18] so that it might be said this day [*kědê šeyē'āmēr hayyôm*] by all generations

[16]Which is exactly what Abraham Ibn Ezra does. See Joseph Bonfils, *Sāpnat Pa'nēah* Vol. 1 (Heidelberg: Carl Winter, 1911) 112, for an explanation of Ibn Ezra's position. Note also Levi ben Gershom's unfounded speculation on this point (*Commentary on the Torah*, Venice ed., 31a), rightly rejected by Abravanel.

[17]Some changes of vocalization are generally suggested. See the commentaries.

[18]Rashi's source explictly mentions Rosh Hashanah, the New Year, which is traditionally regarded as the date of the Akedah. Rashi's vagueness allows *hayyôm* to remain open to interpretation.

who come to the Mount of the Lord [bĕhar YHWH],[19]
"May Isaac's ashes be seen [yērā'eh] heaped up as an offering of atonement."

Rashi's conclusion weaves the text into a prayer which captures
the essence of the Akedah for the Jewish community. The Akedah is
the paradigmatic act of selfless sacrifice, and the merit earned in the
performance of that act benefits the community perpetually
(Spiegel, 1967: 73–76, 86–89). The merit of the Akedah is now
invoked in a prayer for divine mercy, actualizing for every believer
its "imperishable essence" (Buber, 1968: 41–42).

Now I am not advocating Rashi's exegesis as such. I regard it,
rather, as a sort of prolegomenon to the *appreciation* of a recalcitrant
biblical text. Rashi has followed a procedure which is, in my view,
fundamentally compatible with the literary-critical study of the Bible. First, he has assumed that the text has something to say—that it
must mean something. The fact that meaning does not spring to the
surface of the text on the first (or fiftieth) reading does not obviate
the search for it, or justify the argument that the text is meaningless.

Second, in our example Rashi has adhered strictly to the language of the text throughout his interpretation. That fact explains
the cogency of his initial interpretation in contrast to the Targum,
which might be dismissable as a free paraphrase. And it explains his
recasting of the Midrash so that the homily emerges specifically
from the verse and is expressed in the verse's terms.

Third, Rashi *explicates* the text, taking explication as William K.
Wimsatt (1965: 240) defines it: "the realization of the vastly more
rich and interesting implicit kinds of meaning." Rashi, faithful to the
history of intepretation, interprets maximally, striving after nuances
that represent hints or possibilities of meaning. The omnisignifi-
cance of texts was axiomatic for ancient interpreters, and that axiom
gains a sympathetic rehearing in the modern literary-critical emphasis on the ambiguity or openness of texts.[20]

There are, then, three hermeneutical principles here: the assumption that the text is meaningful; the demand that interpretation
be answerable to the text; and the principle that all interpretations
merely realize the text's possibilities: "new" interpretations, if they
adhere to the first two principles, then add to the repository of ideas
that is the history of interpretation.

---

[19] Evidently to be taken figuratively.
[20] I elaborate this point below in my second exegetical example.

All these principles are subordinate to the basic anti-historicist claims of literary criticism. In Richard Palmer's words (1969: 245), "Interpretation is not a taxonomical task of philological reconstruction and restoration (if this were possible). Interpretation calls upon the interpreter to render explicit a work's meaning today; interpretation calls upon one to bridge the historical distance between his horizon and that of the text." This last, as I have stressed, can only be done through the history of interpretation, which is the Bible's history. Thus the permanent relevance of Origen, Augustine, Rashi, and Spinoza (for example) to biblical scholarship.

My second exegetical example is Proverbs 8:30a, in which Wisdom says of herself, *wā'ehyeh 'eṣlô 'āmôn*, describing her relationship with God at the time of creation. The meaning of the word *'āmôn*, crucial for the understanding of the passage, is still debated, although all the basic possibilities have been known since antiquity.[21]

The interpretation of verse 30a is inhibited by its lack of a clear parallel. N.H. Tur-Sinai (1967: 282) claimed that the colon might simply be missing, but that is precisely the kind of claim that I would like to rule out of the discussion. The form *'āmôn* admits various meanings, of which two general kinds have particularly appealed to scholars:

1) Derived from a root meaning "to nurse"; hence, either "nurseling" *(*'āmûn)* or "nurse, teacher" *(*'ômēn)*.
2) A word meaning "artisan" or "vizier", perhaps a loan word from Akkadian *ummānu (*'ômān)*.

The context seems to support both kinds of meaning, and some authorities have tried to reconcile them in one way or another. Heinrich Ewald (1867: 106, 121–122) claimed that verses 30–31 say that Wisdom participated in creation as a beloved child ("mit Gott wie sein liebstes Kind künstlerisch die Welt selbst mit schaffen half. . ."); the interpretation seems to incorporate both senses of *'āmôn*, but Ewald's translation is simply "Künstlerin."

Another view, adopted by F. Hitzig (1858: 80–81) and A.B.

---

[21]See the versions. Also, e.g., *Gen. Rab.* 1:1; *Exod Rab.* 30:9; *Tanhuma Gen.* (beginning); *Seder Eliyahu Rab.* 31 (Friedmann ed., p. 160); *Abot derabbi Natan*, Version A, 31 (Schechter ed., p. 91). For a convenient summary of modern commentaries see Gemser (1963: 46) and Lang (1975: 93–95). Note that the discovery of a possible Akkadian cognate for *'āmôn* only reinforced one of the traditional interpretations.

Ehrlich (1913: 43), is that verses 30–31 are composite,[22] and actually reflect two different interpretations of 'āmôn. Ehrlich thought that v. 31 was a gloss added by an editor who disapproved of the anthropomorphism of v. 30. Hitzig claimed that vv. 30b-31a reflect the interpretation of Wisdom as a child, while vv. 30c and 31b depict her as an artisan. Like the above-cited suggestion of Tur-Sinai, this kind of exegesis makes no sense to me.

The fact that divergent interpretations of 'āmôn are both possible and plausible suggests to me that no single interpretation can contain the "real meaning" of the text. R. Stecher embodies the antithesis of the sort of scholarship I advocate in his rejection of the possible ambiguity of 'āmôn (Stecher, 1953: 431):

> Eine so sprunghafte Kombination der verschiedensten Gedanken und Vorstellungen möchte man dem Dichter von Prov 8, 22–31, den wir als meister seiner Kunst kennen lernen, nicht gerne zubilligen.

Against Stecher and his ilk, I would first cite the general remarks of Meir Weiss (1984: 75):

> Sometimes the poet intends the word to be understood in several senses simultaneously. However, in these cases the different meanings . . . are rather like separate threads twisted together . . . alternately revealed and concealed. . . .[T]here *is* no primary and no secondary meaning. The composition is polyphonic and all the voices are equal.

Weiss's position is, in turn, compatible with both traditional biblical interpretation and modern literary criticism. The best-known literary-critical authority on ambiguity, William Empson, even suggests that biblical language, with its "unreliable tenses, extraordinary idioms, and a strong taste for puns," inspired some of the ambiguity of English poetry (Empson, 1966: 193–194). The 'āmôn of Proverbs 8, I would suggest, falls squarely into Empson's third type of ambiguity, "when two ideas, which are connected only

---

[22] Cf. Adler's suggestion concerning Onkelos on Gen. 22:14 (above, n. 14). Note the implication that ambiguity, multiple meaning, or uncertainty must be explained as conflation or corruption (not artistry).

by being both relevant in the context, can be given in one word simultaneously." (1966: 102).[23]

Once the principle that 'āmôn might be ambigious is accepted, various interpretive possibilities open up. Apparent contradictions or anomalies in vv. 30–31 no longer need to be explained as the work of a glossator; nor need contradictory passages be reconciled in a forced manner. So, for example:

> 30a-b: wā'ehyeh 'eṣlô 'āmôn; wā'ehyeh ša'ăšû'îm yôm yôm[24] (i.e., I was constantly delighted to be his 'āmôn—in whatever sense).[25]
> 30c: meśaheqet lĕpānāyw bĕkol 'ēt (i.e., Wisdom as a child playing in God's presence).
> 31a: meśaheqet bĕtēbēl 'arṣô (i.e., Wisdom as artisan, playing on/with God's earth).
> 31b: wĕsa'ăšû'ay 'et bĕnê 'ādām (i.e., Wisdom as nurse or teacher, delighting in humankind).

Each colon of Proverbs 8:30–31 may be interpreted in the light of a different connotation of 'āmôn: first, in a general way (v. 30a-b); then, in three particular ways (30c-31b). There are, then, at least three possible interpretations of the 'āmôn in Proverbs 8:30. I reject any exegetical principle (pace Stecher) that would force me to choose among them, since none of the possibilities is unequivocally demanded or excluded by the text. If it could be shown that the author of the text intended it to have but one meaning,[26] it might diminish my appreciation of "him," but it would not affect my reading of the poem.

Stephen Geller (1983: 39–40) has recently argued that "rivalry between historical and literary approaches to the Bible must . . . be seen as . . . intellectual self-destruction." But Geller bases that argument on a sophisticated understanding of "history" which is largely incompatible with the theories and practices of biblical scholars. The end of conventional historical criticism will not mean

---

[23] For some suggestive biblical illustrations, see Schramm (1976: 178–191).

[24] Rejecting the widely accepted emendation to ša'ăšû'ayw (supported by LXX). See Cooper (1976: 119).

[25] Being an 'āmôn is the general way in which Wisdom is "there" at Creation— thus the phonetic play between šAM'ANi (v. 27) and 'āmôn. This point will be elaborated elsewhere in a fuller discussion of Prov 8:22–31.

[26] My imagined author, of course, could have no such intention.

the end of biblical history. On the contrary, a new form of historical consciousness can emerge from the literary-critical model—so that biblical scholars might connect simultaneously with the full history of their discipline, and with the broader world of humanistic discourse they inhabit.

WORKS CONSULTED

Aberbach, Moses and Grossfeld, Bernard
1982   *Targum Onkelos to Genesis*. New York: Ktav.

Adler, Nathan
1973   *Nĕtînâ Laggēr*. Repr. in *Ôṣar Mĕpārĕšê Hattôrâ*, vol. 1. Jerusalem: n.p. [orig. 1875].

Augustine
1958   *On Christian Doctrine*. Indianapolis: Bobbs-Merrill.

Booth, Wayne
1961   *The Rhetoric of Fiction*. Chicago: University of Chicago.

Buber, Martin
1968   "Abraham the Seer." *On the Bible*. New York: Schocken.

Combs, Eugene
1983   "Spinoza's Method of Biblical Interpretation and his Political Philosophy." *Modernity and Responsibility; Essays for George Grant*. ed. Eugene Combs. Toronto: University of Toronto.

Cooper Alan
in press "On Reading Biblical Poetry." *Maarav*.
1983   "The Act of Reading the Bible." *Proceedings of the Eighth World Congress of Jewish Studies* (Panel Sessions: Bible Studies and Hebrew Language). Jerusalem: World Union of Jewish Studies.
1976   "Biblical Poetics: A Linguistic Approach." Yale University Ph.D. Dissertation.

Crosman, Robert
1980   "Do Readers Make Meaning?" *The Reader in the Text*. ed. Susan R. Suleiman and Inge Crosman. Princeton: Princeton University.

Driver, S. R.
1904   *The Book of Genesis*. Westminster Commentaries; London: Methuen.

Ehrlich, A. B.
1913   *Randglossen zur hebräischen Bibel,* vol. 6. Leipzig: Hinrichs.

Emanueli, Moshe
1978   *Sēper Bĕrēʾšit: Hesbērîm wĕhēʾārôt.* Tel-Aviv: Society for Biblical Research.

Empson, William
1966   *Seven Types of Ambiguity.* New York: New Directions.

Ewald, Heinrich
1867   *Die Dichter des Alten Bundes,* vol. 2. Göttingen: Vandenhoeck & Ruprecht.

Fish, Stanley
1980   *Is There a Text in this Class?* Cambridge: Harvard University.

Frye, Northrop
1982   "Literature, History, and Language." *The Horizon of Literature.* ed. Paul Hernadi. Lincoln: University of Nebraska.

Geller, Stephen A.
1983   "Through Windows and Mirrors into the Bible: History, Literature and Language in the Study of the Text." *A Sense of Text: The Art of Language in the Study of Biblical Literature.* JQR Sup.; Winona Lake: Eisenbrauns.

Gellis, Jacob
1983   *Sēfer Tôsāfôt Hashālēm,* vol. 2. Jerusalem: Mifal Tosafot Hashalem.

Gemser, B.
1963   *Sprüche Salomos.* HAT I:16; Tübingen: Mohr.

Greenberg, Moshe
1982/3   "Can Modern Critical Bible Scholarship Have a Jewish Character?" *Immanuel* 15: 10–12.
1981   "The True Meaning of the Bible" (Hebrew). *Shedemot* 79: 88–91.

Hitzig, Ferdinand
1858   *Die Sprüche Salomos übersetzt und ausgelegt.* Zürich: Fussl.

Holub, Robert C.
1984   *Reception Theory: A Critical Introduction.* London: Methuen.

Hoy, David
1978   *The Critical Circle.* Berkeley: University of California.

Jauss, Hans Robert
1982   *Toward an Aesthetic of Reception*. Minneapolis: University of Minnesota.

Kadushin, Max
1972   *The Rabbinic Mind*. New York: Bloch.

Lang, Bernhard
1975   *Frau Weisheit*. Dusseldorf: Patmos.

Levinson, Bernard
1979   "Pentateuch and History in Martin Noth and John Bright." McMaster University M.A. Thesis.

Loewenstein, Mordechai
1972   *Nepeš Haggēr*. Repr. Jerusalem: Makor [orig. 1906].

Long, Burke O.
1968   *The Problem of Etiological Narrative in the Old Testament*. BZAW 108; Berlin: Töpelmann.

Noth, Martin
1972   *A History of Pentateuchal Traditions*. Englewood Cliffs: Prentice-Hall.

Origen
1966   *Origen on First Principles*. N.Y.: Harper.

Palmer, Richard E.
1969   *Hermeneutics*. Evanston: Northwestern University.

Popkin, Richard H.
1979   *The History of Scepticism from Erasmus to Spinoza*. Berkeley: University of California.

Proksch, Otto
1924   *Die Genesis übersetzt und erklärt*. KAT; Leipzig: Deichert.

Rad, Gerhard von
1972   *Genesis: A Commentary*. OTL; Philadelphia: Westminster.

Schramm, Gene
1976   "Poetic Patterning in Biblical Hebrew." *Michigan Oriental Studies in Honor of George G. Cameron*. ed. Louis L. Orlin. Ann Arbor: University of Michigan.

Silberman, Lou
1982   "Wellhausen and Judaism." *Semeia* 25: 75–82.

Skinner, John
1930   *A Critical and Exegetical Commentary on Genesis*. ICC; Edinburgh: Clark.

Smith, Morton
1969   "The Present State of Old Testament Studies." *JBL* 88:
            19–35.

Spiegel, Shalom
1967   *The Last Trial*. N.Y.: Schocken.

Spinoza, Benedict de
1951   *Theologico-Political Treatise. The Chief Works of Bene-
            dict de Spinoza*, vol. 1. Repr. N.Y.: Dover [orig.
            1883].

Stecher, R.
1953   "Die persönliche Weisheit in den Proverbien Kap. 8."
            ZKT 75: 411–451.

Strauss, Leo
1983   "Jerusalem and Athens: Some Introductory Reflec-
            tions." *Studies in Platonic Political Philosophy*. Chi-
            cago: University of Chicago.
1965   *Spinoza's Critique of Religion*. N.Y.: Schocken.

Strickland, Geoffrey
1981   *Structuralism or Criticism? Thoughts on how we read*.
            Cambridge: Cambridge University.

Tur-Sinai, N. H.
1967   *Pĕšûtô šel Miqrāʾ*, vol. 4:1. Jerusalem: Kiryat Sefer.

Weiss, Meir
1984   *The Bible from Within*. Jerusalem: Magnes.

Wimsatt, William K.
1965   *Hateful Contraries*. Lexington: University of Ken-
            tucky.

Zucker, Moshe
1984   *Saadya's Commentary on Genesis*. N.Y.: Jewish Theo-
            logical Seminary.

Chapter 4

THE RECESSION OF BIBLICAL SOURCE CRITICISM

Richard Elliott Friedman
The University of California, San Diego

Source criticism of the Hebrew Bible is suffering a recession currently and is even occasionally in disrepute. The President of the Society of Biblical Literature in his Presidential address at the Annual Meeting in 1982, in referring to source criticism, spoke of the "failure of a fiction," and he depicted source criticism as useful in the sense that the Ptolemaic system was useful (Silberman, 1983: 102). A scholar in modern Hebrew and comparative literature, Robert Alter, described what biblical scholars do as virtually entirely "excavative scholarship," apparently meaning the term *excavation* as slightly pejorative in a context of *Bible* (1974: 70). Thank heavens that Albright did not live to hear it.

Indeed, most biblical scholars of our own generation have studied, but do not practice, source-critical analysis. And the current literary study of the Bible, which is potentially such a useful development in the field, *usually* ignores it. Ignores it without even feeling the need to defend such an approach with so much as an appeal to Derrida or to the intentional fallacy. The worst offenders are the seekers of chiasms. Since our bicameral brains seem to incline toward chiastic expression, it fits virtually every passage in the Bible, the Gettysburg Address, every rock song ever composed, palendromes, and tic-tac-toe. It works even on passages which are composite, presumably because each of the component texts is in some way chiastic, and the chiastically-programmed editor assembled them according to the structural program as well. The sources get lost in the shuffle.

It was not always so. The very term "literary criticism" used to mean source criticism. It was the foundation of the field. The founders suffered for the opportunity to pursue it. The works of

Masius, Spinoza, and Simon, among others, were placed on the *Index Librorum Prohibitorum*. De la Peyere, a French Calvinist, was arrested and informed that in order to be released he would have to become Catholic and recant to the Pope. He did. Simon was expelled from the Congregation of the Oratory. All but six of 1300 copies of his book were burned. John Hampden, the English translator of the work, did not fare much better. As Edward Gray worded it, in proper British understatement, Hampden "repudiated the opinions he had held in common with Simon . . . in 1688, probably shortly before his release from the Tower" (Gray, 1929: 101). Ostensibly for political reasons, De Wette was expelled from his professorship. Bishop Colenso became known as the "wicked bishop." William Robertson Smith was tried for heresy, and cleared, but was expelled from his chair at Aberdeen. And at Marburg, Wellhausen was forbidden to teach Old Testament.

And today: you cannot do historical study of the Bible without source criticism. At minimum, you have to be able to date your evidence. And as for the place of source-critical analysis in literary study of the Bible, you meet a *person* when you read a text. And on the other side of the pen, when you *write* a text, you *are* a person, who acquaints his or her reader, to some extent, willingly or not, with oneself. Carrying the intentional fallacy to extremes is, intentionally or unintentionally, fallacious—a way of avoiding the very difficult task of determining the connections between the writer and his or her product. An indicator of our natural desire to find a *homo sapiens* behind a text is the fact that so many scholars and their students refer to J, E, D, and P as people: "J tells *his* story," "E thinks such-and-such; *his* theology is so-and-so." J, E, D, and P were originally sigla that stood for texts, not people.

Beside source criticism's usefulness to historical and literary study, there is also the matter that we really want to know who wrote the Bible. (It is the Bible, after all.) In my experience, lay audiences are fascinated by this subject; and students who have first read the text of the Torah and other narrative books and then go back to look into who produced them, when, and why, also are interested, only apprehensive as to how they can ever master it for an examination. I have also found, among colleagues who do not normally work on source critical matters in their primary scholarly interests, that when they are drawn into a discussion of the sources and who produced them and why, they become interested, often enthusiastically so, in the pursuit.

If source criticism is still useful, and usually necessary, for historical and literary study, and if it is still interesting to scholars, students, and laypersons, why then has it diminished in the field? I think that the reason, first, is that we really were stymied. The initial successes of the enterprise were the proof that sources really did exist, the identification of those sources, and at least some relative chronology, and occasionally more specific placement of sources in their historical moment. After these initial successes however, which after all took hundreds of years, the biblical source critics arrived at a stone wall. It was fine to be able to identify sources, but the more interesting literary-historical questions remained un-answered and perhaps seemingly unanswerable: What was the rela-tionship of the sources? *Why* were they produced? Why were they combined in this way? The clearest answer to any of these questions was the *why* of the production of the book of Deuteronomy, which even Hobbes, long before De Wette identified with the Josianic reform of 622 B.C. (Hobbes, 1651: Part 3, Chapter 33, 201; De Wette, 1805). But in time, fewer scholars regarded D as having been written on or for that occasion, but rather as having been older and merely *promulgated* in 622. The sources remained largely myste-rious in themselves and relative to one another. Without this infor-mation, the potential contributions of source critical inquiry to historical and literary study were necessarily limited.

I believe that sufficient work has now been done to make it possible to deal with these matters successfully. Following is a sketch of the primary sources of the Pentateuch in terms of their literary relationship to each other.

To begin with J and E: Scholars have often viewed them as being products of the divided kingdoms of Israel and Judah following the reign of Solomon, with E deriving from Israel and J from Judah. Let me review the J and E narratives with an eye to confirming this view of *where*, and to answering the questions of *who, why,* and *what was their relationship.* What follows is a synthesis of a body of previous scholarship and my own observations.

The Abraham traditions begin with J, with key events occurring at Mamre/Hebron. Hebron was of course David's capital for the first seven years of his reign. It was the principal city of Judah, and it was a major center of the Aaronid priesthood, which appears to have long been the dominant priestly house of Judah following Solomon's expulsion of Abiathar from his position of shared leadership in the priestly hierarchy at Jerusalem. J's advocacy of the Davidic kingdom seems also to be reflected in the Abrahamic covenant's promised territorial boundaries: "from the river of Egypt to the Euphrates," which correspond to David's sphere of influence. What is promised to Abraham is fulfilled in David. The Abrahamic covenant is in fact emphasized more than the Sinai covenant in J. E, meanwhile, does not *have* an account of an Abrahamic covenant. The E source makes *Moses* the turning point, the age of the revelation of the divine name, the age of the first covenant. In sheer quantity, J has more material on the patriarchs; E has more on Moses at Horeb.

It is also J that contains the account of Sodom and Gomorrah, which also were located by tradition in the territory of Judah.

In the accounts of Jacob, northern and southern interests again fit characteristics of the E and J texts respectively. Both J and E have Beth-El stories, and both north and south had *claims* on Beth-El. Located near the border between the two kingdoms, Beth-El was one of Jeroboam's two primary religious centers for Israel, but Judah's interest in it is reflected at the very least in Josiah's reacquisition of that town at the arrival of an opportune moment. Certainly Israel's interest in Beth-El was greater than Judah's, and E in fact emphasizes the significance of Beth-El far more than does, J, both in terms of space and of detail.

In E Jacob sees face-to-face and wrestles with ʾĕlōhīm, and is named yiśrā-ʾēl, as a result of which he names the place of the theophany pĕnîʾēl. It was Jeroboam, King of Israel, who built the city of Peniel (1 Kings 12:25); and this story is, after all, the etiology of the name of the northern kingdom, despite Judah's former place under that broad appellation.

The key accounts of Jacob's supplanting his brother Esau/Edom appear in J; Judah bordered Edom, Israel did not. Yahweh's prediction to Rebekah that "two nations are in your womb, and the greater will serve the younger" squares with the reality that the young kingdom of Judah, under David, came to dominate the older kingdom of Edom. Isaac's deathbed promise of Jacob's supplanting of Esau also presumably reflects David's conquest of Edom (2 Samuel 8:14); and J's portrayal of Isaac's compensatory blessing to Esau, that Esau one day "will break [your brother's] yoke from your neck" (Genesis 27:40) seems to reflect either Edom's rebellion under Haddad against Solomon or the final independence of Edom from Judah at the time of Jehoram. J's special interest in Judah presumably accounts for the presence of the Edomite king list in Genesis 36, which was one of the first enigmas that medieval commentators identified with regard to the tradition of Mosaic authorship. Spinoza already related it to David's defeat of Edom.

The J and E accounts of Jacob's sons and daughter bring further indications of the proveniences of E and J. In the accounts of the naming of the twelve sons and two grandsons of Jacob, who became eponymous ancestors of tribes, the parent in almost every case makes reference to the deity. If we divide the etiological accounts between those that identify the deity as Elohim and those that identify him as Yahweh, we find that they break into two blocks. Those that use Elohim are Dan, Naphtali, Gad, Asher, Issachar, Zebulun, and Ephraim and Manasseh. That is, the northern tribes. Those that use the name Yahweh are Reuben, Simeon, Levi, and Judah. What was the fate of these four tribes historically, and what is the fate of these four sons in the biblical accounts? These are the four oldest sons of Jacob. Reuben, the firstborn, loses primacy because he sleeps with his father's concubine. The second and third born, Simeon and Levi, lose their places in the succession because of their violent destruction of Shechem in the matter of their sister Dinah. The Genesis 49 blessing of Jacob underlines this. Judah, the eponymous ancestor of the Davidic kingdom, is the recipient of the blessing of primacy and dominion over his brothers. This, of course, corresponds to the historical picture. The Reubenite territory, cut off from the cis-Jordanian tribes by the Dead Sea to the west, and bordered by Moab to the south and Ammon to the northeast, was strategically the most vulnerable of the tribes. It did not survive as an independent entity on its land. Simeon's holdings apparently were assimilated to those of Judah, Simeon, too, losing any independent territorial identity (Joshua 19:1-9). Levi, already in early sources, is understood to be landless. The J accounts thus justify proleptically the rise of Judah to preeminence. It is also interesting to recall in this context that scholars have in the past pointed out similarities of language and concerns between the J source and the Court History of David. In this respect, the concern with *succession* here in J is visibly in kinship to the succession narrative of the Court History, even to the point of there being four sons of David depicted in the Court History as contenders for the place of their father, with the fourth son the victor, and four sons of Jacob depicted in J as in line for the place of their father, with the fourth son the victor. Indeed, the offenses of Reuben, Simeon, and Levi are the offenses of Absalom, who violently avenges a sexual assault on his sister and sleeps with his father's concubines.

The birth and naming account of Benjamin, separated from the other accounts, is arguably J or E, which is reconcilable either way, insofar as the Benjaminite territory was alligned with Judah but nonetheless had a history of being tied to the north, with the Benjaminite Saul the first king of all Israel and his son Ishbaal the king of the initially separated northern kingdom.

The portrayal of Simeon's and Levi's violent destruction of Shechem, for which their father criticizes them, serves another purpose for J in casting aspersions on the background of Shechem itself, which Jeroboam had built as his capital (1 Kings 12:25), and which had been the site of Israel's rejection of Rehoboam's kingship. The E version, meanwhile, simply reports that Jacob purchased it.

The naming of Joseph contains a clear doublet, one deriving his name from the root *'sp* and one from the root *ysp*, one referring to the deity as Yahweh, one referring to him as Elohim. Joseph's importance in the tradition as the mechanism that brings the Israelites to Egypt would account for his significant role in both J and E, but their respective *treatments* of Joseph again reflect their proveniences. As is often pointed out, in E it is Reuben, the first-born, who saves Joseph from death at the hand of his brothers, but in J it is Judah. In E it is Reuben who offers surety for the safe return of Benjamin to Jacob; in J it is Judah who takes responsibility for Benjamin. This last item may also reflect the overlapping northern and southern interests in the tribe of Benjamin to which I have already referred.

Whereas the birthright passes to Judah in J, in E it passes to Joseph. The double portion of the firstborn is Joseph's, expressed in the promotion of his two sons, Ephraim and Manasseh, to the status of their eleven uncles. When Jacob thus promotes Ephraim and Manasseh, moreover, he reverses his hands so as to place his right hand on the head of the younger of the two, Ephraim, declaring that Ephraim will be the greater. Ephraim is the tribe of Jeroboam, the location of Shechem. Indeed the author of E, who puns regularly, expresses Joseph's double portion as: *škm 'ḥd 'l 'ḥyk* (Gen 48:22). The fact is that, of all the sons of Jacob, the only two who have extended narratives about them are Joseph, the ancestor of the tribe from which Jeroboam comes, and Judah, the eponymous ancestor of the home tribe of David, Solomon, and Rehoboam. The apparently competing throne names of *yārob'ām* and *rĕḥab'ām*, moreover, may also be fodder for paronomasia in J, in which the root *rḥb* occurs five times (Gen 13:17; 26:22; 34:21; Exod 3:8; 34:24), connoting the expansion of the nation. It never occurs in E.

The extended narrative regarding Jacob's son Judah to which I have referred is also worth noting in the context of the tie of J to the Davidic kingdom. It is, first of all, the story of the origin of the Judahite clans, and it concludes with the report of the bursting forth of the second born Peres, the eponymous ancestor of the clan of David. According to this account in Genesis 38, further, Judah marries a Canaanite woman who is identified only as *bat šûaᶜ*. David marries a woman named *bat sĕbaᶜ*. Did the ancient Judean's ear hear a similarity between the names *ba šûaᶜ* and *bat šebaᶜ*? The former, certainly, is spelled with a *mater lectionis* which was pronounced even consonantally as a *waw*, not as a *vav*. Still, the only *vav/bet* spelling error in the Hebrew Bible is the reference in 1 Chronicles 3:5 to the wife of *David*, who is identified there as *bat šûaᶜ* instead of *bat šebaᶜ*.

The story of Judah and Tamar which follows manifests further examples of affinities of J to the Court History of David, including the pivotal role of a Tamar in each, and, again, a concern with succession in each, and a patent, significant role of sexual relations in each, both involving a sexual rejection of a victimized heroine.

The J and E accounts in the book Exodus further contribute to identifying the background and character of the two sources. It is difficult to determine the sources of Exodus 1, though in it the deity is referred to *by the narrator* only as Elohim, which J never does. That is one reason for seeing it as entirely or partly E. There is another ground for seeing E here in light of the likelihood of a tie of E to Israel and J to Judah. Probably the most offensive of the Solomonic economic policies which led to the alienation of the northern tribes and the division of the kingdom was Solomon's establishment of the *missîm*, the forced labor programs. The requirement, beyond monetary taxation, of annual physical labor in the royal *mas*, or corvée, must have been a bitter pill to swallow for a people who had a tradition of having been slaves in Egypt. And, indeed, the precipitating act of northern rebellion against the house of David and Solomon was the stoning to death of Adoram, Solomon's and Rehoboam's officer *ᶜal hammas*. It is therefore interesting that in Exodus 1 the usual term for the Egyptian taskmasters, *nogĕśîm*, is not used. Rather, the term for the labor enforcers is *śārê missîm*. The term hardly seems likely to have been the choice of an author who favored the Judean court.

That is the first datum of the account of the exodus. The last datum mentioned with regard to the exodus is that Moses took Joseph's bones with him. The concern with the eventual removal of

Joseph's remains from Egypt to the promised land is also the last thing expressed in the book of Genesis. Both passages are generally identified as part of the E source, and that, too, fits with the northern provenience of E, because, according to Joshua 24:32, the traditional burial site of Joseph was in the north, specifically at Shechem.

In a subsequent E text, at the mountain of God, Moses, Aaron, Nadab and Abihu, and seventy elders see God. The inclusion of Nadab and Abihu is enigmatic. They are never mentioned before or after this in E or J. According to P, they are Aaron's sons. Their mention in E is interesting because Nadab and Abiyah are the names of Jeroboam's sons. Admittedly, the names Abihu and Abiyah are not identical. Still, the similarity of the names of the sons of the two makers of golden calves in the Hebrew Bible, together with the other signs of E's interest in the affairs of the northern kingdom and the southern priesthood, contribute to our perception of this datum as also relating to the respective backgrounds of E and J.

Nowhere is E's interest in the affairs of the northern kingdom and the southern priesthood more visible than in the golden calf episode. Its derogatory depiction of the golden calf, with its associations with the religion of Jeroboam, has led a few commentators to regard the account as being J, i.e. Judean. But it is E. It refers to the deity as Elohim in narration, which never happens in J, and it naturally flows from the preceding E account (Exod 24:12–15a, 18b), which pictures Moses ascending the mountain (har ha'ĕlōhîm), taking Joshua with him, and leaving Aaron in charge—as opposed to the preceding J account (Exod 19:24f), in which Moses takes Aaron up with him. The E source elsewhere does not seem to attack Jeroboam, his heirs, or the legitimacy of the northern kingdom's independence. On the contrary, we have observed its etiological interest in the cities that Jeroboam built up: Beth-El, Shechem, Penuel; and' it favors Jeroboam's home tribe of Ephraim. The E author's acceptance of the political existence of the kingdom of Israel, however, does not include support of its religious structure as well. At the same time, in picturing Aaron as the villain of the episode, E shows no affection for the dominant priestly house of the southern kingdom either. Those who regard the E source as deriving from northern Levitical circles have good grounds here. The northern Levites had seen Abiathar, their representative in David's dual priesthood, expelled by Solomon after supporting the losing brother in the battle for the succession to David's throne. This left the southern, presumably Aaronid representative, Zadok, in sole possession of the priestly prerogatives. The Gershonites of the north found themselves first set in a Solomonic taxation district which was possibly administered by an Aaronid; and later they saw some of their cities ceded to Phoenicia in Solomon's sale of the Cabul to Hiram of Tyre (Halpern, 1974: 519–532). They had come a long way down from the days when they had administered the place where Yahweh caused his name to dwell at the Tabernacle in Shiloh. It is no wonder, therefore, that it is a Shilonite, Ahijah, who is credited with having instigated Jeroboam's rebellion against the Judean royal house. They had reason to be hostile to both the royal and the priestly houses of Judah, which were tied closely together in any case, as indicated by the Priestly report that Aaron's wife was the sister of Nachshon ben Amminadab, the *nāśîʾ* of the tribe of Judah. The northern Levites, therefore, certainly had good reason to break with the south. The establishment of the northern kingdom itself was in their interest. The disappointment came, however, when Jeroboam established a non-Levitic priesthood for Israel, ministering at the golden calf sanctuaries of Beth-El and perhaps Dan. E does not oppose the Ephraimite kingdom of Jeroboam. How could it? It remained the only real hope of the out-of-power Levites; but the *religious establishments* of both the north and the south, symbolized by the young bulls and the person of Aaron respectively, are censured. Other items in the golden calf episode coincide with this picture. First, there is the involvement of Joshua in the account. Joshua is much more involved in E than in J generally, and in fact he may not be mentioned in J at all. He is associated with the Tabernacle, and he is the only Israelite who is dissociated from the golden calf event. Joshua is an Ephraimite hero, buried in *har Ephraim,* the mediator of the inaugural covenant ceremony in the land at *Shechem*. Second, the golden calf account pictures the *Levites* as loyal and zealous. Third, in E, Moses smashes the tablets of the Decalog and is not reported to have carved another set, thus possibly suggesting that the tablets that are supposed to be in the Temple in Jerusalem are either a fiction or unauthentic.

Both J and E, it seems, cast aspersions on the iconography and sacred implements of the other. The J laws of Exodus 34 forbid *molten* gods; and the calves are molten, while Judah's cherubim are carved of olive wood and gold-*plated*. The E commandments, meanwhile, forbid gods of silver and gold generally (Exod 20:23). Only J refers to the ark, which was within Judah's borders. In the conclusion of the J version of the spies episode, the Israelites suffer military defeat when they enter battle without the ark, thus implying that a nation cannot be militarily secure without it. Meanwhile, only E refers to the Tabernacle, the symbol of the great days of the northern religious establishment. And finally, in the J account of the events in Eden. Yahweh sets cherubs as the guardians of the tree of life, an appropriate choice for a Judean to make for a protector of something sacred.

In referring to the J spies episode, we should also note that the spies go to Hebron and to the Negeb. That is, they never go farther than Judah. The hero, moreover, is Caleb; and the Calebite territory was located in Judah, and it included Hebron (Josh 14:6–15).

While J extols the Judean hero Caleb, it denigrates, in the succeeding episode, the villains Dathan, Abiram, and On—all Reubenites.

E meanwhile denigrates Aaron once again in the snow-white Miriam episode, with the deity personally appearing and declaring that Moses' experience of God is superior to that of Aaron, Miriam, and all others. Indeed, the picture of Moses in E *throughout* is stronger than that of J. Its wording emphasizes Moses' personal agency in the liberation of the people from Egypt, while J rather emphasizes the role of Yahweh himself. In the J account of the burning bush, Yahweh says, "*I* am going down to save them from the hand of Egypt and to bring them up from that land." But in the E version, he rather tells Moses. "I shall send *you* to Pharaoh, and [you] bring out my people the children of Israel from Egypt." There is in general more development of Moses' personality in E than in J. J has nothing to compare with Moses' plaintive cry in Numbers 11, with its extraordinary intimacy with the deity. For E, which has no Abrahamic covenant, the era of Moses is the turning point of history, the age of the first covenant, the age of the revelation of the personal name of God, the age of the rise of the Levites, the age of the giving of a body of law. In fact the presence of the laws of the covenant Code, embedded in E, is a further indicator of E's deriving from Levitical circles, insofar as legal material in the Hebrew Bible is regularly embedded in texts by priests; namely: P, D, and Ezekiel, J, meanwhile, includes virtually no law beyond the decalog, and virtually no concern with matters of priesthood. J does not save the revelation of the divine name for the age of Moses, because for J the age of *Abraham* and above all the Abrahamic *covenant*—which is to be fulfilled in *David*—cannot be treated as in any way inferior to the Mosaic covenant.

The E source is thus to be traced to the northern Levitical establishment, probably of Shiloh and Nob. The priests and prophets of the old religious establishment of northern Israel had experienced hope followed by disenfranchisement, first by the royal house of Judah, then by the royal house of Israel. Thus Ahijah of Shiloh, the initiator or Jeroboam's secession, later rejects Jeroboam's house. The J source, meanwhile, is to be traced to non-priestly, pro-Davidic circles in Judah, probably following the reign of Jehoram, given the references to Edomite independence and to Assyrian Calah as *hāʿîr haggĕdôlâ*, which suggests the reign of Assurnasirpal II.[1]

E and J were alternative versions of the shared national traditions of patriarchs, exodus, Sinai/Horeb, and wilderness sojourn. Each consistently reflects the concerns of its day, its country, and its sponsors. It is commonly claimed in our field that E is hopelessly fragmentary, and it is occasionally in vogue even to deny its existence as a continuing source. Presumably this is because E has no primeval history or Abrahamic covenant and is less represented in the book of Genesis than is J; and scholars, working through the Pentateuch, read Genesis first and, at least since Martin Noth, follow an unwritten law derived from the evidence of Genesis that "When in doubt, it's J." If the same scholars would fairly read Exodus first, they would have to conclude that E is the more complete source.

In any case, after the Assyrian dispersion of Israel in 722, the expanded population of Judah found itself in possession of two versions of one historical sequence. The E version, with its denigration of Aaron, the eponymous ancestor of the Jerusalem priesthood, could hardly have been a welcome arrival in Jerusalem. The J version, as we have it, on the other hand, contains nothing that would necessarily be offensive to the E Levitical group. The two were combined editorially, retaining the material that deprecated Aaron, suggesting that the redactor was either himself of the Levitical group, or in any event no friend of the Jerusalem priestly establishment.

What was the response of the Jerusalem priestly establishment

---

[1] The Calah reference was suggested to me by W. H. Propp.

to the existence of the combined JE work in Judah, a work that pictured Aaron as the designer of the golden calf and as being reprimanded by the deity in the matter of Moses' Cushite wife, a work that suggested no special priestly role for Aaron's descendants? I think that their response was to produce an alternative composition of their own. Specifically, P.

In Martin Noth's treatment of the Pentateuchal sources in *Überlieferungsgeschichte des Pentateuch,* he observed that the extent to which the Priestly narrative parallels that of JE, both in sequence and in specifics, suggests that the author of P drew the narrative material from those sources (Noth, 1948). Noth's general observation received a more thoroughgoing demonstration in Sigmund Mowinckel's treatment, a careful comparison of P and JE at each unit of their respective accounts (Mowinckel, 1964: 26–43). Mowinckel still was cautious in his interpretation of the data, concluding that P depended on JE "directly or indirectly." While we can admire Mowinckel's sense of scholarly caution, we are nonetheless left understandably dissatisfied with this state of things. I mean to argue that the relationship of at least the *narrative* portion of P to JE is direct indeed, that P was intentionally composed as an alternative to JE.[2] Mowinckel's observations are manifest, I believe; that is, the correspondences of facts, specific language, and narrative sequence suggest that the P text is following JE. But, even more striking, the differences between the two, differences of detail, sequence, and omission, can be explained quite in the same way as the differences between J and E, i.e. in terms of a relatively small, consistent group of concerns which reflect the political and ideological situation of the authors, in this case the Jerusalem priesthood. Namely:

There is continuing emphasis upon the Tabernacle and the prerogatives of the Aaronid priestly house there. In P there is not a sacrifice prior to the erection of the Tabernacle and the consecration of the priesthood in Exodus 40. Only an Aaronid priest may perform a sacrifice or enter the Tabernacle. No term for repentance or mercy occurs in P—the roots *rḥm, ḥnn, šwb,* and *ḥsd* do not occur—and divine mercy is rarely depicted in its narrative accounts, the point being apparently that forgiveness is to be acquired through formal cultic channels, i.e. through sacrifice, mediated by a priest, at the

---

[2]This is a synthesis of the analysis that I began in my *The Exile and Biblical Narrative* (1978: 76–118).

Tabernacle, not merely by repentance. (Repentance is free.) The priest's mediation itself is to the point as well. The Priestly source develops the priests and Tabernacle as the only potent agencies of divine communication. The Priestly narrative thus includes no portrayals of angels, no portrayals of Yahweh so blatantly anthropomorphic as the JE portrayals of Yahweh's walking in the garden of Eden, standing on the rock at Meribah, wrestling with Jacob. P does not even use the word *prophet* (with one exception, where it is used figuratively and is applied to *Aaron*).

A comparison of the Priestly accounts with their JE counterparts demonstrates that Priestly narrative reflects these concerns consistently. A number of JE accounts in which angels figure occur in P as well, but minus the angels. The story of Lot and the destruction of Sodom and Gemorrah is reduced to three verses, and the angels who are catalysts of the action in J do not figure in P. Likewise in comparing the accounts of Hagar and the birth of Ishmael, the P version is reduced to three verses, and the angel who is of some importance in the J and E versions is gone in P. The long account of the arrangement of Isaac's marriage to Rebekah in J, which includes two references to Yahweh's angel, is a one-verse notice in P, no angel. Jacob's experience with angels at Beth-El and his change of name to Israel after wrestling with ʾĕlōhîm at Peniel are collapsed into a single Beth-El account in P in which no divine creatures figure. The Priestly account of Jacob's promotion of Ephraim and Manasseh (Genesis 48) likewise omits the E depiction of Jacob's blessing them with the protection of an angel. The account of the first meeting of Yahweh and Moses, too, eliminates the burning bush and the angel in it. The P Red Sea account eliminates the angel, as does the P Balaam account. Nor does P include the story of the bĕnê ʾĕlōhîm and human women. The P account of Meribah does not portray Yahwek as standing on the rock in the wilderness, nor does the deity personally make clothes for the first man and woman and personally seal Noah's ark in P. In J, Yahweh personally descends upon Sinai; in P, he does not.

The channel of communication to God is not angels, but priests, and Tabernacle; and this interest governs much of the character of the narrative. Thus P is hardly a narrative source at all in the material prior to the recounting of the age of Moses and Aaron. It is not just the presence of angels in the JE versions that is responsible for the brevity of the P accounts of Lot, Hagar, and Rebekah. The longer, anecdotal JE accounts in Genesis are generally eschewed in

P, though P does offer fuller narrative from the exodus on. Thus the Jacob-and-Esau and the Jacob-and-Joseph materials in JE are no more than a few verses each in P; and the Cain-and-Abel story, the Patriarchal wife/sister stories, and the Isaac-and-Abimelek account are gone.

All accounts of sacrifices prior to the consecration of Aaron and the Tabernacle are missing in Priestly narrative. Thus the sacrificial component of the Abrahamic covenant in J (Genesis 15) is not present in the P version (Genesis 17). Again, two stories in JE are collapsed into one in P. The covenant story, with its sacrifice, and the Mamre revelation, with its three angelic visitors, merge into a single, short depiction of Abraham's divine communication in P. Abraham's (near) sacrifice of Isaac likewise does not occur in P. Nor does Noah's sacrifice following the flood. This is presumably the reason why in J Noah takes seven pairs of clean animals in the ark and one pair of unclean, while in P he takes only one pair each of all kinds. In J, Noah must have more than one pair each of clean animals or his sacrifice would wipe out a species. In the Priestly point of view, the righteous Noah cannot possibly be portrayed as offering a sacrifice, and therefore no extra sacrificable animals are necessary.

In E Aaron fashions the golden calf, while merit is attributed to the zealous Levites. Not a welcome story to an Aaronid, the golden calf event does not occur in P. The other E account that deprecates Aaron, the story of snow-white Miriam, likewise does not occur in P.

What we are observing in all these cases is the impact of a basic set of priestly concerns upon the form which this group's literary product takes. It may result in abbreviation or elimination of an account, modification, elimination, or even addition of detail. An example of the last of these is the case of the spies episode in Numbers 13 and 14. In the J version, Caleb is the only spy to oppose the negative report of the others, and it is on this merit that he is to survive to arrive in the new land. The only other Israelite who is born in Egypt and survives to enter the land is Joshua. Joshua's merit in JE is clear. He is the only Israelite to dissociate himself from the golden calf incident, and he is the faithful *měšārēt* of Moses who remains in the Tabernacle. But these two sources of Joshua's merit in E can have no place in an Aaronid priest's composition. The golden calf episode, with Aaron at its center, was eliminated; and the presence of a non-Aaronid in the Tabernacle is an offense punishable by death in P. The presence of Joshua in the P version of the spies episode is apparently a Priestly writer's solution to the problem that he could not portray the merit of Joshua along the JE lines, and yet he could not deny the place of Joshua in Israel's national tradition as the successor of Moses.

While observing the spies and golden calf episodes, we should note that in both these accounts in JE there is initially a divine condemnation of the nation, which is then rescinded in response to an appeal by Moses to Yahweh's mercy. In P, the element of appeal to divine mercy is not present in the spies episode, and the golden calf episode of course is not represented. Not only is this consistent with the lesser concern with mercy in P; it at the same time eliminates the role of Moses as the human champion who saves his community.

The shifts in the treatment of Moses and Aaron in P especially point to the writer's concern for enhancing the reputation of Aaron and his descendants. The common line "and the Lord spoke unto Moses . . ." in JE often has become "and the Lord spoke unto Moses *and Aaron*. . ." in P. In JE, Moses' rod can become a snake (Exod 4:1–5); in P it is the rod of Aaron which becomes a snake before Pharaoh (7:10). In JE Moses is told that he is to be a god to *Aaron* (4:16); in P Moses is told that he is as a god *to Pharaoh*, and Aaron is his prophet! (7:1). In JE Moses is portrayed as concerned that he is *kbd ph wkbd lšwn;* whatever that means, the Priestly author has chosen another, perhaps pejorative, idiom, casting Moses as concerned that he is ʿrl *šptym* (6:12). The picture of Moses in the P version of the striking of the rock at Meribah is troubling as well. Moses' beneficial act in the E version is cast as his ultimate act of disobedience in P, for which he suffers the ultimate punishment— death before entering the land—a punishment which Aaron shares even though he is portrayed as an innocent bystander.

The P treatment of the seduction at Baal-Peor does Moses no honor either. The Moabite seductresses in JE have become Midianite seductresses in P, an unfortunate substitution given that Moses' wife is Midianite. And when an Israelite prince and a Midianite princess enter the Tabernacle in the sight of Moses—who does not act—to perform what is perhaps a fertility rite, it is the Aaronid Phinehas who kills the offenders in a portrayal that is perhaps the etiology of shish kebab. His zeal results in an eternal covenant of priesthood for his family.

The defense of the priestly house of Aaron is of course at the heart of the Korah episode as well, which in some way was perceived as corresponding to the Dathan/Abiram episode in J. In P, Moses is portrayed as specifically denouncing those Levites who seek the prerogatives of *kĕhûnâ*, which are exclusively Aaron's and his sons'. He says, "You have plenty, Levites" (Numbers 16:7), and in response to their claim that all of the people are holy he declares that Yahweh will make known those whom he will bring near to himself as holy. The test is the offering of incense—a responsibility of the holy—in which Korah and his company's claims are rejected. The subsequent Priestly materials further treat the relative prerogatives of the Aaronids and Levites. The bronze incense burners of Korah's company are beaten into a covering for the altar as a reminder that no non-Aaronid may offer incense (17:5). When a plague strikes the congregation as Yahweh's response to their complaint that Moses and Aaron have killed "people of Yahweh," it is arrested by Aaron's use of incense (17:11f). The singular status of the Levites is then confirmed by the miraculous blossoming of their tribal staff, on which the name of Aaron is inscribed; then the Aaronids are assigned the responsibility of the Tabernacle, the Levites are assigned to the service of the Aaronids, and all others are warned not to approach the Tabernacle on pain of death (18:4,7,22). In the place of the Dathan/Abiram account in J, which depicts a challenge to the authority of Moses, P offers us an account of a challenge to the house of Aaron as well.

P follows E in developing the revelation of the divine name as occurring at the time of the exodus, which also fits this overall picture, because that is the age of Moses and of Aaron, the age of the construction of the ark and Tabernacle and of the establishment of the priesthood. Since the P source, nonetheless, also develops the Abrahamic covenant, like J, P ascribes a special new importance to the name El Shadday, which in P stands as an important middle stage in the deity's self-disclosure. That is, in the Noahic covenant he is *'ĕlōhîm*, in the Abrahamic covenant he is El Shadday, and in the Sinai covenant he is Yahweh.

Finally, in reporting the death of Moses, P does not include the JE notation that the deity personally buries Moses. The Priestly text does, however, note the number of days that the people mourn Moses—thirty—the same as that of Aaron.

What one observes in all of this is that the Priestly narrative is following that of JE—in sequence, particulars, and language—but the Priestly writer has introduced *systematic* changes, the changes are at points polemical, and most of these changes are not stylistic but ideological. P was conceived and produced as an alternative version of Israel's sacred national traditions to that of JE. JE was known to the author of P—and not just in a general way. It was on the table—either literally or figuratively—when P was composed. If there had been no JE, there would have been no P source either. There might still have been some legal and literary materials produced within the house of Aaron, but not the Priestly narrative that we know. The relationship between the sources JE and P is intimate.

As Ziony Zevit and I have discussed in recent studies, the Priestly narrative is quoted in Dtr[1], Jeremiah, and Ezekiel—which would make it pre-exilic and presumably pre-Josianic (Zevit, 1982: 502–509). The important linguistic studies by Robert Polzin, Ziony Zevit, Gary Rendsburg, A.R. Guenther, and Avi Hurvitz collectively, and on most points nearly unanimously, confirm that at least P-*grund* is composed in pre-exilic biblical Hebrew (Polzin, 1976; Zevit, 1982: 493–501; Rendsburg, 1980: 65–80; Guenther, 1977; Hurvitz, 1982). My work on the Priestly Tabernacle and its relationship to the First Temple likewise points to pre-exilic composition of the P narrative and much of the P legal material, as do the analyses of Priestly law by Zevit, Menahem Haran and Jacob Milgrom. (Friedman, 1978: 48–61; Zevit: 485–93; Haran, 1978; Milgrom, 1976). This places the composition of much of P in an era of considerable growth of the kingdom of Judah in the wake of the Assyrian destruction of the kingdom of Israel, an age of competing Levitical groups for the priestly prerogatives and income. It is not at all difficult to picture an Aaronid priest of this age perceiving it to be necessary to compose a Torah which would be an alternative to the JE characterization of the tradition.

It is also not difficult to picture how the other, non-Aaronid priestly houses would respond to the P portrayals. Beyond Jeremiah's polemic, there is the Deuteronomist's clear favoritism of the JE version. This is not the place for a detailed analysis of the relationship of D and P, but at least we can note the obvious; namely, that the Deuteronomist (Dtr[1]) recounts history with continual reference to the words of JE, but no more than one or two allusions to P. Second, Deuteronomy only mentions Aaron three times, twice to say that he died and once to say that he made the golden calf. Third, Deuteronomy does not distinguish between priests and Levites; all Levites are priests. Fourth, there is the full range of differences between D and P on points of law. Conclusion: in the last years of the kingdom of Judah, the character of the nation's literary products

continued to reflect fundamental religious and political conflicts
which were centuries old.

It is customary to comment on the brilliance of the redactor's
synthesis of the sources. It was an extraordinary task. Given the
alternative and antagonistic character of the sources to one another,
the redactor fashioned, in the Torah, probably the most ironic work
in all literary history. As Alan Cooper and I have discussed
elsewhere, it is, as a synthesis, richer than the sum of its components (Cooper, 1981; Friedman, 1987).[3] Combining P, with its absence of references to divine mercy, with J, with its depiction of God
as

$$^{\jmath}l \; rhm \; whnn \; ^{\jmath}rk \; ^{\jmath}pym \; wrb \; hsd \; w^{\jmath}mt$$
$$nsr \; hsd \; l^{\jmath}lpym \; ns^{\jmath} \; ^{c}wn \; wps^{c} \; wht^{\jmath}h \ldots$$

results in an account of a God continuously in tension between his
justice and his mercy in a balance that was not intended by the
authors of either of the sources. We might have wished for a less
skillful redactor. The New Testament's separation of its four gospels
is cleaner. And having a God who is so torn between justice and
mercy has been no picnic for Jews and Christians. But I think that
the redactor had no choice. He had no four separate persons to
whom to ascribe his "gospels," because by his day all had apparently
come to be ascribed to Moses. Scholars often claim that he was
bound to retain all of his sources by respect for the written word.
The fact that none of the sources is complete makes this claim
doubtful. More probably, all of the sources had to be retained
because all of them contained materials which had become *famous*
and had acquired a body of supporters. One could not successfully
promulgate a text as the Torah-which-God-gave-to-Moses that did
not include the story of Adam and Eve, the story of the golden calf,
and the story of Phinehas' spearmanship—because the audience
would not allow it. Thus the redaction of the work was no less tied to
the life of the community than was the composition of the components.

I suggest that this sketch which I have drawn of the relationship

---

[3] This is not to suggest that Cooper and I are in agreement on the place of source
criticism in literary study of the Bible. See his discussion of this question in this
volume.

of the sources—and of course the more complete analysis of which it *is* only a sketch—means that it is now possible and, I think, important to utilize source-critical study more productively than ever in our work. We have reached a stage at which source criticism can mean synthesis, and not merely division, of the text. Analyses that fail to provide such synthesis will no longer satisfy. Now that we are close to the solution, this is not the time to confuse the issue with new fragmentary treatments of J and E as non-continuous sources; this is not the time to break off large portions of J and E and place them after the exile;[4] (van Seters, 1975; Rendtroff, 1977) and this is especially not the time for literary critics of the Bible to ignore source criticism disdainfully, thinking that they are doing something higher than Higher Criticism, when they are in fact losing the dimension that this could give to their apprehension and appreciation of the text. And, as for the source critics, it certainly is no longer sufficient to identify a passage as E because it calls a maidservant an *ʾāmâ* instead of a *šipḥâ* and be done with it, or to add a short, purely descriptive discussion of the theology of J or of E. One must attempt to present a picture of the place of that text in its corpus; in a larger treatment, one must deal with the place of the corpus in relation to the other corpora. One must have some conception of the world that produced each of the works and of the world that produced the *combination* of those works. Then—now—source criticism can be, instead of a useful fiction, a revealing and enlightening study of the creation of the Bible.

And it can give us a richer sense of the text itself. We can appreciate the qualities of the text as it stands, and at the same time we can appreciate the chains of historical situations and events, the happy coincidences, and the remarkable ironies that produced those qualities. Whatever one learns about the mind of the author in literary analysis of other works, one learns about the complex *meeting* of minds (intended or not) that were brought together to fashion this work.

That is not merely excavation—any more than digging for gold *and making a strike* is merely excavation—so long as we treasure what we have found.

---

[4] See also the collection of discussions of the suggestions of van Seters, Rendtorff, and H.H. Schmid in *JSOT* 3 (1977); and see the important critique by J.A. Emerton (1982).

WORKS CONSULTED

Alter, R.
  1975   "A Literary Approach to the Bible," *Commentary*,
              (Dec.).

Cooper, A.
  1981   "The Act of Reading the Bible," *Proceedings of the
              Eighth World Congress of Jewish Studies*.

Emerton, J.A.
  1982   "The Origin of the Promises to the Patriarchs in the
              Older Sources of the Book of Genesis," *VT* 32, 14–
              32.

De Wette, W.M.L.
  1805   *Dissertatio critico-exegetica, qua Deuteronomium a
              prioribus Pentateuchi libris diversum, alius
              cuiusdam recentioris auctoris opus esse monstratur.*

Friedman, Richard E.
  1978   *The Exile and Biblical Narrative* (HSM 22; Chico:
              Scholars Press)
  1987   "The Hiding of the Face: An Essay on the Literary
              Unity of Biblical Narrative," in *Judaic Perspectives
              on Ancient Israel*, J. Neusner, ed.

Gray, E.
  1929   *Old Testament Criticism* (New York: Harper).

Guenther, A.R.
  1977   "A Diachronic Study of Biblical Hebrew Prose Syntax,"
              diss. University of Toronto.

Halpern, B.
  1974   "Sectionalism and the Schism," *JBL* 93, 519–32.

Haran, M.
  1978   *Temples and Temple Service in Ancient Israel* (Oxford:
              Oxford University Press).

Hurvitz, A.
  1982   *A Linguistic Study of the Relationship Between the
              Priestly Source and Book of Ezekiel*, Cahiers de la
              Revue Biblique: Paris.

Milgrom, J.
  1976   *Studies in Levitical Terminology* (Berkeley: University
              of California Press).
  1976   *Cult and Conscience* (Leiden: E.J. Brill).

Mowinckel, S.
    1964   *Erwägungen zur Pentateuch Quellenfrage* (Trondheim: Universitetsforlaget).

Noth, Martin
    1972   A *History of Pentateuchal Traditions* Prentice-Hall. [*Überlieferungsgeschichte des Pentateuch* (Stuttgart: W. Kohlhammer Verlag, 1948)];

Polzin, R.
    1976   *Late Biblical Hebrew-Toward an Historical Typology of Biblical Hebrew Prose* (HSM 12: Chico: Scholars Press).

Silberman, L.H.
    1983   "Listening to the text," *JBL* 102.

Rendsburg, G.
    1980   "Late Biblical Hebrew and the Date of P," *Janes* 12, 65–80.

Rendtorff, R.
    1977   *Das Überlieferungsgeschichtliche Problem des Pentateuchs* (BZAW 147).

van Seters, J.
    1975   *Abraham in History and Tradition* (New Haven: Yale University Press).

Zevit, Z.
    1982   "Converging Lines of Evidence Bearing on the Date of P," ZAW 94, 502–9.

Chapter 5

BIBLICAL OR ISRAELITE HISTORY?*

Baruch Halpern
York University, Toronto

I.   Some schismatic semantics

For the past 15 years, a semantic gnat has nettled scholars who study the archaeology of Israel: are they Biblical or Syro-Palestinian archaeologists? The name "Biblical archaeology" reflects the field's history and captures its current constituency—interest in the Bible underwrites and staffs much of the professional fieldwork; and the term parallels "classical archaeology" in denoting research centered on the world of a defined literary corpus. But some archaeologists are leery. The name associates them with amateurs, who quest for the Ark of the Covenant and, periodically, find Noah's. It lumps them together with uncritical enthusiasts who thirst to prove what archaeology cannot—that "the Bible is true." It invites carpetbagging by inspired non-archaeologists.

Plainly, were professional standards uniform and high enough to command respect from colleagues in other branches of archaeology, there would be no issue. The substantive problem shapes the semantic one: can "Biblical archaeology" be brought to conform to the most rigorous standards of archaeology-in-general? The answer, given the vigilance of Departments of Antiquities watchdogs, is probably positive. So there is no pressing need to cut "Biblical archaeology" loose from its cultural, intellectual and emotional roots. Yet one cannot blame the archaeologists who hope by changing names to dissociate themselves from unprofessional colleagues, as scientists from alchemy.

Replace "archaeology" and "archaeological" with "history" and

*This study was conducted with the support of the Alexander von Humboldt-Stiftung and the Social Sciences and Humanities Research Council of Canada.

"historical" and you disclose a related, latent controversy. Interest in Biblical history stems historically from the seminary, and those who write that history often confuse it with homily. Biblical history in this sense represents a confession central to the common identity of a sect, or even to the self-conception of an individual. To take the Bible as "true" simplifies getting hold of that identity or self-conception; it cuts right through the hard questions of critical historical study. To let the glow of Biblical history eclipse the reality and immediacy of all else, to skip lightly back to antiquity for the history from which one sculpts an identity—this also makes it easy to get a grasp on the past.

But simple faith does not afford an avenue to historical evidence. It cannot cogently meet demands for "proof". This is the challenge, in fact, that drives the "Biblical archaeologist" to the spade: to "prove" in the face of skeptics that Joshua conquered Canaan, that Jericho fell to his onslaught, that Moses led Israel to Sinai, that Abraham once lived. The same motivation actuates much "critical" work in the history of Israel. "Biblical history"—the study of Israel and Israel's world by modern scholars—too often reflects a yearning to find "the Bible is true," to identify "Biblical history" with the narratives of the Bible. This is legitimate as a confessional enterprise, in the church or Sunday school. Such is the power of faith that it transforms even the Ivory Tower into a rood steeple.

To call the study of Israelite antiquity "Biblical history" mirrors, thus, the history and nature of the field. Even the most scrupulous practitioners consider their historical work "Biblical." Yet one wonders whether they do not carry this self-conception, this common identity, to excess. Contrast the names of major journals in classical history with those in "Biblical": *Klio*, the *Journal of Roman Studies*, the *Journal of Hellenic Studies*, *Greek and Byzantine Studies*, the *Zeitschrift für die alttestamentliche Wissenschaft*, the *Journal of Biblical Literature*. There are broader journals covering ancient Israel's environs: the *Journal of the Economic and Social History of the Orient*, the *Journal of Near Eastern Studies*, the *Journal of Asian and African Studies;* only rarely do they carry pieces with Biblical content. Again, Martin Noth's *Geschichte Israels*, for all its deficiencies one of the most critical textbooks in wide circulation, is catalogued by academic booksellers under "Theology". The field of Israelite history has been institutionally isolated from its siblings in History and Near Eastern Studies. It is an illegitimate child of Exegesis: when graduate students emulate their *Doktorväter*, they absorb Theology, Philology, even Epigraphy, but almost never History. Despite professions to the contrary, History has been king of "Biblical Studies" only as a sort of Louis. Theology has been its Richelieu.

Over the last generation, the most important work in "Biblical history" has come from students of scholars themselves sensitive to historical concerns and method.[1] The number of such scholars is small: historical sense must be born, apparently, not cultivated. Yet the scarcity of critical historians has not led them to rally together or, beyond linking hands with Assyriology on occasion, to establish guild-centered ties (the *American Historical Review* carries no studies in Israelite history). History in Israel's case remains the handmaiden of Theology, Hagar to the harsh Sarah of Exegesis.

The isolation of "Biblical history" from history-in-general has been elective. It expresses the sociology of a milieu, Biblical scholarship, in which literary, theological and confessional concerns enjoy an extensive natural constituency. Yet prolonged association with this constituency has affected the character of "Biblical history", differentiating it in fact as well as focus from other historical fields. Historical work on ancient Israel has been addressed to and assessed by scholars whose primary interests and occupations are not themselves historical. In one sense, this has been salubrious—rendering the historian answerable to concerned colleagues. But it has engendered predictable confusion over professional standards: what is legitimate method? What is a publishable study? Clarifying these questions is a task that will require decades, if it is ever undertaken. In the meanwhile, it is worth addressing issues symptomatic of the confusion. Those taken up below fall into the familiar categories of the historiographic and the historical. They involve pressing methodological problems, but by no means all or even the most basic of them.

II.   Some scholastic schematics

A. *An Issue in Biblical Historiography*
Anyone who has undergone training in logic, and many who have not, will have encountered the puzzle involving two tribes of

---

[1] To name individuals would necessarily be invidious. I allow myself the luxury of pointing to the single example of treatises emanating from scholars who took their doctorates at the Hebrew University in Jerusalem.

scribes: the Israelite scribes always lie, while the Philistine scribes (who publish much less, in accordance with the Biblical injunction), always tell the truth; encountered on the road, the two are by any outward criteria—dress, accent—indistinguishable. The task, which is that of the scholar, is to elicit, by a single question of a single scribe met by chance, the truth about some issue, such as "Was David keen with a sling?" or "How do I get to Toledo?" Corresponding to the two tribes of scribes, there are two families of scholars. Simple Simon and Naive Nellie always ask their question directly and assume the answer is true: every scribe is a Philistine! Their colleagues, Crafty Cathy and Shifty Bill, identify by painstaking analysis of the answers every scribe as an Israelite. Either pair or both could be right in the case of a given encounter, and here is the difficulty with the study of Israelite historiography. When do we trust our sources?

Critical Biblical scholarship cut its teeth on source-criticism in Genesis. Since, it has stubbornly attempted to recapitulate its pattern of development on nourishments less susceptible to such mastication. The Naive scholar, thus, is one who assumes (by extension, believes) that his sources represent essentially accurate accounts originating ultimately in the era they describe. Shifty Bill, however, assumes a more convoluted path from event to report: report mediates event, if at all, only through the hazy recollection, always shaped by partisanship and often by unbridled imagination, of a later writer; most reports are in fact unreliable.

When this dichotomy first arose, over Homeric epic and the Pentateuch, Craft won the day, for these works do not involve historiography of the same order as that in Herodotus and the Former Prophets. Yet inevitably, the controversy came to embroil the latter reports as well. The cause was the fact that historiography does not reflect history. It refracts one through the other an author's understanding of what happens generally and his understanding of what happened specifically in a particular, significant and coherent sequence of events. Simple Simon tends to be a bit too Naive, Crafty Cathy a touch too Shifty where it is in point.

The Simple confront the Shifty at every scholarly turn. Thus, Naive scholars cite Joshua to claim that Israel conquered Canaan, if in a period more extended than the narratives imply, at least in the course of a single movement. Their Crafty counterparts insist such claims are concoctions of a later, united Israel, projected into an otherwise unremembered past. Here, their skepticism is warranted.[2] The two camps clash again over the existence of a pre-monarchic league, where the Crafty dismiss Judges 5 and other early evidence—by denying its broad significance or by dating it late—and evaluate later reports as maximalizing retrojection. Naive Nellie, by contrast, sees the emergence of the Saulide state as evidence of earlier affiliation, and the recollection of a premonarchic tribal system as sufficiently unnatural to warrant its accuracy. The evidence vindicates neither view decisively.

For misplaced Shiftiness, Assyriology in the last century pro-vides a *locus classicus*. G. Maspero persuaded himself that Sargon of Akkad represented nothing more than a late retrojection of Sargon II of Assyria, a view subsequently disproved (Millard, 1983: 36). A candidate for comparison in Biblical history is not difficult to find. Crafty scholars have persistently denied the historicity of Hezekiah's reform. The main source in this case is the Chronicler, and the Chronicler *always* prevaricates (he is the archetypal Israelite scribe). Simple Simons defend the Chronicler's reputation, citing corroboration from 2 Kgs 18:8. Archaeological results, although exiguously, now tend to sustain the conservative view.[3]

These disputes illustrate the characteristics of the two scholarly camps. The first is most important. At the extremes, Shifty Bills and Naive Nellies are effectively Pyrrhonists (what I have elsewhere called negative fundamentalists) and fundamentalists; individually, their positions coincide with those of the modernist and the con-servative. But on a given issue, a scholar elsewhere disposed to Craft may elect Simplicity. Except among ideologues, who by defi-

---

[2] The (forthcoming in ASORDS) dissertation of Z. Gal on the settlement of the Galilee and the dissertation of I. Finkelstein ("The Izbet Sartah Excavations and the Israelite Settlement in the Hill Country," 1983) are two important links in the ever-stronger chain of evidence. Israel did not control any part of lowland Canaan until after Deborah's nation-shaping victory (Judges 5) [B. Halpern, 1983: 95–106, 205–221].

[3] Historical considerations (hinging around Sennacherib's inscriptional evidence) demand that the destruction of Lachish III be attributed to Sennacherib's third campaign in 701, with implications for the dating of Beersheba II, though the issue is not without serious complications: see Y. Yadin (1976: 5–6) and the response in M. and Y. Aharoni (1976: 73–90), esp. on the unusual potter's mark on the 8th–7th c. store-jar singled out by Yadin, p. 83. On the *bāmâ* or temple (more likely the former), see Y. Aharoni (1972: 32–42; 1974: 2–6), and the rejoinder by Yadin (pp. 7–14), much of which is correct. The dating of the strata is the only germane issue here; the advantage would seem to lie with Aharoni. Secondary use of altar stones probably implies cultic reform. But this is not certain, and the central issues are all contro-verted. It should be noted, too, that the skeptical view on Hezekiah's reform is probably more reasonable than the case its proponents have so far made for it.

nition abuse history in the way that diggers of the lost ark abuse archaeology, the individual historical problem and not an overarching dogma is ideally at issue. By excluding the ideologues even from Biblical history, we evade, perhaps unwisely, the issue the archaeologists confront. But among professional Biblicists, the state of the field is such that even Simple Simon has his critical moments.

Second, Craft is sometimes unavoidable. Contradictions in testimony, with which Biblical historiography is replete, demand it. 1 Samuel 17, for example, attributes Goliath's demise to David, 2 Sam 21:19 and 1 Chr 20:5 to Elhanan ben-Dodo.[4] Some efforts at harmonization betray a yearning for Simplicity—Elhanan as another name for David—but this, too, involves Craft.

Again, Crafty scholars maintain that 2 Kgs 18:17-19:36, a miraculous version of Jerusalem's preservation from Sennacherib, represent a midrashic elaboration of events recorded in 2 Kgs 18:14-16 (where Hezekiah pays the Assyrian off, as Sennacherib's annals claim). Naive scholars counter by offering the theory that Sennacherib campaigned against Hezekiah *twice;* in 701, as the annals and 2 Kgs 18:14-16 suggest, he was paid off, while in the later campaign he suffered a military catastrophe (recently, Shea, 1985: 401-418). Yet even the Naive solution involves Craft: it presumes that the historian in 2 Kgs 18:13-19:37 mistakenly (or maliciously) conflated two different campaigns into one, in Hezekiah's fourteenth year. The improbability of this scenario is perhaps greater than that of the Crafty one (the date of Sennacherib's first campaign being preserved, that of the second entirely lost, when first-hand sources are hypothesized). But the point is, even the Naive approach to the problem requires a measure of Shiftiness.

Inconsistency, thus, elicits Craft. So, too, does the assessment of reports as folkloristic. It is the nature of eponymic lore that justified Shiftiness in treating the Pentateuch. Admittedly, scholars Naive in ilk during the second third of this century thought that such an attitude toward the patriarchal narratives verged on negative fundamentalism. They vindicated the text by pointing to recollections of early practice the texts retained, situating Abraham as a donkey-caravaneer in Bronze-Age Canaan.[5] This approach is crypto-

---

[4]The patronym has been corrupted by the influence of *mnwr 'rgym;* but as widely recognized, the Bethlehemite hero of record was probably the original subject. On this scenario, association from Elhanan's patronym, *d(w)dw,* sparked the displacement to David *(dwd).*

[5]See G.E. Mendenhall (1965: 36–39) for a typical maximalist account.

fundamentalist, seeking literal truth at the literal level in a literature whose truth-content lies elsewhere: for the most part Genesis addresses in an eponymic idiom the relationships among later kingroups and their institutions; the need to structure the narrative as a whole also leads to the inclusion of certain elements (so, the need to associate Abraham with various shrines makes him seem itinerant, not migrant). At the larger level, T.L. Thompson (1974) and J. van Seters (1975) have compellingly demonstrated how frangible the case for patriarchal research has been. It must be so. The sources do not deal with political leaders or integrate their protagonists into an identifiable political framework; and donkey caravaneers have as yet no archaeological reflex.

From the Abraham story, we can learn something of Israelite views of contemporary or more antique ethnology. It is another matter, however, to lift one or another element (migration, life in tents) from the author's global view of Israel's past and to assume that it is an isolated survival in reliable memory, unshaped and unaffected by the folklore in which it is embedded. This is effectively to return to a view that the Bible is "true", literally "true", that the narrative itself is not organic and unified, but a collection of isolated statements from which the devotee can pick at will. The patriarchal histories are precisely national folklore, whether traditional or not: any historically accurate information they preserve has survived by accident, because it serves a narrative function, and not by virtue of hypothetical antiquarian scruples.

This sort of story—the myth of origins—has from Niebuhr through Heidegger captured the imagination of creative scholars. Scholars are, after all, no more proof against the genre's charm than is the public. But the type of text involved confounds responsible exploitation, a rule to which Biblical historians have provided no exception. Certainly the Niebuhrian road has led nowhere but to fantasy. One is reminded of K. Sethe's attempt to chart pre-dynastic Egyptian history from myths, foredoomed to solipsism and blessed by eventual obscurity (Sethe, 1930). Similar applications to the patriarchal material, even including Alt's, have suffered from identical flaws. Whatever literal or metaphorical historical information has survived in it has been homogenized with later concerns.

One can travel farther in the company of Crafty scholars, who put cultic and kerygmatic texts, like the narratives in Exodus, Numbers and Joshua, into the same boat. Contemporary concerns shape these cycles as much as antiquarian. Even when the narratives

themselves are antiquarian in genre, as seems to be the case in
Joshua, their sources and avenues of transmission resemble those of
Genesis: materials whose claims to truth lay at metaphorical levels
have undergone modal metamorphosis: the later historian takes
them as literally true (Halpern, 1983: 41–73).

Genre is thus a central element in justifying Craft. Even the
tentative naivete of "demythologization" meets consistently with
disastrous results, because it, too, assumes that narrative whose
truth-content is metaphorical can be translated one-to-one to literal
reality. Typical was Paul Haupt's conviction that the revelation at
Sinai was volcanic, and the miracle at Jericho seismic.[6] The relative
sophistication of LB/Iron I culture makes these views unlikely. But
they misconstrue the narrative intention involved in each case by
attempting to reduce surds—the basic units of metaphorical, not
literal, discourse underlying the accounts. At this level of discourse,
in folklore, legend and myth, Craft is indispensable. Perhaps the
only scholar to draw the appropriate conclusions for Israelite history
has been the historian, Abraham Malamat.[7]

Certain other cases call for Shiftiness. Texts touching only individuals or narrow localities, that do not make significant national
claims or that make such claims about eras for which the historian
lacked sources (Joshua), fall naturally under suspicion. Here subject
matter joins genre as a criterion of whether a memoir can *a priori* be
held to be unreliable. Seemingly antiquarian accounts—1 Samuel 7
may be an instance—can carry concoctions meant to glorify a
character *qua* literary persona, or to detract from some historical
character's achievements.[8] But in proportion to their loyalty to
historical records, and in inverse proportion to their injection of
contemporary political interests into individual pericopes, they are

---

[6] See P. Haupt (1909) 354–369. His claim that "Monotheism can have originated
only in a highly civilized country as a reaction against excessive polytheism" (p. 356) is
a monument to the philosophical and theological bias actuating his views.

[7] A. Malamat (1983: 1–16) now in *Israel in Biblical Times. Historical Essays*
(Jerusalem: Bialik and I.E.S., 1983) 3–22, in altered form; esp. germane here are pp.
3–9, 21–22. Cf. J.A. Soggin (1978: 44*–51*).

[8] On 1 Samuel 7, see A. Weiser (1962: 22–23) with the argument that the claims
of victory there detract from David's accomplishments. I am dubious: 1 Sam 7:11–13
are intended to establish that Samuel's stewardship retrieved the territory lost to the
Philistines by the house of Eli: he restored the old border of Ebenezer, where the
battle that led to Eli's fall was joined (1 Sam 4:1, 5:1). This is clear from his
declaration, "It is to this point that YHWH has succored us," not farther, and from
the statement that the Philistines no longer intruded into Israelite territory (which

less liable altogether to be skewed from historical social reality. The limitations affecting their use are correspondingly less debilitating.

The foregoing discussion may seem to concur with the skeptic's view that stylization, or conformity to a genre vindicates Shiftiness. This is untrue. Historical narrative, the form in which history is presented, employs literary tropes; it is often highly stylized (as are the annals of the Assyrian kings, which by and large are fairly reliable). It adopts in these cases the literary and cultural patterns its authors think appropriate to the events—that is, because the author, say, of Judges 3–8 *sees* the "judges" as YHWH's avatars, *he portrays* them as such, framing them in the mold of the Divine Warrior (Liverani, 1973: 178–194; Halpern, 1981: 111–123). Still, close attention to genre is the more vital in that the genre of the extensive work—history—involves the collection of sources. The sources are uneven: the broken ground of Biblical historiography calls for caution in crossing.

Yet Shifty Bill and Naive Nellie share one folly, that of crediting to a historical text's author the whole of its content. This makes him, for Nellie, a better historian than ever lived—relying only on accurate sources. Shifty Bill errs equally in making the historian a fraud and a distributor of taffy. The authors of Kings, at least, and probably those of Chronicles and the rest of the Former Prophets, were trying to write history, to capture the essence of Israel's past as a nation. They believed that historical facts justified their views, and adduced some that did not, out of antiquarian interest. Shifty Bill thus impugns the historians all too often. But the view of neither scholar allows for the sometimes creative, sometimes conservative role of the undeniable tradition of folk entertainment in Israel.

Storytelling is the source of at least some of the seemingly folkloristic segments in Kings. The author of 2 Kgs 8:4f., for exam-

would be nonsense had the Israelites conquered the Philistines, as the standard interpretation of v 14 has it). I wonder, therefore, whether we should not read v 14 as claiming that Israel recovered the (highland) towns taken by the Philistines, who lived "from Ekron to Gath" (the inland towns that would have expanded at Israel's expense in the aftermath of the rout at Ebenezar). In that case, no conquest of Philistia is claimed—indeed, it is questionable whether any occurred even under David. The tradition is intended only to glorify Samuel, if it is not accurate, and conceivably to detract from Saul's accomplishments. For the latter view, see J. Blenkinsopp (1972: 79). My reading of v 14, which is preferable because philologically possible and more in accord with the surrounding verses and the political *status quo* being portrayed (esp. 1 Samuel 13–14), would invalidate the criticism levelled at Blenkinsopp by T.N.D. Mettinger (1976: 81 n. 4); but the theory wants further historiographic analysis before it is proved.

ple, identifies the storytelling tradition as the natural *Sitz im Leben* of the Elisha cycle, citing it implicitly as his source. Equally clearly, storytelling forms the kernel of Judges and 1 Samuel. A striking instance is the doublet 1 Sam 23:19–24:22//26:1–25, where the historian incorporates in his account two versions, inherited in different literary contexts, of David's final reconciliation with Saul. The historian incorporated both versions because differences in location and content, taken literally, implied that two separate events were involved; yet the similarities in plot, in development, in characterization, in literary bearings within the Saul-David cycle and in verbiage strongly suggest we have a doublet. Had the historian not been interested in preserving his inherited materials as literal, historical sources, the demands of plot unity would have led him to jettison one of the versions (the same applies to many of the other doublets he retained). The point here, however, is that the availability of the variants reflects the operation of oral tradition.

Storytelling about Davidic exploits falls into the genre of the Ehud story and parts of the Samson cycle, bordering on the picaresque. This literature centers on tactical accomplishments through individual cleverness—at least in its popular manifestations (Ehud; each story undergoes a different transformation in genre as it is integrated into larger narratives with larger concerns). In reduced form, such tales are preserved about David's heroes; indeed, the story of 1 Sam 24//26 most closely resembles and probably drew its inspiration from that in 2 Sam 23:13–17.[9] Integrated into narrative, they occur elsewhere in 1 Sam 14:1–14; 17 (one could include, among others, 19:11–18; 21:10–16; 2 Sam 2:12–23)—defining the genre precisely in its literary and oral dimensions is unnecessary here, except to note that instances are lacking in Kings.[10] What wants emphasis is that these tales were bruited about, not stored in archives. Parts of the cycle of stories about David, which naturally mixed fact with invention and easily displaced accomplishments of subordinates to the great man himself (Elhanan and Goliath, at a minimum), underwent a transition in genre over time, underwent

[9] On the role of the water-ritual in 2 Sam 23:13–17, cf. 1 Sam 7:6; see my *Constitution* (1981: 341, n.24). The former may be a folk-etymon of the ritual. On the probable triplet, cf. 165–167.

[10] Audience determines what tropes apply in which tales. In Judah, for example, Joab's assassination of Abner may have been transmitted in such a context, in Jerusalem, Hushai's duping Absalom. Thus, we cannot judge a story's genre in folk-entertainment strictly from its literary form. But literary forms do indicate what sorts of tales were transmitted, and how they could be framed.

modal metamorphosis at historians' hands. Like cultic metaphor, they were treated as though they were accurate sources and thereby entered the literature afresh.

What this means is that most often, Craft should be directed at the sources, and Naivete at the historians themselves. This is not a hard rule, but as a guideline is not rude.[11] Its central ingredient is the claim that Craft requires a historical dimension that Shifty Bill and Crafty Cathy rarely give it. The implications for Simpletons, though similar, are less severe.

This analysis of the conditions that call for Craft wants qualification in a fourth observation on the relationship between Craft and Naivete: when conditions do not plainly justify Shiftiness—as in the instance of Hezekiah's reform or in that of the premonarchic league—it represents a "What if?", a "Let's suppose." To the extent that this reflects conscientious skepticism, it arises unexceptionally from the critical approach to antiquity. "What if, in his zeal to tar Jeroboam as an apostate, the author of 1 Kings 12 misrepresented the theological status of the calves in the north?" The insufficient deployment of this tool reduces the study of historical Israel to a mindless parroting of biblical assertions: it fuels the tradition in the literature, reinforced by the longstanding legitimacy of exegetical commentaries, in which such parroting replaces history, a tradition often represented in standard historical textbooks, and asymptotic to that of the Sunday school.

But in the grasp of negative fundamentalists or of scholars whose Craft stems from naivete about history, "What if?" is prone to get out of hand, just as it does when wielded by students. "What if, in hopes of rehabilitating David, the authors of 2 Samuel suppressed memories of his primary devotion to the chief god of Jerusalem, Salem?" "What if"—to this we shall return—"David's high priest,

[11] In deploying doublets in storytelling-like patterns of repetition, how did historians evaluate their truth claims? R seems to have been actuated by a desire to avoid literal contradiction, or to minimize it, while retaining his sources: see R.E. Friedman (1981: 24–34); this conclusion is borne out by experiments I have conducted by having students generate alternative assemblies of JEP. R in Samuel seems to slip into a folkloristic mode by using the technique of repetition to climactic effect (but, I think, drawing on sources to furnish the material), as esp. in 1 Sam 18–20, then 23–26. At the same time, he, too, evinces an interest in minimizing formal contradiction in his arrangement of the accounts (for which, see my *Constitution*, chap. 6). This contrasts with the prevailing conditions in 1 Chronicles 2–4, where the "editors" seem more tolerant of formal contradiction, presumably because they do not believe it to involve real contradiction (the components of each case being supposed to have different reference).

Zadoq, was a Canaanite syncretizer?" "What if, without apparent
motive and out of the blue hundreds of years after the fact, the
Chronicler invented Hezekiah's reform?" What if the improbable,
what if something no more likely than the next possibility, is in fact
what occurred?

Crafty "what ifs" are legitimate expressions of scientific skepticism. Indeed, the distribution of borderline cases (and cases well
beyond the border) refutes the thesis that they are uniformly inspired by negative fundamentalism. The problem arises when Shiftiness degenerates into solipsism (as in denying the historicity of
Josiah's reform: see Hoffmann, 1980; van Seters, 1983). A Crafty
"what if" is solipsistic when presented in a distorted probabilistic
context, when remote possibility is treated as genuine, and genuine
possibility as probable. This engages an inherently evidential field,
history, with possibility instead of likelihood. Moreover, we must be
on guard against the ingenuousness of Crafty claims that this or that
text advances the author's prejudices, and is therefore suspect: any
assertion in the text can be seized on as evidence of the author's
bias—indeed, the text as a whole usually is—so that the argument is
liable to arbitrary application. In historiography, the author believes
that facts confirm his point and therefore cites them in corroboration; how one distinguishes evidence from concoction at this level
remains subjective. These are problems perpetuated by tradition
and example. Budding scholars grow overenthusiastic, often, at the
prospect of "criticism." How sensibly they learn to use it turns on
the examples furnished by their teachers and on how clearly the
teachers delineate when application is apt.

To this point, the discussion has run as follows. The opposition
between Crafty Cathy and Simple Simon cannot be equated with
that between the Pyrrhonist and the fundamentalist; some Shiftiness, and some Simplicity, is necessary to responsible work in
Israelite history; yet, Shiftiness, which can precipitate us into the
maelstrom of Pyrrhonism, is apt to get out of hand, just as Naivete,
sometimes in the form of cryptofundamentalism, often has done. It
remains to situate the problem, and its solution, historically.

The contrast between Naive and Crafty scholars expresses the
historiographic nature, and the theological and exegetical past, of
Biblical history. Internal evidence, textual matter, is paramount.
The issue of what sorts of questions are most appropriate under the
circumstances is taken up in the succeeding segment. But preoc-
cupation with the (in)accuracy of textual claims, and the unconscious

identification of these claims, for good or ill, with revelation, have made some solipsism inevitable. Interpretation of the narratives depends on their socio-political contexts, which scholars identify by analyzing internal evidence. Given such introversion, an infinite regress of Crafty "what ifs" cannot be proscribed, and it is in fact a credit to the field that, when one has occurred, it has been given relatively restricted play.

One consequence of this condition, though, is that of falling out among scholars without progress in method. There is no clear sense of what constitutes a basic professional standard, no "codification" beyond philological competence. The recent studies arguing the unity of the Deuteronomistic History follow Noth's lead in basing themselves on interpretative consistency in consecutive texts, on literary patterns and so on. The same scholars would no doubt repudiate this tactic when employed by opponents of the Documentary Hypothesis in the Pentateuch, who claim that plot unity and literary patterns across sources could not come from editors. The poverty of the evidence, simply, beggars method. It also leads us to exaggerate the import of historiographic issues concerning which research cannot produce certainty. Words, usage assume grotesque dimensions: they can, with a certain moderate probability, help to determine authorship; this, in turn, with its own compounded, moderate probability, can be used to justify Craft (Hoffmann, 1980; van Seters, 1983). Indeed, an over-emphasis on words has also had profound repercussions in the actual reconstruction of Israelite history, as we shall see.

How can we ground, or make more fully dialectic, the relationship between Craft and almost exclusively literary evidence? Efforts underway to elucidate ancient scribal practices and society—the latter as providing the scribe's audience—will ultimately make important contributions (see A. Lemaire, 1981; Millard, 1982; 1983; Naaman, 1976; Cogan, 1977, 1980; and Cogan and Tadmor, 1977). The proposals here are related. Our first step should be to determine the historical intentionality of the authors of the Former Prophets and Chronicles. Based on a survey of numerous cases, my own impression is that this was sincerely historical, authentically antiquarian: the authors were prey to bias when interpreting evidence;[12] and they wrote the history germane to them—about Is-

---

[12] As in 1 Chr 14:12//2 Sam 5:21, for treatment of which see M. Cogan (1974: 116). For partisan error in transmission, note 1 Sam 10:27 where *kmḥryš* eliminates

rael's relations with YHWH and how they could be repaired. But they seem to rely on sources for their data, rather than *ad hoc* concoction (the argument to this point is complex, and cannot be made here). By paying heed to their historical orientation—exemplified, after all, by the genre, history, that they chose to write (*not* pseudepigraphic memoir, *not* direct revelation)—we can begin to lend historical dimension to the exercise of Craft and the closely-related analysis of redaction-history.

Every historical hypothesis has or makes historiographic assumptions, and every historiographic hypothesis has converse implications. Scholars need to explore these implications before coming to fixed conclusions about the literature. It does not follow that they should publish full-dress studies of sociology in order to deal with redaction-history; but in light of the threat of solipsistic Shiftiness, indication of consciousness in this regard would help coordinate professional standards and expectations. This, in turn, is pivotal to the coherent development of the discipline.

The problem for analysis is simple: assume, against Tom Paine, who characterized the compilers of the Pentateuch as "some very stupid and ignorant pretenders to authorship" (1945: 521) because of the apparent aporias the Enlightenment uncovered, that Israel's historians were neither blackguards nor blunderers: by what intellectual processes did they arrive at the conclusions they communicate? Except when they answer this query satisfactorily, Shifty Bill and Crafty Cathy should be banned from print.

The renowned "all-Israel" redaction in Judges furnishes a serviceable example. Here, the editor has often been derided for generalizing the relevance of local events. How, then, did the "redaction" occur? Naturally. It took place over generations of the stories' retelling to audiences who, as Israelites, identified with the protagonists. The property that led them to take pride in the accomplishments related was not that they were denizens of the Jezreel or Benjamin, still less that they, too, were Hebrews (as Ammonites), but specifically that they were Israelites. The "all-Israel redaction" did occur, but was not tendentious. In its final form it consists of historical expressions of socio-political unity with a reasoned and probably partly sound historical reconstruction (of an Israelite political community before Saul). Bad faith is not involved.

---

the embarrassing extra month of *kmḥdš* and provides a connection to the silence of 1 Sam 10:14–16.

To observe, as Hoffmann has done, that the Deuteronomistic Historian interested himself in cultic history and that his history displays lexical and structural coherence is not to make a case that he worked with complete latitude, unconstrained by sources. This view is possible—remotely, because dependent on a monolithic view of P as post-exilic and without pre-exilic heritage; dependent, too, on understanding Dtr's post-exilic context as unique, discontinuous from pre-exilic culture, and cynical about the veracity of the history it used as a guide to policy: after all, stylistic homogeneity does not imply the absence of sources, some of which shape the style (Herodotus; Deuteronomy in Jeremiah; JE in Deuteronomy; Exodus everywhere, and on). But what proponents of such a view should feel it incumbent upon themselves to produce is a detailed accounting as to why each particular, on their hypothesis, is disposed as it is. Why is reform attributed to this king, not that? Why is this, not that text embellished? Why are miracle stories prominent in accounts of Ahab's and Joash's period, but not some others? Why is the weight of Solomon's temple donations recorded, but not others'? Why has the historian written this lie, not others? Why does the "redactor" intervene here, not elsewhere?

Historically-minded scholars have on occasion satisfied this demand. Martin Noth's Deuteronomistic Historian worked in good faith with his inherited sources. J. M. Miller's treatment of the traditions concerning Ahab and his sons in international affairs is paradigmatic.[13] These cases have been exceptions, however, rather than the rule. Crafty historiographic analysis has in general not prefaced the question, "How did the historian come to believe this?" to the conclusion that "this" is his confection. This is to move from literary characteristics to pronouncement on history without providing historical argument. Craft *vis-à-vis* historiography demands a genealogy of false claims, an explanation as to why *this*, not some other false claim is registered there. Finding a literary scheme in the historiography is not enough to warrant skepticism—the scheme may derive from sources, or be imposed on data derived

[13] See M. Noth (1943); J.M. Miller (1966: 441–454; 1967: 307–324). These are only examples, which could easily be multiplied, as with M. Weinfeld (1964: 396–420; 1967: 93–113) For a clever historical argument to Naivete, see Wright (1967: 58*–68*). For a typical failure to meet the standards promoted here, see Würthwein (1970: 152–166). Würthwein sees 1 Kgs 19:11–13 as secondary, marked off by an epanalepsis, reflecting the cultic "theophany". But this clever suggestion is never measured against the question, why an editor chooses to insert a posited cultic pattern in historical narrative only here and just here.

from sources. The same is true of bias or *"Tendenz":* it may have entered the narrative with a source, or it may be founded on the author's evaluation of the sources. To show that a certain claim was made insincerely, one must minimally establish why it is just and only where it is, and why it takes the form it takes, and no other.

The process of establishing such a norm should begin with our form of publication: in addition to noting the verbal hints that lead to Crafty analysis or redaction-history *(Spannungen),* scholars should be writing short histories of how the text began and how it got the way it is. This has long been the custom in the Lower Criticism, where professional standards, though imperfect, have been consistently higher than those in the Higher. The implementation of the same test in historiographic research would eliminate from print a large number of proposals, including all those dreadful reconstructions of the growth of prophetic books in which the *ipsissima verba* recovered amount to a few fragments of verses from each chapter. To require such discipline of graduate students would be to make a major beginning.

B. *An Issue in Israelite History*

The second order of problem confronting students of Israelite history is higher than the first: having sorted out his historiographic problems—abandonment of them, at least formally, has often been more fruitful—how devious or straightforward should the scholar be in attempting to reconstruct history? This brings us back to Bill, Cathy, Simon and Nellie in their encounter with the unidentified scribe. Training in logic can help to guide them: with an introduction to truth-tables, the four scholars apply themselves differently to their informant, whom each pair suspect of a different national or tribal affiliation. The question they *now* ask is: If I asked another member of your scribal tribe whether the pellet with the poison's in the flagon with the dragon, what would he or she say? If the informant is a truthful, Philistine scribe responding for hypothetical kindred, he will repeat the truth his kindred would tell. And if the informant is a diabolical Israelite scribe, responding for hypothetical kindred, the truth will anyway out: the kindred would lie, and the informant, wishing to lie about what these liars would say, would therefore tell the truth. Israelite or Philistine, the Scribe tells the truth!

The obvious difficulty with the solution—and I am sure Crafty Cathy would bring it up—is that history is not a logical puzzle.

Knowing full well what question it is in which his interrogators are interested (what do they care what a kinsman would say?), the treacherous Israelite scribe lies into the *intent* of the question, not into its formal frame. This is not even to raise the possibility that the Philistine scribe may be "stupid and ignorant" or think his kindred are, or any other minor quibbles. Logical constructs will not work mechanically to ground historical conclusions. Only hard work in historical—not logical or exegetical—trenches will.

This is most obvious in the era of what Malamat astutely calls Israel's proto-history (1983: 1–16). The demography of Biblical studies has dictated that scholars spend precious resources groping longingly toward those prehistorical origins the evanescence of which dimly lights the historical horizon. We suffer from an excess of historical reach over grasp. There is nothing inherently wrong with such a condition, which has been known to produce breakthroughs in theoretical physics. Only, the obstacles to exploiting the Biblical material—with its decoction of folklore and literary convention—still await solution. At the same time, it must be remembered that metaphorical interpretations of the proto-historical narratives, which, for example, take patriarchs to stand for population groups, are even more dangerous (Malamat, 1983; Halpern, 1983: 146–163). Alt may have been right to see in these materials reflections of Israel's LB/Iron I piecemeal entry into Canaan; but this can never be proven. His attempt to penetrate through to authentic "patriarchal" religion was also shaky. Conversely, his analysis of the later cultic implications and use of the materials was penetrating (Alt, KS 1.89–125, 1.1–78, 1.79–88). One can mine this literature for the era depicted only in the company of external controls; with patient application, it can be a source at least of corroborative inference about later eras.[14]

These conditions attach, too, to materials later than the proto-historical. Problems in evidence beset even the history of the monarchy. Skeptics dismiss much testimony hastily, confusing indications, say, of Deuteronomistic authorship with proof of late

[14] What is reflected is Israel's later views of her proto-history. Thus portrayal of a migrating community dependent on pastoralism reflects the economic relations of the Iron I settlers in the central hills and the model of pastoral elements contemporary, say, with J. Israelite Primitivism (Nazirites, Elijah in popular legend, the Rechabites, among others) attests that the view is old. Note J.W. Flight (1925: 158–226) and S. Nyström (1946). More recently, see U. Worschech (1983) for an effort to situate the patriarchs in the Bronze Age.

invention. But such errors are diagnostic: scholars have yet to establish
a historical context broad and detailed enough to allow them to
adjudicate the sources' claims. Thus, even concerning an era for
which useful sources survive, questions of import resist reply: e.g.,
the extent and nature of Ahab's cultic innovations; the character of
Jehoshaphat's reform; the essence of the Naboth incident. Some of
these questions will never be answered: unless a letter signed by
Jezebel turns up in a secure archaeological context instructing the
jury as to its verdict and ordering payment for perjurers, the real
story of Naboth is beyond our power to recover. The same is true of
other private acts. This illustrates the challenge for the next years'
study of Israelite antiquity. What questions *can* we hope to answer,
and what sorts of evidence expect to adduce? In writing about
Naboth, the Israelite historian had thematic concerns, different
from our own: Ahab's and Jezebel's wickedness, the justice of their
fate. How can we extract information relevant to our own historical
agenda from such accounts? These queries should *guide* our professional agenda.

Disproportionately represented among the best work in Israelite history have been efforts to connect important developments
in Israelite politics to external affairs. Working out from these
efforts, one can even produce a fairly gross sketch of Israel's political
history (the gaps in it larger in depth than in breadth of analysis).[15]
Here, external evidence furnishes control over the use of Biblical
information. Almost in the same breath, one might mention studies
that use the history of pre-Israelite Canaan, where relevant, and, by
bringing it into comparison with early Israelite materials, shed light
on the latter (Alt, KS 2.1–65; Mendelsohn, 1956:17–22; Mazar,
1980: 152–173). These are less sturdy, but still productive for other
scholars. But the corpus of external information is limited, and
appeals to parallels or to sociological models as substitutes—and
their deployment always entails injustice to the particularities of
Israelite and Canaanite history—have not led to secure advances
(e.g., Noth, 1930; Mendenhall, 1962: 66–87; Gottwald, 1979).

Nor does archaeology hold great promise. Germane texts have
in the main eluded us, and promise to continue to do so. Architecture

[15] See generally Malamat (1983); H. Tadmor (1961: 232–271); and R. Borger and
H. Tadmor (1982: 244–251) to illustrate a different type. There are a number of
sterling instances in Malamat (1979). These are cited only as some of the examples
available.

is mute—at best, moot—on such subjects as the administration of justice, or even what went on in the "house of Baal" that Ahab built. Historiographically, we sometimes believe we can prove that this or that datum derives from a source—a favorite technique is to demonstrate that the text's claim contradicts the "redactor's" bias. This is not to establish that the source was right; and the instances in which the trick can be turned are limited, in part by the state of redaction-criticism. Altogether, we stand very nearly at an impasse.

In 1957, G. E. Mendenhall confronted retrospectively what seemed to him a similar situation regarding Hebrew origins. The key to rehabilitating the Pentateuchal reports, he wrote, was getting at the culture of the eras they portray and comparing it with the culture the texts reflect (1965:37–39). This prescription had been anticipated in practice roughly a century earlier in the work of such luminaries as Jacob Burckhardt and Theodor Mommsen. Moreover, Mendenhall, caught up in the contemporary flush of Albright school exuberance over proto-history, naively prescribed the approach as an anodyne to skepticism about myths of origins. Burckhardt and Mommsen had in their time adopted it to lead the scrutiny of classical antiquity out of the quagmire of Niebuhrian obsession with origins, and away from the potentially infinite regress of source-criticism of legend: theirs was the model Wellhausen tried, but failed, to follow.[16] Still, Mendenhall's intuition into the exigencies of historical method had some merit.

Five years after this formulation, Mendenhall made his foremost contribution to scholarship by implementing it, in an assault on a major problem. The resultant essay rekindled enthusiasm for the sociological study of Israelite antiquity,[17] though this approach enjoyed a strong tradition stemming at least from the work of Alt and Weber. It should be noted, Mendenhall's sociological hypotheses, like Alt's contrast between charismatic kingship in Israel and institutionalized kingship in Judah, have proven to be without adequate

[16] I will develop this view in a forthcoming volume. For another aspect of the intellectual influences on Wellhausen—those that actuated him as opposed to those that, in my view, he hoped to emulate—see R. Oden, *supra,* and the literature cited there.

[17] "Hebrew Conquest," the most important consolidation of which has been Gottwald, *Tribes.* For the intellectual antecedents of Mendenhall's thesis, note Mendelsohn (1932; 1941: 36–39; 1942: 14–17; 1949); and esp. J. Lewy, (1939: 615–617). Note also Reisner (1897: 145) and Kraeling (1941: 240). Against Mendenhall, see M. Weippert (1969) and Halpern (1983).

basis (Alt, 1951:2–22; ET, Alt, 1968: 311–335; Buccellati, 1967; Ishida, 1977; Halpern, 1981). Nevertheless, if much of the best work in the field arises from integrating Israelite reports with external data, it is the study of Israelite social reality that has produced results of the broadest implications and scope.

Not unnaturally, Biblical scholars have been prone to fix their attention on salient events and movements. History is change, and conflict precipitating change—by scholarly natural selection—rivets historians' gaze. The effective restriction of the evidence to transmitted text and the resultant proliferation of editorial hypotheses and Crafty judgments make this behavior less than normally adaptive. Without archaeological (including documentary) corroboration, one is hard put to forge a hard consensus on such issues.

Theoretically, the same difficulty attaches to a crab-like approach to history. But our sources are less likely to have been consistent or even conscious about cooking the data concerning social, institutional relationships, or concerning customs, topography, material culture and so on. Distortions do occur, depending on the source's genre (e.g., material culture in "Jack and the Beanstalk"). But based on the whole of the evidence (and on a sense of physical reality), these should remain readily identifiable. Crafty Cathy justifiably suspects that the ancients falsely attribute victories to their kings or falsely associate unrelated events. To extend such skepticism to the realms of constitutional relationships or house-plans entails much greater risk. And knowledge of the latter can provide a perspective on claims in other arenas.

In short, our historical quest should center on the background, the abiding institutions and patterns of culture, against which the quicker movements that catch the scholarly eye are visible. We cannot deterministically "predict" on this basis developments the sources do not register. But *Kulturgeschichte* and sociology can afford us what they did classical history: a means to evaluate specific reports about specific events. Just as archaeology is best equipped to provide data concerning village structure, kinship, herding ratios and the like, the textual evidence is most solid when exploited to discover what its authors *assumed*. The extent to which R. H. Kennett's study of Israelite social life has anticipated subsequent archaeological discoveries confirms such a claim resoundingly (1933). This work, like that of de Vaux and Pedersen—not source-criticism focussed on the history of theology—is the real prolegomenon to the history of Israel.

Again, in the absence of such studies, the historian consciously or unconsciously hypothesizes his results; his work always presumes and implies a certain social reality. In many instances, and increasingly as the scholar is unfamiliar with historical reality, the scholarly work—be it even a study in literary art—can involve exceedingly improbable historical presumptions. Attention to the institutional and cultural aspects of Israelite life enhances control over more specific reconstructions, cultivating a better sense of the limits—real, not merely logical—of historical hypothesis. It particularly helps to orient us as to what impact to anticipate from the developments of which we do know, such as the combination of Assyrian and Aramean pressure after the battle of Qarqar leading to the overthrow of the Omrides by a complex Israelite coalition.

Thus, it is one thing to follow Kings' accusation that Ahab's wife instigated judicial murder in order to acquire a plot of land for her husband, although, in a vacuum, the claim seems far-fetched. It is altogether another to argue that David made a Jebusite priest-king YHWH's and Israel's highest cultic functionary. Hints dispersed through the literature may tantalize us to associate a *hypothetical* (but illusory) god *ṣedeq* with Jerusalem, and with cult paraphernalia that seem heterodox in the light of 8th c. reformist theology; and, discounting Chronicles, Zadoq's late appearance in Samuel makes it *possible* to assign his rise to the aftermath of Jerusalem's capture. His name then makes it *possible*, although names with *ṣdq* are fairly far-flung, to associate him with Jerusalem.[18] Only the implications for Israelite political culture, however, afford grounds for assessing the full improbability of this heady mixture: in the climate of contemporary xenophobia, which, along with the rise of cataphractic combat, had led to the inauguration of the monarchy (Halpern, 1981: 216–249), not even David, that most ecumenical of Israelite kings, could have elevated a non-Israelite to the highest Israelite cultic rank. Not even David would at the time have dared make a priest of another god and another ethnos Israel's and YHWH's chief minister; less would he have needed to secure the loyalties of a Canaanite population already propelled into his camp by Saulide persecution; less still would he have done so at the very moment when he had secured the submission of his xenophobic northern subjects and reduced a non-Israelite fasthold to demonstrate how

[18] From here, it is only a small step to making him *king* of Jerusalem, based, again, on his name. See H.H. Rowley (1939: 113–141).

well he represented their interests.[19] Understanding the patterns of Israelite culture and politics better places us to assay such postulation. Conversely, no matter how well-versed we are in Israel's culture, we shall never know the truth about Naboth.

C. *The Issue of the Historical Imagination*

What the sorts of activities commended in the preceding segments can supply is the discipline needed for the exercise of the historical imagination. Disciplined historical imagination is what has characterized all the best work in the study of Israelite history, and what has been lacking in all the worst. The need for it is pressing in a field whose principal source affords no hint of events such as Shishaq's devastation of the north—one of the major archaeological markers of the Iron Age—or the epochal coalition at Qarqar and Jehu's equally epochal policy reversal and contribution to Shalmaneser III, or the extent of Omri's or Uzziah's influence, to name only a few instances (Sarna, 1979:3–19). William Foxwell Albright, as often, grasped the situation masterfully. Evaluating a volume that in methodological terms grafted Gressmann on to Niebuhr, that he himself termed "a historical romance," Albright closed with the generous verdict that the volume was not to be missed, and commended it "highly to all who would have their historical imagination quickened, for creative history can never be written without imagination." (1925:182–184). That *obiter dictum* has as much force for Israelite history as for any other.

On this point, the methodological problems addressed in the first two segments of this section come together. Redaction-critics, for example, who do not reconstruct plausibly the reasoning and motivation of their hypothetical redactors are guilty of failing to exercise historical imagination. They therefore tend to reconstruct redaction that implies that a somewhat labile author contradicted sources willfully, changed them at certain points while leaving them alone at others where the conditioning factors were to all appearance identical, and in general worked idiosyncratically and erratically. In such cases, the method resembles that of Rowley in identifying Zadoq as a Jebusite: exegetical hints and patterns of literary

---

[19]Was ever victor so vanquished? The equivalent to Rowley's scenario would be Louis IX installing a Moslem adversary as Pope. On Zadoq, see S.M. Olyan (1982: 177–93); my "Sectionalism and the Schism," (1974: 519–532) and *Emergence* (1983: 221–231); all this work inspired in part by F.M. Cross (1973: 195–215).

juxtaposition are parlayed into historical conclusions, without the conclusions being checked to see how they fit into Israel's wider sociocultural context. Only a few hypothetical redactors—Wolfgang Richter's Rdt in Judges is a parade example—make any sense at all as historical individuals. [20]

Here again we see the vestiges of scholarly paradigms taken over from exegesis and theology, whose concerns are synchronic and atemporal. Attention to literary hints, to words, not contextualized in an appropriate historical reality, inevitably leads to misprision of editorial activity and to the treatment of textual claims at the wrong level of reconstruction. The word assumes exaggerated dignity, becomes more symbol than sign. Folklore is confused with historiography, historiography with history. Haupt's reconstruction of the Sinai and Jericho experiences falls into this category, as does Rowley's eccentric identification of Zadoq.

A similar case, involving an even more talented scholar, is Richter's association of the noun, *nāgîd*, with the pre-monarchic north. Without direct attestation, the theory rests ultimately on a distinction between what is alleged to be the office, *nāgîd*, in 1 Sam 9:1ff. and the indubitable office, *melek* (Richter, 1965:71–84). Yet Richter denies the historicity of 1 Sam 9:1ff. He attempts, thus, to draw specific historical information concerning the earliest monarchic era from a document exhibiting no other recollections of it. This is not impossible, whatever other considerations militate against the specific proposal; but it means picking the historical ingredients out of a folkloristic puree, and guaranteeing that the folklorist dug them up from archival soil. Even where the object of this exercise is to reconstruct institutions, rather than events, the procedure is dangerous: one assigns Element X of a later text to the 11th c. B.C.E. because it can be used to illuminate an otherwise unclear era; one matches the unknown circumstances of the 11th c. to a hint, taken from the folklore, that may *possibly* belong to some historical social milieu, that milieu *possibly* the one to which it is being matched.

More important, Richter's approach applies literary relations directly to history: Saul's anointing in the folklore to be *nāgîd* proves that the term describes an office once different from *melek*; the

[20] This is the case for almost all reconstructions of Dtr$_2$, for example. Only R. Smend (1978) has since Noth come meaningfully to grips with this problem, in his case by denying systematic redaction in favor of successive and similar adjustments. See, however, W. Richter (1966).

difficulties are that the anointing may be a literary topos, that the two words may in fact represent two different aspects of the same office, that language and metaphor, in short, must not be reified. This error is common in biblical history, and one to which the present author has succumbed.[21] Indeed, its perpetrators number among them some of the most distinguished professional practitioners: T.N.D. Mettinger, for example, sees the report of David's nominating the *nāgîd* in 1 Kgs 1:35 as evidence of a *nāgîd*'s not being chosen by YHWH (1976:151–184); Richter's position is similar. But this is a narrative relating how the *nāgîd* in a certain situation was "really" chosen. At a different level of discourse (more theological), one would without hesitation refer to Solomon's election as YHWH's act. Indeed, the anointing in 1 Kgs 1:32–40 was meant to express to contemporaries, and even to readers of this text, *YHWH's* naming Solomon *nāgîd*. The narrative's analysis is secular; the position of *nāgîd* cannot be judged secular on that basis (Ishida, 1977:35–51; Halpern, 1981:1–11, 111–118, 171–174).

This is rather a sophisticated instance. A more widespread one is the view that the Minor Judges were different from the Major, which rests on the dubious argument that the nature of the sources concerning each differs. Another probable case is the use of prophetic polemic against the cult and against social injustice to prove that Israel's society was characterized by idolatry and economic oppression. At a minimum, these conclusions are moot: the nature of such polemic is often to persuade the converted to eliminate fringe phenomena, to implement accepted social norms, on which the polemics are based, ever more completely. One is hard-pressed, for example, to find parallels to American rhetoric of the late 1960's and the 1970's about inequality, racism and poverty either in Russian or in Third World literature. The openness of the society has much to do with what sorts of charges are regularly aired. In Israel, the theoretical limitation of centralized power, part of it the special status of "prophecy," promoted social criticism. That some of this survives does not mean that its targets were as rampant or as degenerate as it claims.[22] Language is language. When it is

---

[21] In Halpern and Levenson (1980: 507–518), in the suggestion that Caleb's replacing Nahshon as a *nāśî'* mirrors his supplanting Nahshon in the Chronicles genealogies. A similar case flaws the contribution of D. Edelmann (1984: 195–209), which takes treaty-related verbiage in 2 Sam 2:6f. to imply that Jabesh-Gilead was in a vassal relationship to Saul different from that of his other subjects.

[22] *Constitution* (1981). Note K.W. Whitelam (1979) for the dominant ethic of

mistaken for reality, the confusion signifies our failure to apply historical imagination.

Even when contextualizing historiographic or historical reconstructions does not lead to outrageous cacaphony, scrupulous application of historical imagination can be a powerful evaluative tool. The Albrightian view of the Conquest as a single military movement furnishes a concrete example: at the physical and political level, it strains credulity to reconstruct a unified, politically-centralized Israel consciously setting out from southern Transjordan to reduce all Canaan to its service, let alone its then dispersing to the farther reaches of its later dominions without maintaining superiority, unity, or a grip on the best lands. Conversely, a revised Altian scenario entails only small-scale homesteading of regions relatively distant from imperial control, with ethnic solidarity giving rise to political, leading to coalescence into nationhood. The adoption of monarchy supplies another illustration. The old, Wellhausenian view has the royal administration striving consciously toward Wittvogelian despotism from Day 1. But Israel's response to the advent of heavy-armored champions and lowland Philistine cooperation must be understood in terms of traditional patterns of thought and administrative ethics. The early kingship must also be conceived in terms of domestic political configurations, with the king intellectually, emotionally and culturally integrated with his popular constituents: he *was* one of them, a consideration the import of which was not lost on the author of Deut 17:15.[23]

A failure to apply historical imagination with discipline leads not only to improbable reconstructions, but also to the imposition of alien categories on ancient Israel. Thus, scholars have habitually spoken of a "prophetic party", as though the prophetic literature were not rife with indications that every party had its prophets. They have placed "the prophets", all of them, into opposition with "the priests", deploying a historic Protestant canard against empty, ritualistic Catholicism to tar the Israelite establishment. And they have even founded such analyses on a distinction between "true" and "false" prophets, although "false" prophets are historically speaking indistinguishable from "true." This last represents a collapse of history into homily, an inability to surmount the confessionally-

---

administration; esp. M. Weinfeld (1982: 491–519). On the social roles of the prophets see R.R. Wilson (1980); cf. D.L. Petersen (1981).

[23] The views laid down here are argued in *Emergence, Constitution*, respectively.

created framework for viewing the past. Probably the most insidious related case has been the tendency to apply the theology of Josiah's reform as normative even for earlier eras (as well as contemporary). This has, among other things, led to a drastic exaggeration of syncretistic tendencies and of the accuracy of prophetic rhetoric against cult imagery. Israelite religion has always been the cynosure of professional and amateur interest. That study of it so frequently flouts historical standards is a source of some embarrassment to the field as a whole.

Work in Israelite antiquity demands a shrewd combination of historiographic and historical analysis. It demands careful attention to the properties of language, anterior to the formulation of historical conclusions. The differences between the historian's viewpoint and the viewpoints of various characters in his narratives, between actual event and cultural patterns shaping narrative convention, between such convention and ritual reported in narrative—to name a few—all need to be borne in mind.[24] All interpretations of language demand contextualization of the historiography in a vision of Israelite reality, then movement to a similarly contextualized interpretation of what events the historiography reflects. The process is delicate, demanding the right mix of Craft and Naivete, and a disciplined historical imagination. That it is beyond the capacity of the Pyrrhonist and fundamentalist is plain.

This brings us back to our two families of scholars trying to learn from an informant, who may be from a tribe of scribes that lies, if the chalice from the palace holds the brew that is true. The puzzle's lesson resembles that of the foregoing reflections: Simple Simon, Naive Nellie, Crafty Cathy and Shifty Bill cannot work effectively as separate teams; Craft must strike a balance with Simplicity, Nellie get together with Bill. The problem at hand will also require that beyond exercising their customary proclivities, they exercise their

---

[24] So, in 1 Samuel 11 we have a report of what was probably the battle that confirmed Saul's grasp on power after a ritual inaugurating him as king, a report that the confirmatory part of the kingship ritual followed his victory (though no doubt it was executed either exclusively or as well before the battle, at the ritual of his royal designation), a narrative use of the victory as the "test" of his divine election and worthiness to be king, and historical elements passed over in silence—the crossing of the Jordan to Gilgal—which played on contemporary mythopoeic sensibilities and helped, ultimately, to structure the kingship ritual and conceptions of the kingship as history passed into cultural pattern. These different levels of valence are not mutually exclusive. See also Porter (1970: 129–131) on double (divine and human) appointment of royalty; Halpern (1981).

imagination, and adopt a lateral approach to boot. But between the four of them, there is one rather simple way they can discover overpowering evidence as to whether their scribe is an Israelite or a Philistine. I leave it to the reader to imagine how.

III.   Some sociological sciomantics

The foregoing section points to some of the deficiencies in contemporary scholarship and, not systematically, indicates types of remedies that might be apt. The tonics prescribed are not untested. Some, if not all, are now being applied; in particular, an increased energy has for the past decade characterized the assault on Israelite sociology. This makes it doubly ironic that today it is the sociology of Biblical scholarship itself that affords cause for concern.

The "schismatic semantics" with which this contemplation opened are not frivolous. The last twenty years have witnessed a widening split between Biblical historians, mostly of the Crafty variety, and those whose work lies in ancillary disciplines, such as archaeology, epigraphy, and philology. One sees the tendency in a proliferation of journals, for example, defining themselves as philological, rather, or more, than Biblical. Often, the divide is attributed to an "information explosion" that, to my mind, has been exaggerated. One contributing factor as yet uncited is symptomized in the success of a journal like *BAR*: constitutionally Naive scholars—fundamentalists, conservatives, and some moderates—feel driven from Biblical history; they move most comfortably into the ancillary disciplines when called on to make their primary scholarly contributions. For this reason, the constituencies of the respective areas have a tendency to skew. *BAR*, with its conservative readers hoping for light on the Bible from professional archaeologists, will not attract the same audience or circulation to its sister-journal, *Bible Review*. The reason? Shifty Bill has no readership in the Bible Belt.

A second factor exacerbates the situation. Scholars whose primary training and vocation lies in the ancillary disciplines quickly develop the feeling that their fields are more "scientific" than Biblical history, and to the extent that one defines science as natural science and as quantification they are right. They frequently see their materials mishandled or ignored by scholars whose primary interest is exegetical, historical or theological. Speaking broadly, the predictable result is that individuals among them develop and socialize an attitude of scorn toward such exegetical postures and techniques as Crafty Cathy's historiographic anaylsis. The effect is self-reinforcing: members of the community are discouraged from learning why Craft is indispensable, and the scorn grows.

Comparable currents affect the bearers of critical orthodoxy, the more traditional Biblical critics. They see the cavalier attitude affected by Naive scholars toward the history of their Craft; they observe that the factors enumerated above combine with orientation in training to dispose those scholars against practising Shiftiness even when conditions call for it, or to practise it arbitrarily, in accordance with preformed theory. In short, they see their soft data—which has its own, humanistic logic—mishandled by the masters of the hard data. The result: they begin to regard these colleagues as technicians. In the aging Biblical Archaeology—Syro-Palestinian Archaeology controversy, this development is well underway.

This cleavage, though schematic, can have only deleterious consequences. Two forces palliate it. First, most practitioners of orthodox Biblical criticism accept that the weight of proof in the ancillary disciplines exceeds that of historiographic hypothesis. Indeed, they accord evidence in these disciplines an exaggerated respect. Simultaneously, the scholars of the ancillary disciplines are not homogeneously conservative—many, perhaps most of them remain open to orthodox criticism; some are even versed in it, although the day when an Albright or a de Vaux could dominate both has passed into a mournful twilight. Disrespect for fundamentalism has also been socialized in academic circles to the extent that pressure against exhibiting it is strong. So the polarization of the disciplines is, and will always be, incomplete. Second, the two sides bear too heavily on one another to make for clean separation in publication. The process of give-and-take in journals and books is centripetal, compelling readers to attend to both, and scholars to protect their flanks. That both communities are striving toward similar goals, ultimately, necessitates communication and reconciliation. This is a conviction enshrined in the Albrightian program for the field.

What is unfortunate is that the process shows signs of being lengthy. Scholars have a tendency to accept the parting of the ways between "technical" and humanistic work as natural, on the lines of natural scientific specialization. The authors of the Biblical Archaeology—Syro-Palestinian Archaeology controversy in fact want to avoid confusion between the two that they feel dilutes their standards; they hope to *discourage* facile exploitation of archaeology by Biblicists. They envision the distinctions and barriers as permanent, irreversible.

There is considerable merit in this view, taken substantively rather than as a wrangle about names. Unless strong measures are taken, its call for and prediction of compartmentalization will, when realized, have an inhibitive impact on synthesis beyond its natural force. One must bear in mind that the last hundred years—even the last forty—have seen inscriptional and archaeological data increase at dizzying rates; the increase in publication and publication outlets and in the population of scholars has matched it. But this has generated a great deal more *Biblical* scholarship, even speaking proportionally, than technical.

Bibliographically, the result has been chaos, and the few efforts to stem the tide, though brave, have been flawed—one thinks of *OTA,* whose format is ideal, but whose diffusion is too great; every 25 years or so, such a tool needs to be re-mounted and synthesized as a sort of bibliographical dictionary. Comprehensive tools are called for that can be easily maintained. It is hard to see that they will effectively be developed—eliminating fringe publications and centering on Israelite antiquity itself—before the middle of the next century.

What makes such tools so valuable is that their organization and digestion of scholarship transforms the field to the degree that it makes a standard body of scholarship open and accessible; all scholars can reasonably be expected to familiarize themselves with the state of learning so canonized. Given more powerful levers, the current segregation of archaeology from text-work need not prove permanent, just as the *CAD* promises in the end to open up the hitherto esoteric world of Assyriology to a slightly larger community. New Albrights and new des Vaux are to be anticipated. The problem in critical Biblical scholarship has not been an information explosion so much as a failure to develop sufficiently powerful reference works. Computerization of the literature, a prospect unfortunately more distant than many of us believe, would of course simplify the task considerably. Encouraging the development of new models, and the dissemination of detailed study in the history of scholarship, side by side with synthesis—encouraging activities already being carried out but insufficiently general—would prove ameliorative.

All these measures would have the common effect of increasing the socialization of scholarship. This, in turn, affects the rate at which professional standards are codified. It is possible to stipulate literally hundreds of issues and tasks that offer themselves for execution in the interim, ranging from sophistication of redaction-criticism and of attention to the different languages of historiography,[25] to examination of the interstices of Israelite history, such as the forms and rhythms of economic and political interactions, and including, ideally, the assembly of a synchronic picture of Israelite culture in a limited era—the 7th c. being the most promising.[26] It was, significantly, such a synchronic purchase that afforded Mommsen a means of evaluating claims concerning earlier history. But these undertakings can bear mature fruit only in an environment in which standards have been clarified, the basis of discussion agreed. They will be most productive, that is, in the sort of environment "Syro-Palestinian archaeologists" express their longing for by retitling their collective endeavor. It remains to be seen if "a rose is a rose is a rose" and that's final, or if it can make itself even sweeter, by using its Latin name.

The science of Israelite history set out in the 20th c. speculating about Abraham's peregrinations, figuring out when the Rachel tribes met the Leah tribes, and explaining how desert life and the sight of a volcanic eruption created monotheism. By the late 1920's, in the work of such scholars as Alt, it assumed the proportions of a branch of history-in-general. Grown out of theology, whose procedures, concerns and scientific framework are quite different from those of history, the field retains traces of its ancestry—especially in the proclivity to confuse literary issues with historical. The task for the coming century will be to discard these vestiges of a promising youth: keeping theology to the side,[27] yet without ceasing to be a Biblical historian, the scholar must become an Israelite and Canaanite historian. Without ceasing to control the sources' literary properties, and, in whatever measure possible, the history of their composition, the scholar must wean himself from the barbiturate of

[25] And where their truth claims lie. It should be noted that we altogether lack royal inscriptions—Arad 88 the possible exception, for which see D. Pardee (1978: 289–336) esp. p. 290; A.R. Millard (1978: 23–26), esp. p. 26—to guide us in stratifying thought and vocabulary chronologically, and in assessing the impact of copying, as training and as method, on Israelite literature.

[26] Or roughly 722–580. This is the time wealthiest in extant texts. Sennacherib from below and Nebuchadrezzar from above also seal off a relative treasure of archaeological detail.

[27] For its impact on scholarship intended to be antiquarian, see the esssay of J.D. Levenson, supra, and Weinfeld (1979).

literary possibility to confront instead historical reality, and especially its meaning for its principals. This agenda seems straightforward; it will not so soon be fulfilled.

History, say the wags, is the agreed-upon lie, and in this caricature there is found much truth. What the wags keep to themselves, truth be told, is the scarcity of lies agreed on. No professional historian expects it to be otherwise: history in this sense consists of scenarios, divers and not all mutually exclusive. What we must strive toward, however, is a different sort of history—in the instance, Biblical, or Israelite—an agreed-on set of standards geared to produce the sorts of lies around which consensus can form. The greatest service this generation could render its field would be meaningfully to contribute to this end. Exposing Israelite and Philistine scribes is delightful, an occupation to be savored. Developing an explicit etiquette to govern the sport would improve the results; by reducing injury and injustice to its objects, it would also heighten the entertainment.

WORKS CONSULTED

Aharoni, M. and Y.
1976   "The Stratification of Judahite Sites in the 8th and 7th Centuries B.C.E.," *BASOR* 224, 73–90.

Aharoni, Y.
1974   "The Horned Altar of Beer-Sheba," *BA* 37, 2–6.
1972   "Excavations at Tel Beer-Sheba. Preliminary Report of the Fourth Season, 1972," *TA* 1, 32–42.

Albright, W.F.
1925   Review of E. Sellin, *Wie wurde Sichem eine israelitische Stadt?* Leipzig: Deichert. *JAOS* 45, 182–184.

Alt, A.
1951   "Das Königtum in den Reichen Israel und Juda," *VT* 1, 2–22 (= KS 2.116–134) [ET *Essays on Old Testament History and Religion*. Garden City, N.Y.: Doubleday, 1968].
1953   "Die Landnahme der der Israeliten in Palästina" KS 1.59–125.
1953   "Die Wallfahrt von Sichem nach Bethel" KS 1.79–88.
1953   "Der Gott der Väter" KS 1.1–78.
1953   "Die Staatenbildung der Israeliten in Palästina," *KS* 2. 1–65;

Berger, P. R.
Forth-   *Die neubabylonischen Königsinschriften*. AOAT 4/3.
coming   Neukirchen: Neukirchener.

Blenkinsopp, J.
1972   *Gibeon and Israel. The Role of Gibeon and the Gi-
beonites in the Political and Religious History of
Early Israel*. SOTSMS 2; Cambridge: Cambridge
University.

Borger, R. and Tadmor, H.
1982   "Zwei Beiträge zur alttestamentlichen Wissenschaft
aufgrund der Inschriften Tiglatpilesers III," ZAW 94,
244–251.

Buccellati, G.
1967   *Cities and Nations of Ancient Syria: An Essay on Political Institutions with Special Reference to the Israelite Kingdoms*. SS 26; Rome: Istituto di Studi del
Vicino Oriente.

Cogan, M.
1980   "Ashurbanipal Prism Inscriptions Once Again," *JCS*
32, 147–150.
1977   "Ashurbanipal Prism F: Notes on Scribal Techniques
and Editorial Procedures," *JCS* 29, 97–107.
1974   *Imperialism and Religion: Assyria, Judah and Israel in
the Eighth and Seventh Centuries B.C.E.*. SBLMS
19; Missoula: Scholars.

Cogan, M. and Tadmor, H.
1977   "Gyges and Ashurbanipal. A Study in Literary Transmission," *Or* 46, 65–85.

Cross, F. M.
1973   *Canaanite Myth and Hebrew Epic*. Cambridge: Harvard University.

Edelmann, D.
1984   "Saul's Rescue of Jabesh-Gilead (1 Sam 11:1–11): Sort-
ing Story from History," ZAW 96, 195–209.

Flight, J. W.
1925   "The Nomadic Idea and Ideal in the Old Testament,"
JBL 42, 158–226.

Friedman, R. E.
1981   "Sacred History and Theology: The Redaction of
Torah," in *The Creation of Sacred Literature: Com-
position and Redaction of the Biblical Text*, (ed.)
Friedman, R. E.; Near Eastern Studies 22;
Berkeley: University of California.

Gottwald, N. K.
1979   *The Tribes of Yahweh.* New York: Orbis.

Halpern, B.
1983   *The Emergence of Israel in Canaan.* SBLMS 29; Chico: Scholars.
1983   "Doctrine by Misadventure. Between the Israelite Source and the Biblical Historian," in *The Poet and the Historian. Essays in Literary and Historical Biblical Criticism,* (ed.) Friedman, R. E.; HSS 26; Chico: Scholars, 41–73.
1981   *Constitution of the Monarchy in Israel.* HSM 25; Chico: Scholars.
1974   "Sectionalism and the Schism," *JBL* 93, 519–532.

Halpern, B. and Levenson, J. D.
1980   "The Political Import of David's Marriages," *JBL* 99, 507–518.

Haupt, P.
1909   "The Burning Bush and the Origin of Judaism," *PAPS* 48, 354–369.

Hoffmann, H. D.
1980   *Reform und Reformen: Untersuchungen zu einem Grundthema der deuteronomistischen Geschichtsschreibung.* ATANT 66; Zurich: Theologischer.

Ishida, T.
1977   *The Royal Dynasties in Ancient Israel. A Study on the Formation and Development of Royal-Dynastic Ideology.* BZAW 142; Berlin: de Gruyter.
1977   "*ngyd:* A Term for the Legitimation of the Kingship," *AJBI* 3, 35–51.

Kennett, R. H.
1933   *Ancient Hebrew Social Life and Custom as Indicated in Law, Narrative and Metaphor* (Schweich Lectures, 1931); London: Oxford University.

Kraeling, E. G.
          "The Origins of the Name Hebrew," *AJSL* 58, 237–253.

Lemaire, A.
1981   *Les écoles et la formation de la Bible dans l'ancien Israël.* OBo 39; Göttingen: Vandenhoeck & Ruprecht.

Lewy, J.
1939   "Habiru and Hebrews," *HUCA* 14, 615–617.

Liverani, M.
1973   "Memorandum on the Approach to Historiographic Texts," *Or.* 42, 178–194.

Malamat, A.
1983   "Die Frühgeschichte Israels—eine methodologische Studie," *TZ* 39, 1–16 [*Israel in Biblical Times. Historical Essays*. Jerusalem: Bialik and I.E.S., 1983, 3–22 (in altered form)].

Malamat, A. (ed.)
1979   *The Age of the Monarchies: Political History.* WHJP 4/1, Jerusalem: Massada.

Mazar, B.
1980   "The Philistines and the Foundation of the Kingdoms of Israel and Tyre," *Canaan and Israel. Historical Essays.* Jerusalem: Bialik and I.E.S., 152–173.

Mendelsohn, I.
1956   "Samuel's Denunciation of Kingship in the Light of Akkadian Documents from Ugarit," *BASOR* 143, 17–22.

1949   *Slavery in the Ancient Near East.* New York: Oxford.

1942   "State Slavery in Ancient Palestine," *BASOR* 85, 14–17.

1941   "The Canaanite Term for 'Free Proletarian'," *BASOR* 83, 36–39.

1932   *Legal Aspects of Slavery in Babylonia, Assyria, and Palestine: A comparative study 3000–500 B.C.* Williamsport: Bayard.

Mendenhall, G. E.
1965   "Biblical History in Transition," in *The Bible and the Ancient Near East. Essays in honor of William Foxwell Albright*, (ed). G. E. Wright; Garden City, N.Y.: Doubleday.

1962   "The Hebrew Conquest of Palestine," *BA* 25, 66–87.

Mettinger, T. N. D.
1976   *King and Messiah. The Civil and Sacral Legitimation of the Israelite Kings.* CBOTS 8; Lund: Gleerup.

Millard, A. R.
1983   "The Old Testament and History: Some Considerations," *Faith and Thought. Transactions of the Victoria Institute* 110, 34–53.

1982   "In Praise of Ancient Scribes," *BA* 45, 143–53.

1978   "Epigraphic Notes, Aramaic and Hebrew," *PEQ* 110, 23–26.

Miller, J. M.
1967   "The Fall of the House of Ahab," *VT* 17, 307–324.
1966   "The Elisha Cycle and the Omride Wars," *JBL* 85, 441–454.

Na'aman, N.
1976   "Two Notes on the Monolith Inscription of Shalmaneser III from Kurkh," *TA* 3, 89–106.

Noth, M.
1943   *Überlieferungsgeschichtliche Studien*. Halle: Max Niemayer, 1943; reprinted Tübingen: Mohr, 1957 [ET, of pp. 1–110, *The Deuteronomistic History*. JSOTSups 15; Sheffield: JSOT, 1981].
1930   *Das System der zwölf Stämme Israels*. BWANT 4/1; Stuttgart: Kohlhammer.

Nyström, S.
1946   *Beduinentum und Jahvismus: eine soziologisch-religionsgeschichtliche Untersuchung zum Alten Testament*. Lund: Gleerup.

Olyan, S. M.
1982   "Zadoq's Origins and the Tribal Politics of David," *JBL* 101, 177–193.

Paine, Thomas
1945   *The Complete Writings of Thomas Paine*, (ed.) P.S. Foner; N.Y.: Citadel.

Pardee, D.
1978   "Letters from Tel Arad," *UF* 10, 289–336.

Petersen, D. L.
1981   *The Roles of Israel's Prophets*. JSOTSups 17; Sheffield: JSOT.

Porter, J. R.
1970   "The Succession of Joshua," in *Proclamation and Presence: Old Testament Essays in Honor of Gwynne Henton Davies*, (ed.) J. I. Durham and J. R. Porter; Richmond: John Knox, 102–132.

Reisner, G. A.
1897   "The Habiri in the El Amaina Tablets," *JBL* 16, 143–145.

Richter, W.
1966   *Traditionsgeschichtliche Untersuchungen zum Richterbuch*. BBB 18; Bonn: Hanstein (2nd ed.).
1965   "Die *nagīd*-Formel," *BZ* N.F. 9, 71–84.

Rowley, H. H.
1939   "Zadok and Nehushtan," *JBL* 58, 113–141.

Sarna, N. M.
1979   "The Biblical Sources for the History of the Mon-
            archy," in Malamat (ed.), *Age of the Monarchies:
            Political History*, 3–19.

Sethe, K.
1930   *Urgeschichte und älteste Religion der Ägypter*. Leipzig:
            Brockhaus.

Shea, W. H.
1985   "Sennacherib's Second Palestinian Campaign," *JBL*
            104, 401–418.

Smend, R.
1978   *Die Entstehung des Alten Testaments*. Stuttgart:
            Kohlhammer.

Soggin, J. A.
1978   "The History of Ancient Israel—A Study in Some
            Questions of Method," *EI* 14, 44*–51*.

Tadmor, H.
1961   "Azriyau of Yaudi," *SH* 8.

Thompson, T. L.
1974   *The Historicity of the Patriarchal Narratives*. BZAW
            133; Berlin: de Gruyter.

Van Seters, J.
1983   *In Search of History. Historiography in the Ancient
            World and the Origins of Biblical History*. New
            Haven: Yale University.

1975   *Abraham in History and Tradition*. New Haven: Yale.

Weinfeld, M.
1982   "'Justice and Righteousness' in Ancient Israel against
            the Background of 'Social Reforms' in the Ancient
            Near East," *Mesopotamien und seine Nachbarn.
            XXV Rencontre Assyriologique International,
            Berlin*, (ed.) H. J. Nissen, J. Renger; Berlin: Reimer,
            491–519.

1979   *Getting at the Roots of Wellhausen's Understanding of
            the Law of Israel on the 100th Anniversary of the
            Prolegomena*. Report 14/79; Jerusalem: Institute for
            Advanced Studies.

1967   "The Period of the Conquest and of the Judges as Seen
            by the Earlier and the Later Sources" *VT* 17, 93–117
            [version of his Hebrew paper, "The Conquest of the
            Land of Canaan and the Destruction of its Inhabi-
            tants: Two Different Viewpoints in the Bible"].

1964   "The Awakening of National Consciousness in Israel in the 7th Century B.C.E.," *Oz le-David. Biblical Essays in Honor of D. Ben-Gurion*. Jerusalem: Kiryath Sepher, 396–420.

Weippert, M.

1967   *Die Landnahme der israelitischen Stämme in der neueren wissenschaftlichen Diskussion*. FRLANT 92; Göttingen: Vandenhoeck & Ruprecht [ET, *The Settlement of the Israelite Tribes in Palestine*. SBT 2/21; London: SCM and Naperville: Allenson, 1971].

Weiser, A.

1962   *Samuel. Seine geschichtliche Aufgabe und religiöse Bedeutung. Traditionsgeschichtliche Untersuchungen zu I. Samuel 7–12*. FRLANT 81; Göttingen: Vandenhoeck & Ruprecht.

Whitelam, K. W.

1979   *The Just King. Monarchical Judicial Authority in Ancient Israel*. JSOTSups 12, Sheffield: JSOT.

Wilson, R. R.

1980   *Prophecy and Society in Ancient Israel*. Philadelphia: Fortress.

Würthwein E.

1970   "Elijah at Horeb: Reflections on I Kings 19:11–13," in *Proclamation and Presence: Old Testament Essays in Honor of Gwynne Henton Davies*, (ed.) J. I. Durham and J. R. Porter. Richmond: John Knox, 152–166.

Worschech, U.

1983   *Abraham. Eine sozialgeschichtliche Studie*. Europäische Hochschulschriften 23/225; Frankfurt: Lang.

Wright, G. E.

1967   "The Provinces of Solomon," *EI* 8, 58*–68*.

Yadin, Y.

1976   "Beer-sheba: The High Place Destroyed by King Josiah," *BASOR* 222, 5–6.

Chapter 6

WOMEN'S STUDIES AND THE HEBREW BIBLE[1]

Jo Ann Hackett
Indiana University

It is gratifying to me that women's studies is included in this volume on the future of biblical studies, although it is something quite different for me to be working on ways to deal with real people and situations instead of tracing the changes in the letter *dalet* over the centuries. It is, of course, completely appropriate that we should be considering women's issues within biblical scholarship because these issues are finally being addressed in most fields, a sign, among other things, of the influence of feminism on academics. It is, in fact, hitting our field a little later than most. Even though within Judaism and Christianity the ordination of women is more attainable and at the same time more a current issue, more controversial, than it has been in the recent past, the interest that issue generates probably spills over more into master's programs and seminary curricula than into doctoral programs aimed at producing scholars.

K.D. Sakenfeld's (1982) excellent article (which grew out of a SBL session on women's studies and biblical studies) outlines this same phenomenon. She brings up the gap between the way the "scholarly guild" treats the Bible and the impact the Bible has on the culture as a whole, a gap she especially experiences as a seminary professor (1982: 13-14).

In the following paper, I will, first of all, mention some of the

[1] Part of the research included in this paper was completed during the summer of 1983, with the help of a Summer Stipend from the National Endowment for the Humanities, and I would like to take this opportunity to thank the NEH for its support.

Substantial portions of this paper, specifically much of the methodological summary and the results as applied to Judges 3–16, have appeared in a slightly different form as "In the Days of Jael: A Model for Reclaiming the History of Women in Ancient Israel" (1985).

work that has already been going on within the field. I will also suggest, however, that scholarship on women is developing in certain very definite directions these days and will, I think, continue to do so for years to come. It is my further goal, then, to outline those directions, and to indicate some of the applications women's studies methods are being given in work in our field, and I will include my own work here.

If people know anything at all about scholarship on women in the field of biblical studies, the work they know is most likely that of Phyllis Trible. Trible spelled out very clearly in an article in *JAAR* in 1973 her dilemma and her solutions. The article is called "Depatriarchalizing in Biblical Interpretation," and in the beginning of the article she says:

> I face a terrible dilemma: Choose ye this day whom you will serve: the God of the fathers or the God of sisterhood . . . . Yet I myself perceive neither war nor neutrality between biblical faith and Women's Liberation. . . .Let me not be misunderstood: I know that Hebrew literature comes from a male dominated society. I know that biblical religion is patriarchal, and I understand the adverse effects of that religion for women. I know also the dangers of eisegesis. Nevertheless, I affirm that the intentionality of biblical faith, as distinguished from a general description of biblical religion, is neither to create nor to perpetuate patriarchy but rather to function as salvation for both women and men. . . .The hermeneutical challenge is to translate biblical faith without sexism (1973:31).

One of Trible's solutions is to emphasize certain biblical themes, for instance, that Yahweh is above sexuality: although Yahweh is generally referred to with masculine words, there is also feminine imagery used about the deity in the Hebrew Bible, and so Yahweh is unlike "fertility" gods who are male or female. She also affirms the commonly-made argument that biblical faith is largely about liberation (1973).

Trible works from her personal stance as both a feminist and a believing Christian and thinks there is a way out of that dilemma. She especially tries (as have many feminist New Testament scholars) to reveal oppressive interpretations of what were, in her scheme, originally liberating texts. Her approach is basically exegesis and literary interpretation, not historical research.

Another scholar in our field, Phyllis Bird, published an article several years ago in *HTR* that can be seen as a refutation of Trible's interpretation of Gen 1:27, even though Trible is rarely mentioned in the article. Where Trible says that the clause "male and female created he them" should be taken seriously as parallel to "God created *ʾādām* in his own image" and that ancient authors also saw it that way, Bird maintains that the P writers were not feminists, that the passage was not meant to comment at all on the equality or inequality of the sexes, and that the "male and female" part of v. 27 simply leads logically into the blessing in v. 28: "Be fruitful and multiply." In other words, as one of my students summarized it, Trible sees v. 27b as connected logically with what immediately *precedes* it, while Bird sees it connected logically with what immediately *follows*. That is not to say that Bird thinks the deity prefers men to women, and as a theological point she will emphatically deny such an interpretation, of course. But she cautions against interpreting the P writers as if *their own* theology or anthropology included any doctrine of equality or inequality of the sexes (Bird, 1981; Trible, 1978: 12-23).

I actually bring up Bird's work for two additional reasons: first, to call attention to her article in *Religion and Sexism* (1974: 41-88). The article is titled "Images of Women in the Old Testament," and it is a marvelous source for students who express an interest in women in the Bible—accurate and clearly laid out. Secondly, I want to include a footnote of hers from p. 133 of the *HTR* article I mentioned earlier, a note that is a very nicely worded explanation of what she and others are doing:

> By "feminist" theology or critique I refer to that work which is characterized by an awareness that traditional theology and biblical interpretation have been dominated, in one way or another, by "patriarchal" or androcentric perspectives, values and judgments. Awareness of this persistent bias has led to various attempts to expose, explain, and reinterpret texts that have traditionally carried the patriarchal message and to identify, where possible, sources which qualify or contradict it. . . .Much is the work of amateurs, for the origins of the critique and the new constructions were almost entirely "outside the camp"—precisely because those within the scholarly guilds lacked the necessary experiential base, or, for other reasons of restricted environment, failed to recognize the problem.

Robert Oden echoes this sentiment when he writes above about our "amateur" status when we turn to fields outside our initial training.

One thing I would like to do in this paper, then, is to provide a number of tools to help us broaden our "restricted environment," by explaining some of the methods and some of the common terminology being used in the new scholarship on women, in particular, women's history and sociology/anthropology.

The New Scholarship on Women

One of the unusual facets of women's studies research within biblical studies or any other field is that the goal of such research is to render the specialty obsolete. The aim of the kind of work I am doing is that the results should be integrated into our research and our teaching.

Whatever the success of such idealism, one thing I do believe is that scholarship on women in our field is not going to go where it has been. While I have found the more theological and literary work useful in many of my classes, it is most useful for those students with the same dilemma as Trible: those aware that feminism can, among other things, be a threat to a strong or literalistic biblical faith. For students who have an interest in and knowledge of women's studies, however, there are very different questions to be asked these days.

Carol Newsom, among others, has pointed out to me that doing women's history is interesting in part because it calls into question our previous ideas of historiography. Another observation I would like to make about the possible impact of women's studies on biblical studies is that to do it one has to retrain, to be willing to move the boundaries of "our field" out a bit: to accept some of the new scholarship on women, some sociological and anthropological work, the new women's history. In a field that seems to me only recently to have discovered political history instead of religious or theological or sacred or biblical history, we are now being pushed headlong into social history, especially those of us doing research on women.

In an effort to explain where I see this type of work heading in the future, I will use a scale worked out by Peggy McIntosh, the Program Director of the Wellesley College Center for Research on Women. Dr. McIntosh spoke at a conference at Claremont in 1983, a conference that addressed the problem of working women's studies research into the curriculum. Dr. McIntosh suggested that there are five stages in which women's studies consciousness can find itself, and, luckily for me, she used precisely women and history, my very interest, as her model.[2]

[2]The following summary of McIntosh's discussion is taken from "Stages of

The first stage she calls "womanless history." This is history as I was taught it, throughout high school and college: history construed, as McIntosh says, to exclude those who did not possess a good deal of power. After that, we have what she calls "women *in* history," what others have called "compensatory" history, that is, pointing out that we have had, after all, Joan of Arc, Deborah, Indira Gandhi, and Margaret Thatcher. This stage can also be observed with histories of people of color. One simply goes through and inserts those people who have done "significant" things but who have been left out of traditional history. McIntosh says this stage implies that there is nothing wrong with the system of thought, that it simply needs a little trimming or sprucing up here and there, so that from our superior position, we will take the disadvantaged into account—where they truly deserve our notice.

One can question whether stage two is better than stage one, or simply more devious.

The third stage is "women as a problem or anomaly in history." We realize that we "can't simply 'include in' those who by accident were left out, who were 'denied opportunity' to be studied," as if the problem has been simply misogyny on the part of historians. It was no accident we were left out. We are a problem, if the standards for excellence are so defined as to exclude the contributions of most women and, for that matter, people of color. McIntosh says we should ask ourselves: who defines a "major" turning point in history, a "major" theology or religious tradition? And who is best served by that definition? Obviously those who define excellence and those who benefit from the definition are one and the same.

Stage four for McIntosh is "women *as* history," and this is where I would put my own work or what is known as the new women's history. That is to say, women have a history as well as anyone else. We have been around just as long as they have. Our "history" is a lot harder to get at, but it is there. Furthermore, this stage involves giving up the definition of women (or lower-class people or people of color) as victims and losers, because the "victim" attitude accepts the old self-serving norms and standards while this fourth stage involves accepting multiple norms. Rather than having only one standard of excellence and defining everyone else as deficient or not

---

Curricular Re-Vision," the text of her talk as it was distributed to interested participants in the Claremont conference, "Traditions and Transitions: Women's Studies and a Balanced Curriculum," February, 1983.

important enough to consider, at this level we include many defini-
tions of significant. McIntosh gave an example of what a stage four
class in 19th century literature might be like. We should ask, she
says, not "Did the women write anything any good?" but rather,
"What did the women write?" Not "What great work by a woman
can I include in my reading list?" but rather "How have women used
the written word?" This is what I, and others, are beginning to ask of
Israelite history. Not "Did women do anything 'of significance'?" but
rather "Just what did the women do?" "What did the women believe?" And we even go on to ask "What, in fact, can we know about
what most people actually did and believed, outside of the edited,
relatively pristine theologies and history we confront in the Hebrew
Bible?"

McIntosh says doing this kind of research feels as if we are all
making it up together—and that is not a good solid feeling. We are
asking different questions than we were trained to ask, looking for
new ways of doing research, for new categories to describe experience, for new ways of teaching. These tasks are especially difficult,
and sometimes may not even be possible, with an ancient text—we
have almost no journals or letters on which to rely, unless we dig
them up, no underground newspapers to read to give us information
about what people really thought. Here, boundaries between disciplines start to break down. We learn wherever we can. The teacher
or researcher becomes less an expert. The field is experimental.
There *are* no experts. It is interesting to me that McIntosh here is
echoing Bird's and Oden's observation that we are all amateurs at
this.

There is a fifth stage in McIntosh's scheme, a stage she calls
"history redefined as inclusive," and as I indicated above, it is the
aim of much women's studies research to redefine the mainstream
within a given field. This stage is, I would suggest, well beyond our
reach at the present. We do have, however, good "stage-four" work
on which to build and it is to that work that I will turn next.

As I have noted, one finds in doing research in a new area that
people in other fields have developed methods and have suggested
new categories to employ that help us to look at our sources with a
new eye. This paper is particularly concerned with the new women's
history, a movement within history-writing going on for the last
fifteen years or so, that aims to portray women's lives in a way that
goes beyond the earlier "compensatory" women's histories. Recent
histories of women have tried to report the day-to-day lives of

women of all classes and to explore women's responses to societal upheavals and changes, as well as even to redefine the turning points of history, from women's points of view.[3] It is the prevailing view among anthropologists that women are not, and have not been, dominant in any known society. Their subordinate position, then, and their relationships among themselves and with the dominant males in their societies should be important features of any study of the women in a society. Joan Kelly-Gadol (1976: 816) explained: "We have made of sex a category as fundamental to our analysis of the social order as other classifications, such as class and race." Within this broad understanding of sex as a category of analysis, there are many other categories scholars have found useful in describing and illuminating the position of women of various classes within a given society. These categories are based upon societal features that have been seen to be accurate indicators of women's status. For instance, it appears that hierarchical and centrally-structured institutions have been less open to participation by women in most societies than have local and non-hierarchical institutions. As with many other categories, this exclusion need not occur, but in fact when institutions accrue structure and specific standards women seem to be excluded. This means that an increase in the centralization of a society's institutions will often coincide with a decline in participation by women within those institutions.

One example often cited of this kind of situation is the growth of medical schools in England and in this country. Apparently, before medicine became organized as a scientific, professional discipline, when more medicine was what we might call "folk" medicine, in other words, women were fairly commonly the practitioners. The decline in women's participation comes, according to one study, along with the rise of medical schools and specific professional standards, necessary bodies of knowledge, and so on. Once it took a formal education to be a doctor, women became excluded (Smith, 1976: 382).

A similar issue involves determining the amount of decision-making done within a "domestic" context, as opposed to decision-making removed from the domestic sphere and placed in a "public" or "political" sphere, which organizes and regulates several private

[3]There are a number of excellent scholars in this new field, and I will list here only a few works that give an overview of this branch of social history: B.A. Carroll (1976); J. Kelly-Gadol (1976); C.N. Degler (1975); and C. Smith-Rosenberg (1975).

domestic units. Studies have shown that women tend to have more status within a society when the public and domestic spheres are not widely separated, if at all, i.e., when important decision-making is often done within or near the home.[4]

I think one of the more interesting recent applications of this kind of analysis, this time using New Testament, was made by Elisabeth Schüssler Fiorenza (1983) in her book *In Memory of Her.* There is a section in the book on the house church in early Christianity. Fiorenza examines other sects in the Greco-Roman world that used houses as meeting places, points out that they were often largely or totally female, and goes on to say that, based on the usual domestic/public arguments, this is not surprising. She wants to make the point, of course, that it is reasonable to take Paul at face value when he seems to greet several women as leaders in his communities. In the case of early Christian house churches, she argues, the "public" or "political" domain was, in some cases, precisely the domestic sphere—the home. Little or no separation of the two spheres often points to a higher level of participation of women. This is really an ideal test case for anyone who does women's studies (1983: 175–184).

Use of the public/domestic category assumes certain domestic responsibilities for most women in a given society because of the amount of time spent bearing, nursing, and raising children. The last, of course, is not necessarily done by women rather than men, but in fact the norm is that in most societies most child-raising is done by women. Because of these responsibilities, women are less mobile and may have less freedom to pursue extra-family, "political" or "public" activities, when those activities are clearly separated from the domestic sphere. Consequently, the political sphere becomes a male sphere in so far as it becomes separated from the domestic, that is, decisions are not made within the family, but outside the family unit, and in groups which link several family units.

Although the domestic/public category is one of the most commonly used categories in women's studies, M.Z. Rosaldo (1980), one of the scholars who best articulated the consequences of a division in public and private spheres, published a thoughtful article in which

---

[4] For examples of the use of this category in analyses of women's lives in several cultures, see the articles by Rosaldo, Ortner, and Lamphere in M. Z. Rosaldo and L. Lamphere (eds.) (1974), and R. R. Reiter (1975).

she suggested this category has been misused in writing about women. Her point is worth noting: even though this is a common model, its use actually simply assumes that women are primarily responsible for the domestic sphere. It does not illuminate that fact, and it is not subtle. What are the real workings of gender within a society? They are not as simple as women staying home with the kids and men doing the important work. One of my goals in this paper is to explain some of the current women's studies terminology, and this domestic/public category is common in the literature, but it is merely descriptive: it says nothing about the origins of or even the subtleties of gender relations within a given society.

The Marxist concept of "social" labor is a similar category. Marx and Engels argued that work takes on prestige according to its value to the entire community, that is to say, work done for the society in general (as opposed to work done only for one's family) is "social" work and is the basis of social worth (Engels, 1972: 220–221; Sacks, 1974: 211–213). "Social" labor, then, is comparable to "political" or "public" activities, while labor done strictly for one's family would generally fall within the "domestic" sphere.

All historians deal with social and economic classes. It is clear that one cannot compare by the same criteria a queen and a peasant widow. Evidence of classes within a society, however, has further implications for the analysis of women's status within that society. For instance, upper-class women have often fared better than middle- and lower-class women, not only in terms of the obvious material advantages, but also in terms of their status within their own class. Often class, and consequently ownership of property, supersedes sex as a qualification for leadership roles among traditional elites, so that if a ruling man is absent, or if an elite couple fail to produce a male heir, a woman may take over the duties of governance and the economic responsibilities involved in the family's estate. Simply put, many would prefer a woman of their own class and breeding to a man of a lesser class, when a choice must be made.

Interestingly, and perhaps not surprisingly, periods of social dysfunction or social disruption are actually periods where women's status fares better than in settled times. J. McNamara and S. Wemple (1977) studied medieval Christian women and argued that women had far more leeway before medieval society became stabilized. For instance, they point to the large contribution nuns and monks alike made in the effort to preserve learning, establish monasteries, make conversions, and exercise power over their new rulers during the chaotic period when the Germanic Kingdoms succeeded the Roman Empire. They also chronicle the declining role women had in the church once it got on its feet, an example of a hierarchy systematically either excluding women, or downgrading the type of work allowed them.

Carl Degler was the Harmsworth Professor of American History at Oxford in 1974, and in his inaugural lecture, titled "Is There a History of Women?" he made the following observations about the effects of wars, obviously times of disruption, on women's lives:

> The three major wars of the United States, for example, have been conspicuous in opening opportunities for women to expand the content of their lives. The Civil War saw women move into a variety of occupations theretofore closed to them as well as into other activities. As Clara Barton, the Florence Nightingale of America remarked, when the Civil War ended, 'Woman was at least fifty years in advance of the normal position which continued peace . . . would have assigned her.' . . . The First and Second World Wars also broadened women's roles economically and socially. The First World War is, moreover, properly associated with the enactment of women's suffrage, not only in the United States, but in other countries as well. Women's suffrage was adopted in Great Britain, the United States, and Germany during or immediately after the First World War and in France, Italy, and Japan immediately after the Second. The reason for the acceptance of the suffrage is probably the same reason why new jobs and other opportunities for women were opened during the war. By their very interruptive character in the lives of men, modern wars shake up societies and cause people to think anew about established patterns (1975: 12–13).

This phenomenon, that women's status tends to go up during periods of social dysfunction, follows from some of the points presented earlier. In times of war or other crises, hierarchical structures break down, and groups of outsiders often have the opportunity to exert more power. Or, to quote Peter Machinist, it is at times of social dysfunction "that one can best expect those on the periphery of power at least to be judged on a more flexible range of criteria in terms of access to power" (private communication). This is particularly true of women, since women are usually close to the center of power, by virtue of their relationships with men; even though not allowed into the inner circle of those who exercise power in normal times, they are often the obvious choices to attempt to deal with a crisis situation. Furthermore, men are often absent in these periods, particularly in times of war, so that women are necessarily called upon to perform the work left behind by the men. Finally, in periods of severe dysfunction, centralized institutions might give way to more local handling of affairs, a situation we have already seen to be often advantageous to women's participation.

Concern with a society's setting as rural or urban is not unique to women's history, but is certainly a component of it, for the obvious reason that people's lives are lived in substantially different ways in the country and the city. This is, however, the kind of category that is not easily translated to biblical studies. We often do not have enough of this kind of detail in the narratives we study to formulate appropriate categories.

The kinship system operative in a given society has clear implications for the status of women within the society. Whether inheritance and group identity are matrilineal or patrilineal, whether settlement is matrilocal or patrilocal, affect the amount of contact with and influence allowed the wife's family (and support group) as opposed to the husband's. Evidence of the practice of polyandry or polygyny is important in determining sources of the influence a woman or man may exert in a society. For example, we would like to know whether co-spouses must compete for the attention of and influence over their mate; whether multiple marriage implies a lowering of status for the first spouse; whether inheritance is affected. Other factors that must be considered include the position of people outside the major kinship system, that is, men and women not yet married, widows and widowers, prostitutes. These are some of the most intriguing aspects of societal analysis, because we do get hints of this kind of information in the biblical record.

Robert Oden (1983) has pointed out the importance of kinship relations and proper cross-cousin marriage in the Jacob story, where we are told that Jacob was to take a wife from the family of Laban. The narrator bothers to describe Laban again and again as Jacob's "mother's brother," making sure that we understand the exact kin relationship between Jacob and his wives.

Naomi Steinberg (1984: 180) suggests that the wife-sister stories in Genesis exhibit a concern with genealogy. She maintains that Sarah is treated somewhat differently by the narrator in her two stories than Rebekah is in hers because Rebekah has already given birth by the time the story is told of her; the narrator, then, cannot allow Rebekah to be put in the same danger as Sarah, because of Rebekah's motherhood. And in fact Rebekah does not seem to be abandoned as completely as Sarah was.

The discussion to this point has revolved around issues that are used to describe a society as a whole. There are other categories that can help us to describe and explicate the positions of women within a given society: their social and economic status; their legal status; their religious status; their sources of power.

Concerning women's social and economic status, typical questions that are asked include these: what kinds of occupations are available to women? to what degree are women responsible for the raising and socialization of children? who supplies most of the food for the society? how is the food distributed? do women and men cooperate with each other or do they compete? is there societal propaganda designed to subjugate women to men, and if so, how does it operate? what is the average age of death for women? for men? do women have their own systems of rank and value separate from that of the society as a whole? what happens to women outside the system (for instance, widows and prostitutes)? is the system of pollution fears (biblical *ṭāmēʾ* and *ṭāhôr*) restrictive for women and/ or men, and if so, are these restrictions a source of bonding? who controls a woman's sexuality? is a woman's status dependent upon her social class? how does age affect her status?

The legal status of women is not always easy to discern because so many systems of law (including the Hebrew Bible's) are written by and for the men in a society. There, it is often difficult to determine how many and which laws were actually meant to apply to women and to affect their behavior (Bird, 1974: 48–57). Understanding these restrictions, we would nevertheless like to know: which laws in the Hebrew Bible pertain to women? are women's lives equal to men's under the law? what are the rules regarding marriage and divorce? how is rape dealt with? what legal protection in general was afforded women?

Religious status is particularly difficult to define for women in ancient Israel since many features of people's lives in Israel were seen (or, at least, are reported to us) as "religious," when in the modern world we might choose to classify them as legal or societal features. It is difficult to decide, for instance, whether to group "pollution" beliefs as religious or social features. In my own work I include in this category only those questions which have to do with the cult or cults, and with the evident theological views of women. So, for instance, these questions arise: to what extent are women considered part of the covenant community? what is the theological attitude toward women evident in the various writings? are there female cult personnel? are women involved in the religions considered non-orthodox by the biblical authors? more involved than men? if so, what are the possible reasons for this involvement?

Finally, one must attempt to identify the sources of power available to women in the various societal strata and time periods in question. It may be that a woman's power in a given society comes to her primarily through a man or men—husband, father, brother, son—and not through any features of her own status. That is, she can get what she wants by convincing a man or men that she should have it, by a variety of means. For instance, she can assert or withhold her sexuality; she can call upon family bonds or set family members against each other; she can socialize her sons in such a way as to accomplish her ends; she can refuse to do domestic chores. Kinship relationships are important here also: an extended family with a structured hierarchy increases the complexity of the sexual politics, the struggle to influence the men in the group. For instance, in such a family, a mother's influence over her son is threatened when the son marries; if the hierarchy gives the mother power over daughters-in-law, then the mother is likely to use that power to assure her own dominance over her son, a situation of obvious friction. If polygyny is practised, co-wives become a threat to each other in that no one wife can hope to influence her husband exclusively, and such means as withholding sexual privileges would clearly not be as effective.

We would expect, however, that a woman has her own sources of power, even if most of them stem from her relations to various men in the group. Such other power sources might include: her position in (probably local) institutions; her ability to limit family size; her control over child socialization; role revolts (such as marriage resistance, or vowing virginity for one reason or another); prostitution, if it is the woman's choice; her control of the society's food resources (in many societies, the major source of food is not hunting, but pastoralism and agriculture, and it is often the women who are in charge of producing this food). Certain occupations may bring her status, especially those which involve freedom from dependence on males, either through mobility or economic independence. Finally, there are always the "great women" in a society, women who become famous in spite of their sex. Are they merely out of step with the rest of society, or is it possible that they come from a period of time in which many women had more power than usual, and the only remnant of this situation is the fame of a few women?[5]

In the end, there are several questions that can be asked only after one has examined women's lives through several periods in a society. How does women's status in a given society vary through time? What causes these variations? How do major societal changes (such as in the form of government) affect the women of the society? How do women respond to these changes? What is the status of women vis-à-vis men within specific class lines and time periods?

Women in Judges 3-16

In the final part of this paper, I will present some of the results of my application of various of these methods to the women in Judg 3-16. In many cases, the "results" I can boast of are simply new ways of describing the same old things. The whole enterprise is, moreover, somewhat risky since a later accretion or editorial addition from a totally different time and kind of society would obviously invalidate any conclusion I might want to draw as a social historian based on a given passage. It is even frustrating to try to do something as simple as validate a description of a society in order to proceed with some sort of analysis. I think, quite frankly, we tend to make progress mostly by relying on incidentals. Certainly, however, whatever else we can say about the period of the judges, for example (whenever it was, whether there ever was such a period), it is clearly described as a period of serious social dysfunction. One of the notable features of the social organization of this era is its lack of centralization. In this premonarchical phase of Israel's history, the cry for participation in war, for example, does not come from a standing, centralized, hierarchical "government," but rather from a covenantal agreement that there will be occasions when concerted action is necessary and, in Israelite terms, demanded by Yahweh. The point to be made is that the power *structure* was not centralized, even where concerted effort was possible.

Where such information is available these stories portray a public sphere that does not seem to be widely separated from the private. For instance, from the description of Deborah's duties as

---

[5]This is S. Johansson's (1976) suggestion. She uses Elizabeth I of England as an example and affirms that "she was not just a lucky accident"; rather, her ability to rule was a result of her extensive training, which she received because she lived in a period when many women were educated (pp. 426–27).

judge at the beginning of her story (4:4-5), we assume she is still resident in her own area (whether that was "under the palm of Deborah, between Ramah and Bethel," as 4:5 would have it, or, more likely, within the tribal territory of Issachar, as 5:15 implies), so that her public life as judge need not have interfered with her domestic life. Except when he was at war, Gideon is described as residing in his own house, in Ophrah, during the time that he was judge in Israel. Again, his nonmilitary public duties as judge, although they are not described, were presumably not performed in such a manner as to separate him necessarily from his domestic life. Let me emphasize at this point that I am not simply accepting the details of these stories at face value, but rather am interested in pointing out the incidental information that these stories do not seem to portray a concept of public duty that is widely separated from the domestic sphere.

Admittedly, these are only shadows of the kind of detail we would like to have. The fact that the judges are said to be appointed by Yahweh for their tasks gives us no information about the *societal* bases for authority, or details of the decision-making and settlement of disputes that must also have taken place. The only exceptions are the Shechemite kingship of Abimelek and the emergency recruitment of Jephthah by the "elders" of Gilead and consequent ceremony "before Yahweh" at Miṣpah (if this is part of the original narrative). Abimelek is certainly not the norm among deliverers, and so his story does not really help us in determining how the authentic judges might have been chosen. But Jephthah's story perhaps gives us a glimpse at the human side of the choosing of a judge—we see the fear and desperation of the elders of Gilead and we see that they are led to turn to the only person they think can help them. Yahweh's stamp of approval is delivered only sometime later.

To summarize quickly, Israel in the time of the judges was basically a rural, agrarian society, with some urbanization, as seems probable from the situation in Shechem. During a period of time that is distinguished by its lack of tranquility and by its social upheavals (usually in the text at the hands of an oppressive outside power), there was no central administration and generally ad hoc leadership in localized affairs. There is some evidence that social and economic classes existed (I am thinking here of the wealth of some of the "minor judges"), but the evidence is slim and is mostly a matter of one group accumulating more wealth than another. It is possible that hereditary ruling groups are implied in the Abimelek story, set

in urban Shechem. The marriage customs are what we would expect: patrilineal and sometimes polygynous. Public and private lives
were apparently not widely separated; there is, at least, no evidence
that they were, and some slight evidence that they were not.

Given what we now know about women in different places and
time periods, we are not surprised to find that women could fill
leadership roles in this era of decentralized power and ad hoc
leaders. Women are seldom seen as the ones to make war in a
society, and the same is true for biblical Israel, but we do have in
these stories two women who are intimately involved in a war.
Deborah, as we know, is a prophet and a judge. Her function in the
battle with the Canaanites is to declare the battle a holy war in her
capacity as judge, in other words, to legitimize the battle. Baraq, in
fact, would not go to war without Yahweh's representative with him
(4:8). Deborah also, in chapter 4, delivers the oracle from Yahweh to
Baraq that describes the battle plan.

In the later prose version in chapter 4, Deborah calls Baraq to
summon the troops to battle, but in the earlier song of Deborah in
chapter 5, Deborah is commanded in verse 12, "Awake, awake,
Deborah; awake, utter a song"—not the song in Judges 5, since the
self-reference makes no sense in the middle of the poem, but, as
some commentators have seen, a song to muster the troops, to call
them out for battle (Moore, 1895: 149-50; Miller, 1975: 94). "Awake,
awake," of course, is typical language in the Hebrew Bible for a call
to arms. Isaiah 51 comes immediately to mind: "Awake, awake, put
on strength, arm of Yahweh." The poet is calling on Deborah to get
the battle going and so her song here must be the vehicle for
bringing out the troops. In this case, we might prefer to read with a
Greek variant rather than the MT. The variant reads: "Awake,
awake, Deborah; arouse the myriads of the army (or people)" (see
also Miller, 1975: 92-94).

So although Deborah is indeed the only deliverer who has a
military man working with her, the older version in the song, while
mentioning Baraq, gives an even greater military role to Deborah
than the prose version does. And while we do not see Deborah
carrying weapons and fighting, we do not see Baraq fighting either:
the battle is said to be won by Yahweh's routing of Sisera's troops (in
4:15), or by the stars and the Qishon (in 5:20-21).

In some ways this kind of information does not seem all that
important, but I would like to establish that Deborah and Jael do not
have to be explained away. Albright, in the '20's, got rid of Deborah

altogether, turning her into a city (1921: 61; 1922: 81). And he thought there was no place, metrically, for Jael, toward the beginning of the song in Judges 5, "in the days of Shamgar, in the days of Jael" (1922: 75).

Robert Boling (1975: 95) in his Anchor Bible commentary on Judges refers to Deborah as an "honorary judge" and brings up the old theory that Lappidoth and Baraq were one and the same, that his name was Baraq, "lightning," and that Lappidoth, which Boling translates "Flasher," was presumably a sort of nickname for Baraq.[6] Although he does not say so, the point of this exercise seems to me to be to explain Deborah's position in a way that seems more reasonable to the various authors who have suggested it. She was not really the judge; she was the judge's wife. This relationship could also explain how she could presume to order Flasher around and even to berate him.[7]

Although Jael's killing of Sisera need not be seen as the act of a soldier, it can certainly be said that she coolly and deliberately dispatched the leader of the enemy army. She was also, as I mentioned earlier, remembered in the same breath with Shamgar who was, according to Judg 3:31, a deliverer, although there are problems with this story and its relationship to similar ones elsewhere in the Hebrew Bible (Moore, 1895: 106). One assumes, both from her pairing with Shamgar and from her story itself, that she, too, was remembered as having delivered Israel in a time of crisis. Benjamin Mazar (1965) long ago pointed to the Qenite Jael's possible priestly role and suggested that Sisera sought out her tent not only because her people and his had a peace treaty, but also because her tent was in fact pitched at a sanctuary and Sisera reasonably expected refuge there.

This kind of analysis of the society, by the way, gives similar insight into the leadership of Gideon and of Jephthah. The same evidence of societal upheavals and lack of centralized hierarchical authority can be used to explain the rise to power of these two men, neither of whom could claim a favorable social position within Israel. And both, in fact, themselves question the choice of such lowly or

---

[6] Burney (1970: 85) refers to this theory as a "precarious suggestion," and Moore (1895: 113) gives it as an example of the "conceits" the name Lappidoth "has given occasion to."

[7] W. Richter also concludes that there is no authentic tradition of Deborah as judge, although on different grounds. See Richter (1966: 37–42), esp. the conclusion on p. 42.

outcast characters to deliver their people. As we know, however, it is precisely in troubled times and decentralized systems that such people can wield power, people who in more settled times and structured systems would most likely not be seen as fit to rule.

Alongside these descriptions of heroic acts, women are pictured in what might be termed more traditional roles. Deborah and Jael are identified as the wives of their respective husbands. Jephthah's mother and one of Samson's paramours were prostitutes, and no negative connotations seem to have been applied to this line of work. Jephthah's step-brothers disown him, not because his mother was a prostitute, but because she was a woman "other than" their mother, Gilead's wife.

It is worth noting that it is to Samson's mother that the messenger appears in Judg 13:1–7. His message is a pronouncement of her impending pregnancy, but it also includes instructions as to how the child is to be raised. It was not seen as important that these instructions be given to Manoah, the child's father, and he, in fact, only hears the message because he seems to doubt his wife's story. It would seem safe to conclude that the mother was given the instructions because she would be the one in large part responsible for the child's upbringing. Even if these stories are fanciful, we can still glean the attitude of the story-tellers from the details, and can also learn their understanding of their own society.

Again, speaking in terms of more traditional roles, Jephthah's daughter comes to meet him as he returns from battle "with timbrels and with dances," and we know from other evidence in the Hebrew Bible that women were the ones who met the returning warriors with songs. The story of Jephthah's daughter brings us to another issue, the religious status of women in Israel during this period. There is clearly this one female ritual, described in 11:39–40, where the women of Israel are said to come each year to mourn Jephthah's daughter, whether it was actually the later proscribed Tammuz ritual or whether it was acceptable Israelite ritual. Furthermore, the attitude of Jephthah's daughter is more convincingly faithful than that of Jephthah himself, as has been pointed out by commentators.[8] I would argue that Jephthah's promise of a

---

[8] See Trible's discussion of this story (1984: 93–116), esp. 96–98, and the notes on the nature of the vow on p. 112. This argument was not first made by feminists, of course, and Trible is not the only scholar who discusses the story in this way. See also Boling (1975: 207–8), where Jephthah's "failure to trust" in his judgeship is called his "tragic flaw"; and from a more conservative point of view, cf. A.E. Cundall (1968: 146–47), who notes that Jephthah "showed his lack of appreciation of the character

human sacrifice would not have been viewed neutrally by an Israelite author or audience, but rather would have been judged
negatively, and that Jephthah, rather than being simply unfortunate,
was seen as thoughtless at best and faithless at worst. The story can
be seen, then, at least implicitly, as critical of Jephthah, while his
daughter is shown in an entirely positive light—in Israelite terms, if
not our own.[9] She certainly considers herself part of the covenant
community, and must, therefore, see that a vow to Yahweh is up-
held, whatever the consequences.

It is clear from what we have seen that women in this era had
several sources of power, and did not need to rely strictly on men for
their power. We have discussed Deborah's, and possibly Jael's, position within a decentralized authority structure as being the equal of
that of the men in the same office. Sisera's mother also apparently
had an exalted position, but one in a different society from Israel's.
Although her power source may ultimately have been her son's
position, she may also have been one of the elite women who are
trained to rule when men are absent. Jephthah's daughter, although
she was powerless before an oath to Yahweh, as was her father, still
had the power, and the support of her society, to carry out the vow
and her preparations for it in the manner that suited her.

In other cases, women achieve their ends by working through a
man. Sexual politics is involved in Samson's dealing both with his
wife and with Delilah. Each one plays on her expected feminine role
in order to get information from Samson which she will then use to
her own advantage—the wife to save her life and her family; Delilah
to earn money from the Philistine lords who approach her.

A less transparent, but perhaps real, sort of power is seen in the
wisdom and faith of several women. Deborah is presented as the one
who is certain that the battle against the Canaanites is a proper one
and that Yahweh is in favor of it, while Baraq needs reassurance; it is

---

and requirements of the Lord, and also a lack of confidence in the divine enablement,
by seeking to secure the favour of God by his rash *vow*."

[9] I have worked my remarks about Jephthah and his daughter in response to the
discussion following this paper in San Diego, and specifically to the comments of John
Collins and Michael Coogan; I am indebted to them for the stimulus to rethink. I
hope I have made a stronger case in this version of the argument. I would like to
thank William Propp for pointing out that since the story is an etiological one, it is
necessary for the daughter to die in order that the ritual noted in 11:39–40 be
explained. Although her death is often compared negatively with the rescue of Isaac
in Genesis 22 and of Jonathan in 1 Samuel 14, it should not be; the three stories serve
entirely different purposes.

Deborah's line of reasoning that is followed in this case. Similarly, as I have mentioned before, Jephthah's daughter is clear-sighted about the necessary course of affairs following her father's unfortunate vow, itself a sign that he needed further reassurance of his proper role, while Jephthah can merely whimper; in this case the daughter is able to influence the manner of her death, at least. Finally, Samson's mother is presented as the intelligent half of his parents, while Manoah is lacking in faith in his wife's word and memory, is slow to figure out the identity of their visitor, and in the end is afraid for his life. His wife has to explain to him that Yahweh would hardly have bothered to announce the birth of a son and the grand career of that son, if only to kill them immediately afterwards, something that could have been done at any time. Samson, it might be added, took after his father rather than his mother.

One aspect of a discussion of women's lives in any society is the status of women vis-à-vis men, and it is noticeable that in our stories the major female characters often fare better (as characters in a narrative) than do the men with whom they are involved: Deborah alongside Baraq; Jael vs. Sisera; Jephthah's daughter as opposed to Jephthah; Samson's mother and father; and it is no new insight to say that women certainly got the better of Samson, time and again. One is tempted to suggest that some of these stories actually derive from women's literature, literature composed by, and/or preserved in, women's circles. This line of reasoning seems to suggest, however, that men would not preserve stories favorable to women, and I do not want to make that argument. A more valid criterion for such a suggestion is the observation that women's lives and issues are sometimes central to these narratives: the women's ritual in the story of Jephthah's daughter is one example, and the poem in Judges 5 is another. Judges 5 is really a very female piece of literature. We do, of course, already refer to the poem as the song of Deborah and we know women are credited with singing the battle songs in ancient Israel. Still it is worth re-affirming that this is a women's song. Judges 5, in fact, describes the battle with the Canaanites precisely from the perspectives of the women affected by it: the women involved in the fighting and killing, and the women waiting to hear the results of the battle. Even the women who are assumed to be part of the victor's spoils are mentioned.

In sum, women's status and roles as seen in Judg 3:17–16:31 are more varied than they might be at other times in biblical Israel: their men are not always their sources of power. This is not to say that women were dominant over men, even in this period; still, the characterization of the period as one of decentralized and ad hoc power would lead us to expect wider possibilities for women in public and powerful positions, and this is precisely what we have found.

The purpose of this paper, as was mentioned earlier, has been to point out some of the characteristics of what is known as the new scholarship on women and to indicate some of the areas where it is being applied to biblical studies. I also mentioned that the point of doing such research is finally to see the results and the methods integrated into the mainstream in our field. I realize what this implies, however. I have tried working what I know about research on women in ancient Israel into a basic introductory Hebrew Bible class, and found it very difficult. Methods clash and I find students somewhat taken aback when I switch gears from the religious traditions of ancient Israel into social history. And ours is, of course, basically a rather conservative field; we do not take quickly to new methods and ways of looking at our text, especially when they come from completely different branches of the humanities or social sciences. And so, when pressed, I have to admit that I do not think what some of us are trying to do will make much of an impact on the field in the next few decades. I expect my own work to be of more interest to women's studies scholars than to Bible scholars (except for people teaching in seminaries, of course, where there are more women and more people worried about the effect of the text on their own lives; these scholars have often found that tools for dealing with the stories about women are a welcome addition to their teaching.)[10]

I hope I am wrong in my pessimism. I hope the insights we can scare up from a rather mangled text will make it into the mainstream, and will, of course, at the same time change the definition of and character of the mainstream. Such a process would spell a more lively and more accurate future for biblical studies as a field.

WORKS CONSULTED

Albright, W. F.
1922   "The Earliest Forms of Hebrew Verse," *JPOS* 2, 69–86.

---

[10] Sakenfeld (1982: 13,19) expresses similar pessimism, although she tempers it with examples of the impact women's studies has already made on Hebrew Bible scholarship. See also Trible (1982: 3–4) in the same volume.

1921   "A Revision of Early Hebrew Chronology," *JPOS* 1, 49–
            79.

Bird, P.
1981   "'Male and Female He Created Them': Gen 1:27b in
            the Context of the Priestly Account of Creation,"
            HTR 74, 129–59.
1974   "Images of Women in the Old Testament," in *Religion
            and Sexism*, R. Ruether (ed.), New York: Simon and
            Schuster, 41–88.

Boling, R.G.
1975   *Judges*. Anchor Bible; Garden City, NY: Doubleday.

Burney, C.F.
1970   *The Book of Judges*. London: Rivingtons, 1918, 1920
            [rept. New York: KTAV, 1970].

Carroll, B.A. (ed.)
1976   *Liberating Women's History*. Urbana: University of Illi-
            nois Press.

Cundall, A.E.
1968   *Judges*. Downers Grove, IL and London: Inter-Varsity
            Press.

Degler, C.N.
1975   *Is There a History of Women?* Oxford: Clarendon
            Press.

Engels, F.
1972   *The Origin of the Family, Private Property and the
            State*, E. Leacock, (ed.) New York: International
            Publishers.

Fiorenza, E. Schüssler
1983   *In Memory of Her: A Feminist Theological Reconstruc-
            tion of Christian Origins*. New York: Crossroad.

Hackett, J.A.
1985   "In the Days of Jael: A Model for Reclaiming the His-
            tory of Women in Ancient Israel," in *Immaculate and
            Powerful: The Female in Sacred Image and Social
            Reality*, C. Atkinson, C. Buchanan, and M. Miles
            (eds.), Boston: Beacon Press, 15–38.

Johansson S.
1976   "'Herstory' As History: A New Field or Another Fad?"
            in *Liberating Women's History*, B.A. Carroll (ed.),
            op. cit., 400–30.

Kelly-Gadol, J.
1976   "The Social Relation of the Sexes: Methodological Im-
            plications of Women's History," *Signs* 1, 809–23.

Lamphere, L.
1974   "Strategies, Cooperation, and Conflict Among Women
         in Domestic Groups," in *Woman, Culture, and So-
         ciety*, M.Z. Rosaldo and L. Lamphere (eds.), op. cit.,
         97–112.

Mazar, B.
1965   "The Sanctuary of Arad and the Family of Hobab the
         Kenite," *JNES* 24, 297–303.

McIntosh, M.
1983   "Stages of Curricular Re-Vision," Wellesley College
         Center for Research on Women, Working Paper
         #124 [also delivered as a talk at the Claremont Con-
         ference. "Traditions and Transitions: Women's Stud-
         ies and a Balanced Curriculum," February, 1983].

McNamara, J., and Wemple, S.
1977   "Sanctity and Power: The Dual Pursuit of Medieval
         Women," in *Becoming Visible: Women in European
         History*, R. Bridenthal and C. Koonz (eds.), Boston,
         Houghton Mifflin, 90–118.

Miller, Jr., P.D.
1975   *The Divine Warrior in Early Israel*. Cambridge, MA:
         Harvard University Press.

Moore, G.F.
1895   *Judges*. ICC; New York: Charles Scribner's Sons; Edin-
         burgh: T.&T. Clark.

Oden, R.A.
1983   "Jacob as Father, Husband, and Nephew: Kinship
         Studies and the Patriarchal Narratives," *JBL* 102,
         189–205.

Ortner, S.
1974   "Is Female to Male as Nature Is to Culture?" in
         Woman, Culture and Society, M.Z. Rosaldo and L.
         Lamphere (eds.), op. cit., 67–87.

Reiter, R.R.
1975   "Men and Women in the South of France: Public and
         Private Domains," in *Toward an Anthropology of
         Women*, R.R. Reiter (ed.), New York: Monthly Re-
         view Press.

Richter, W.
1966   *Traditionsgeschichtliche Untersuchungen zum Richter-
         buch*. Bonn: Peter Hanstein Verlag.

Rosaldo, M.Z.
1980   "The Use and Abuse of Anthropology: Reflections on

          Feminism and Cross-Cultural Understanding,"
          Signs, 5 389–417.
1974   "Woman, Culture, and Society: A Theoretical Over-
          view," in *Woman, Culture, and Society,* M.Z.
          Rosaldo and L. Lamphere (eds.), op. cit., 17–42.

Rosaldo, M.Z., and Lamphere, L. (eds.)
1974   *Woman, Culture, and Society.* Stanford: Stanford Uni-
          versity Press.

Sacks, K.
1974   "Engels Revisited: Women, the Organization of Pro-
          duction, and Private Property," in M. Z. Rosaldo
          and L. Lamphere (eds.), op. cit., 207–22.

Sakenfeld, K.D.
1982   "Old Testament Perspectives: Methodological Issues,"
          JSOT 22, 13–20

Smith, H.
1976   "Feminism and the Methodology of Women's History,"
          in *Liberating Women's History,* B.A. Carroll (ed.),
          op. cit., 368–84.

Smith-Rosenberg, C.
1975   "The New Woman and the New History," *Feminist
          Studies* 3, 185–98.

Steinberg, N.
1984   "Gender Roles in the Rebekah Cycle," *USQR* 39, 175–
          88.

Trible, P.
1984   *Texts of Terror.* Philadelphia: Fortress.
1982   "The Effects of Women's Studies on Biblical Studies:
          An Introduction," *JSOT* 22, 3–4.
1978   *God and the Rhetoric of Sexuality.* Philadelphia: For-
          tress.
1973   "Depatriarchalizing in Biblical Interpretation," *JAAR*
          41, 30–48.

Chapter 7

ADONIJAH THE SON OF HAGGITH AND HIS SUPPORTERS: AN INQUIRY INTO PROBLEMS ABOUT HISTORY AND HISTORIOGRAPHY

Tomoo Ishida
University of Tsukuba, Japan

I. Methodological Problems concerned with Interpretation of Works of Biblical History

The Adonijah pericope is integrally related to a larger literary complex called the "Succession Narrative," which consists of most of 2 Samuel and 1 Kings 1–2. Appreciation of this narrative as one of the earliest, as well as one of the finest, historical works in the Bible has long been established in the scholarly world (Wellhausen, 1899: 259–60; Meyer, 1906: 485; Rost, 1965: 119–253). But since the 1960's, and especially in the last decade, this thesis has been attacked by many scholars with different approaches (Conroy, 1978: 1–4; Gunn, 1978: 19–34; Ball, 1982). Of course, there are recent studies which still accept in principle the longstanding thesis of the "Succession Narrative." Generally speaking, they are studies in which historical approaches are employed (Mettinger, 1976: 27–32; Crüsemann, 1978: 180–93; Whitelam, 1979: 123–66; 1984: 61–87; McCarter, 1981: 355–67; Zalewski, 1981: 11–144; Ishida, 1982: 175–87). In contrast, scholars who take either redaction-criticism (Würthwein, 1974; 1977: 1–28; Veijola, 1975; Langlamet, 1976: 321–79, 481–528; 1977: 161–209; 1978: 57–90; 1979: 194–213, 385–436, 481–513; 1980: 161–210; 1981: 233–46; 1982: 5–47) or literary-structural analysis (Conroy, 1978; Gunn, 1978; Fokkelman, 1981; Sacon, 1982) as their method assume a critical attitude toward the accepted opinion about the narrative. The redaction-criticism approach postulates doublets or triplets in the narrative and solves textual difficulties by an assumption of two- or three-fold redactions. In contrast to this diachronic analysis, those who take a literary-structural approach argue for a synchronic understanding of the narrative, describing such patterns as inclusio, chiasmus, concentric structure and so forth. Oddly enough, however, there is a feature that is common between these contradictory approaches: that is, a skepticism concerning the historicity of the narrative. As a result, without regard to the supposition of a contemporary or near contemporary original, the received text is regarded as having been composed either at a time "long after the United Kingdom had ceased to be" (D. M. Gunn, 1978: 33) or in the days between Hezekiah and Josiah (F. Langlamet, 1976: 379) or during the exilic (T. Veijola)[1] or the post-exilic period (J. van Seters, 1981: 166; 1983: 289–91). Inasmuch as we have no effective method for controlling these anarchic postulations, historical studies of the Bible will remain nihilistic, or at best, agnostic.

Our point of departure will be the historical fact that the Bible is a collection of compositions from the ancient Near East that were mostly composed in the first millennium B.C. Of course, disregarding any historical consideration, we may compare 2 Samuel with other texts, for example, with the works of Shakespeare, to gain valuable insight into human nature. This sort of comparison is valid for comparative literature, but is hardly appropriate for historical research, since the cultural milieu of each composition is entirely different from each of the others. Historians also deal with human beings and with human nature, but it is vital in their research to make clear to which definite time and what space the human beings in question were confined.

This method of historical research comes from our empirical understanding that every culture has its own sense of values. Sometimes there is a cultural phenomenon that seems so universal that it must prevail all over the world. But observation of such a phenomenon always remains superficial. In my view, knowledge about foreign cultures is highly abstract even in our present age when all corners of the world are closely connected by a dense network of modern communication. I am very doubtful of the ability of western society to understand the sense of values of Oriental countries, and vice versa. If we feel difficulties in understanding foreign cultures in our modern world, how can we correctly interpret the compositions

---

[1] His thesis of triple redactions by DtrG, DtrP and DtrN suggests that the text in 1 Kgs 1–2 was composed in the exilic period; see *Die ewige Dynastie*.

from the ancient Near East which come to us not only from different
cultures but from different and distant times?
It seems to me that a naive application of modern western logic
and judgement to the interpretation of ancient Near Eastern sources,
including biblical literature, has led us into error. First it is necessary that we establish a set of criteria for interpretation that is free
from the prejudices of our modern society. In other words, the
criteria must be established on an understanding, neutral but sympathetic, of the cultures of the ancient Near East. There, various
peoples lived each with their own rhetoric, customs, outlooks,
senses of values and so forth, which were undoubtedly distinct from
those of other cultures and, of course, from those of our own time.
Naturally, we must be careful about differences among the peoples
of the ancient Near East, but equally we must guard against the
illusion that owing to our inheritance of the Judeo-Christian culture
we can understand the ancient Israelites better than their neighboring peoples. For instance, the concept of the ban (ḥērem) in a holy
war in ancient Israel is quite alien to our society, but it was familiar
to the Moabites in the ninth century B.C., as we know from the
Mesha inscription.[2]

Unfortunately, this historical approach does not seem to be
popular among biblical scholars of today. Neither those who have
employed redaction-criticism nor those who have used literary-
structural analysis as their method have ever made a serious comparison of the Succession Narrative with any extra-biblical sources
from the ancient Near East.[3] Since their argument is essentially
based on the internal analysis of the narrative without any tangible
support from contemporary sources from the ancient Near East,
their conclusions are often inconclusive and remain hypothetical.
This is especially true of the problem of the date of the narrative. As
a result, every scholar suggests any date he likes, as we have
observed above.

On the surface, J. van Seters' (1983) study looks like an exception. On the basis of comparative studies of biblical history writings
with those of Greece and the ancient Near East he maintains that
the first historian of Israel was the Deuteronomist whose work

---

[2] "l ʿštr.kmš.hḥrmth," KAI, no. 181:17.
[3] Mention must be made of R.N. Whybray's study on the Succession Narrative
in which he dedicated a chapter to the comparison of the narrative with Egyptian
literature (1968: 96–116); cf. D.M. Gunn (1978: 29–30).

resembles the Greek prose histories in terms of the scope of subject matter and the themes treated. As for the Court History (i.e., the Succession Narrative), he regards it as "an antilegitimation story" added to the Dtr history, "as the product of an antimessianic tendency in certain Jewish circles" in the postexilic period (van Seters, 1981: 166; 1983: 290). It is strange, however, that he does not make any attempt to examine the literary character of the Court History itself in the light of Greek or Near Eastern sources which he has collected, but draws his radical conclusion simply from his judgement on the relation of the Court History and its view of David to the Dtr history. A good example of his dogmatic argument is found in his failure to produce any evidence to show that there was "an antimessianic tendency in certain Jewish circles" in the post-exilic period, which was, in his view, responsible for the composition of the Court History. All in all, so far as the study of the Succession Narrative is concerned, we can hardly regard his approach as historical.

Recently, P. Ackroyd (1981) has raised a question about the relationship of the "Succession Narrative" to the larger context and has come to the negative conclusion that it should not be separated from the rest of Samuel-Kings. Admittedly, it is important to reconsider the problems of the place of the narrative in the Dtr history together with its unity and boundaries. It seems to me, however, that we still have good prospects for research in proceeding with the thesis of a "Succession Narrative" as a working hypothesis. Moreover, in view of mounting skepticism about the historicity of the narrative, I feel it necessary first to undertake a re-examination of the possibilities of understanding the narrative in its present historical setting, i.e., in the period of David and Solomon. In any case, I will not deal in the present study with the problem of the relationship of the narrative to the larger context.

When we employ historical approaches as our method, the interpretation of biblical sources has to be done after settling the question of the literary genre to which they belong. And, once again, we must look for criteria for the definition of literary genres of biblical sources by comparison with compositions from other areas in the ancient Near East. As such comparative material to the Succession Narrative, I would like to suggest a genre called "Royal Historical Writings of an Apologetic Nature in the Ancient Near East"; for instance, the Telepinu Proclamation and the Apology of Hattushili III from the Hittite archives and the Neo-Assyrian documents of Shamshi-Adad V, Esarhaddon and Ashurbanipal which H. A. Hoffner (1975: 49–62) and H. Tadmor (1983: 36–57) classify under this category. In addition, I have suggested elsewhere that the inscription of Kilamuwa, king of Y'DY-Sam'al in the ninth century B.C., also belongs to this category (Ishida, 1985).

The Succession Narrative is not written in the autobiographical style of these other historical writings, but it is clearly similar to them in its essential character. The following elements are common to these royal historical works as well as the Succession Narrative:[4]

   a) The royal ancestry of the king designate
   b) The unworthiness of his predecessor(s) and/or rival prince(s)
   c) The rivals' rebellious attempt to gain the crown
   d) The counter-attack of the king designate and his victory
   e) His magnanimous pardon and/or purge of his enemies
   f) The establishment of a just kingship.

In addition, one of the most important features common to all is that the kings, who were not usurpers from outside the royal family, ascended the throne either by overruling primogeniture or by taking the place of someone who belonged to the direct royal line. Needless to say, this establishment of the king's connection with the

---

[4] Hoffner (1975: 51) finds the following outline common to the essential structure of the Telepinu Proclamation and the Apology of Hattushili III:
   a) Introduction: T 1, H 1–2.
   b) Historical survey—noble antecedents: T 1–9, H 3–10.
   c) Historical survey—the unworthy predecessor: T 10–22a, H 10–12.
   d) The coup d'état: T 22b, H 12–13.
   e) The merciful victor: T 23 & 26, H 12–13.
   f) The edict: T 27–50, H 13–15.

The apology of Esarhaddon, the most detailed composition among the Assyrian royal apologetic historical writings, called Nin. A by R. Borger (1956: 36–64) is comparable with these Hittite compositions in its general outline in many respects:
   a) Introduction: I 1–7.
   b) Historical survey—the divine election and appointment by his father: I 8–22.
   c) Historical survey—the rival princes' acts against the divine will: I 23–40.
   d) Rebellion: I 41–52.
   e) Esarhaddon's counter-attack and victory: I 53–79.
   f) The establishment of the kingship: I 80–II 7.
   g) The punishment of the rebels: II 8.

With reference to these outlines of the Assyrian and Hittite historical writings together with those of the Kilamuwa inscription and the Succession Narrative we may find the following six elements as common items in all the apologetic historical writings. This is a provisional suggestion. I will deal with the problem in a forthcoming study.

royal family was the fundamental motivation behind the composition
of these narratives.

I have no intention here of making a detailed comparative study
between the Succession Narrative and the apologetic royal histories
from the ancient Near East, but will limit myself to making some
observations of significant points. The fundamental idea in these
histories is nothing less than the royal ideology in the ancient Near
East, according to which the legitimacy of the king was proved by
his royal lineage and divine election as well as by his competence to
rule.[5] It is one of the striking features of the apologetic histories that
the present king's competency as a ruler is put in sharp contrast to
the ineffective rule of his predecessor's or the rival prince's incompetent character as a ruler. This observation will provide us with
criteria for the tendencies of the apologetic historical writings.

Scholars have disagreed on the character of the Succession
Narrative as to whether it is pro-David/Solomonic or anti-David/
Solomonic and some scholars have found pro- as well as anti-Solomonic polemics (Delekat, 1967: 26–36; Noth, 1968: 1–41; Würthwein, 1974; Langlamet, 1976; 1977; 1978; 1979; 1981; 1982). None of
these arguments is conclusive, since they have been made mainly
with the biases of the moral judgement of our modern society. In
contrast, I have suggested in a previous study on the "Succession
Narrative" that the narrative was composed as a legitimation of
Solomon in which David is criticized as the incompetent predecessor and in which the throne of David is regarded as the foundation of
the legitimacy of Solomon's kingship.[6] Therefore, though anti-
Davidic polemics are obvious in some sections, there is neither an
anti-Solomonic element nor any criticism against David's dynasty.
Neither should the report on the court intrigue and the story of
Solomon's political murder be interpreted as anti-Solomonic. In the
structure of the apologetic historical writings, the court intrigue was
the legitimate king's counter-attack against an unlawful attempt by

---

[5] For divine election and royal lineage as the foundation of royal legitimation in
the ancient Near East see T. Ishida (1977: 6–25); cf. also Mettinger (1977: 107–297).
The competence of rule of a king can be regarded as confirmation of his divine
election. A similar situation is found in charismatic leaders called šōpĕṭîm in the pre
monarchical period who could establish their charismatic ordination only through
victories in the field; see T. Ishida (1973: 527).

[6] Ishida (1982). There are scholars who hold that the narrative was composed as a
Davidic apology; see McCarter (1981); Whitelam (1984). On this assumption it is
difficult to explain the nature of the descriptions of David's shortcomings in the
narrative.

an incompetent rival prince to gain the crown. As in these historical writings, Solomon's purge of his enemies shows his competence as a ruler.

In the following section I will analyse the Adonijah passage in 1 Kings 1–2 using a historical approach. In the analysis I will try to differentiate the portrayal of Adonijah from his real figure. In so doing, it will become clear that he is portrayed as a rival prince of the legitimate king designate; he is cast in the villain's role of the royal historical writings of an apologetic nature in the ancient Near East.

II.   An Analysis of the Adonijah Pericope

The Presentation of Adonijah (1 Kgs 1:5–6)

Following the episode of Abishag and the aging King David, which provides a general background as well as a motif for the Abishag episode in chapter 2, the narrative mentions the name "Adonijah the son of Haggith" without any other introduction. Evidently, the readers are expected to know about Adonijah, originally the fourth son, but now the eldest surviving son of David. According to the narrative, Adonijah was recognized by the general public as the first candidate for succeeding David, probably based on the priority of the eldest living son (2:15,22). The principle of primogeniture had been accepted in the royal succession since the inception of the Hebrew monarchy. While Saul expected that Jonathan's kingdom would be established (1 Sam 20:31), David "loved Amnon because he was his firstborn" (2 Sam 13:21b LXX, 4Q Sam^a).[7]

However, Adonijah's attempt to gain the crown is commented upon here as an act of "exalting himself" *(mitnaśśēʾ)*. Though the term *hitnaśśēʾ* does not always have a negative connotation, here it clearly denotes one who exaggerates his own importance.[8] Undoubtedly, this is a biased judgement on Adonijah by his enemy, i.e., Solomon. The comment is followed by a direct quotation of Adonijah's words: "I will be king" *(ʾănî ʾemlōk)*. There is no reason to doubt that they were his true words, but it is difficult to regard them

---

[7] For the principle of primogeniture in the royal succession in the kingdoms of Israel and Judah, see Ishida (1977: 152).

[8] A positive use: e.g., *wĕkaʾarî yitnaśśāʾ* (Num 23:24); a negative use: e.g., *imnābaltā bĕhitnaśśēm* (Prov 30:32).

as his manifesto of a rebellion against David. Judging from the political situation at that time, he had no reason to be in a hurry to seize the throne by force. He was expected by the people to succeed David, and David's remaining days were numbered. We may assume, therefore, that this declaration was originally made to Solomon and his supporters in order to demonstrate Adonijah's determination to be king after David. In that case, a temporal condition such as "after the demise of my father" (ʾaḥărê môtʾabi) should have been included in the original (cf. 1:24). We submit that the conditional phrase was omitted to give the reader the false impression that Adonijah had attempted to attain the throne without David's consent. The supposed omission is further evidence for the Solomonic character of the composition.

The effect of the distortion of Adonijah's words is intensified by the report of his preparation of a rekeb and pārāšîm[9] with fifty outrunners. It immediately reminds us of a similar arrangement made by Absalom when he had schemed to rebel (2 Sam 15:1). An important difference between these almost identical reports is found in the terms used for the items which the two princes prepared. While Absalom provided himself with a merkābâ and sûsîm, Adonijah prepared a rekeb and pārāšîm. Concerning the merkābâ, based on examples in the "Manner of the King" (1 Sam 8:11b), the Joseph story (Gen 41:43) and many other sources from the ancient Near East, Y. Ikeda (1982: 223–25) has shown that Absalom's merkābâ was an imitation of a royal display chariot and that his sûsîm were horses for it; thus, his merkābâ and sûsîm do not stand for chariotry and cavalry. In other words, they formed a ceremonial troop or procession but not a rebel army. Indeed, his preparation of a merkābâ and sûsîm was not regarded as a rebellious act until he raised the standard in Hebron; otherwise, David would have dealt with Absalom before the latter "stole the hearts of the men of Israel" (2 Sam 15:6b).

It seems justified to assume that Adonijah's rekeb and pārāšîm were synonymous with the merkābâ and sûsîm of Absalom. Mention must be made, however, that the pair of terms rekeb and pārāšîm stands, except in the Adonijah passage, for the chariotry and cavalry of Solomon's army (1 Kgs 9:19; 10:26; cf. 5:6; cf. KAI No. 202 B 2

[9]Commentators suggest reading pěrāšîm for MT pārāšîm, a lost form of the plural of pārāš "horse;" see J.A. Montgomery and H.S. Gehman (1951: 83); J. Gray, (1977: 78). For our interpretation of the term as exaggeration see below.

[Zakir]). Since the use of this set of terms rather than the other does not seem incidental, we cannot but suppose that these exaggerated terms were used here to mislead the reader with the false idea that Adonijah not only had followed in the footsteps of Absalom but also had made the decisive step toward a rebellion by gathering a military force. Undoubtedly, the distortion came from the Solomonic historiographer.

The portrayal of the character of Adonijah is completed by three explanatory notes about him. The first tells about David's laxity toward Adonijah: "His father had never displeased him" *(lōʾ ʿăṣābô)*. It calls to mind David's similar attitude toward Amnon (1 Sam 13: 21 LXX, 4Q Samᵃ) and Absalom (18:5, 12). It is worth noting that the same verb ʿṣb is used in the report of David's lament over Absalom's death: "He is grieving" *(neʿeṣab)* (19:3) and in the reconstructed text about David's indulgence towards Amnon: "He has never harmed Amnon's humor" *(wělôʾ ʿāṣab ʾet rûaḥ ʿamnôn)* (13:21b LXX). (Cf. the text-critical notes on the verse in Conroy, 1978). Since David had displeased *(ʿāṣab)* neither Amnon nor Absalom, they eventually hurt *(ʿāṣěbû)* him. Thus the implication becomes clear that it is now Adonijah's turn to hurt David as had Amnon and Absalom. At the same time, we can hardly dismiss a critical tone toward David according to which Adonijah's audacious behavior is understood as a consequence of David's own failure in his paternal duty.

The second note on Adonijah is a comment on his handsome appearance: "He was also *(wěgam-hûʾ)* a very handsome man." The word "also" indicates that he is being compared with someone else. Although we have been informed about the beautiful figure of Saul (1 Sam 9:2) as well as that of David (16:12,18), it is most probable that Adonijah is being compared with Absalom (2 Sam 14:25), for this comment is made here not as a compliment, but as a reason why David had spoiled Adonijah.

The third note reads: "And she bore *(yālědâ)* him after Absalom." Commentators have generally felt a difficulty with the verb *yālědâ*, since no subject is found for it in the sentence.[10] They hold that Haggith in v 5a is too remote to be taken as the subject of the verb (Montgomery & Gehman, 1951: 83). There is an opinion that the phrase "Adonijah the son of Haggith" in v 5a makes an inclusio

---

[10] Noth (1968: 1, 6) holds that an indefinite subject is to be supposed, while Gray (1977: 78 n.g.) suggests that *ʾimmô* has dropped out after the verb.

with the sentence "And she bore. . ." (Fokkelman, 1981: 349). Still, this literary-structural analysis does not explain the reason for the omission of the subject of the verb. In my opinion, the name of Adonijah's mother was omitted from v 6b intentionally. If it had been repeated here, the name of Absalom's mother would also have to be mentioned. Otherwise, Haggith would be taken for the mother of both Absalom and Adonijah. The omission of the name Haggith indicates the purpose of the third note. The message of the note is not to provide the name of Adonijah's mother but the fact that he was born *after Absalom*.

Indeed, the third note is not added here to provide general information. The narrative presupposes the reader's awareness of Absalom and his frustrated rebellion. Up to this point, the historiographer has accumulated parallel action and character traits between Adonijah and Absalom without mentioning the latter's name, i.e., arrogance *(mitnaśśēʾ)*, pretension to the throne *(ʾănī ʾemlōk)* preparation of a royal chariot with horses and outrunners, lack of paternal discipline and a handsome appearance. After having read these parallels, every reader must have had an impression that Adonijah was really a second Absalom. At this juncture, by finally mentioning the name Absalom, the third note confirms the reader's impression and serves as the proper conclusion of the portrayal of Adonijah.

For the above reasons, I am convinced that the portrayal of Adonijah in vv 5–6 was made from the consistently inimical viewpoint of the party opposing Adonijah.

The Alleged Rebellion of Adonijah (1 Kgs 1:7–27, 41–53)

The narrative of 1 Kings 1 is strikingly ambiguous about a crucial question: "What was the purpose of the feast at En Rogel to which Adonijah invited all his brothers and all the royal officials, except Solomon and his supporters?" Two possible answers are: a) Adonijah, like Absalom, called a meeting to revolt against David and to perform his coronation rite; b) Adonijah held the feast only for the purpose of strengthening the unity of his party and of demonstrating his determination to gain the crown. According to my analysis, the second was the reason (Würthwein, 1977: 12–13; Whitelam, 1979: 150–51).

As those who supported Adonijah, the following people are mentioned: Joab the son of Zeruiah the commander of the army, Abiathar the priest, Jonathan the son of Abiathar the priest, all the sons of the king except Solomon, and all the royal officials of Judah except Solomon's supporters. They are also called "the guests of Adonijah" (1:41,49). In addition, Adonijah regarded "all Israel" as his supporters (2:15). In contrast to Solomon's faction, Adonijah's group of supporters certainly was the dominant party. It is entirely conceivable that they did not feel it necessary to prepare for an armed rebellion when they met at En Rogel.

We also have some support within our text for this argument: a) In her plea to David, Bathsheba says: "Otherwise it will come to pass, when my lord the king sleeps with his fathers, that I and my son Solomon will be counted offenders" (1:21; cf. 1:12). If Adonijah had already become king without David's consent, why should he wait for David's death before executing Solomon and Bathsheba? b) As soon as a report of Solomon's accession arrived, Adonijah and his supporters at En Rogel dispersed (1:49). This easy collapse of Adonijah's party shows that they had made no preparation for revolt and were taken by surprise by the court intrigue of Solomon's faction. Otherwise, they would have offered resistance to David and Solomon. c) If Joab and Abiathar had conspired with Adonijah against David, how could they have kept their high positions at the court under the co-regency of David and Solomon (cf. 2:35)? We can see other evidence as well in the Testament of David (2:5–9), with which I will deal later.

Next, how can we interpret the allegation of Nathan and Bathsheba that reports repeatedly about Adonijah's accession at En Rogel (1:11,13,18,25)? It is instructive that a scrutiny of the narrative makes it clear that the credibility of the allegation is problematic: a) Although the alleged coronation of Adonijah is reported only through the direct quotations of the words of Nathan and Bathsheba, it is also suggested that neither Nathan nor Bathsheba can stand as eyewitness for their allegation, since they were not invited to the feast (1:8,10,26). b) Since it was not until Nathan came to her that Bathsheba learned of Adonijah's accession (1:11), her claim obviously had no foundation. c) We cannot expect Nathan's words to be credible, either. He told her the story in the context of his counsel ('ēṣâ) for saving her and Solomon (1:12). The term ʿēṣâ implies here "stratagem" or "scheme," as in the counsel of Ahithophel or that of Hushai (2 Sam 15:31; 16:20,23; 17:7,11,14). Nathan's words must be interpreted in the context of his stratagem.

We may reconstruct Nathan's stratagem as follows: a) To alarm Bathsheba by telling her of the alleged coronation of Adonijah,

based on an exaggeration of the details of the feast at En Rogel (1:11).
b) To make David resent Adonijah when she passed on this report to
him (1:18–19). c) To take advantage of David's senility by inducing
him to believe that he had once sworn to Bathsheba that Solomon
would be his successor (1:13,17) (Noth, 1968: 20; Gray, 1977: 88;
Gunn, 1978: 105–6; Whitelam, 1979: 150–51). d) While confirming
her story, Nathan asks David a leading question in order to elicit a
negative response to Adonijah's adventure (1:22–27). In short,
Nathan's stratagem consisted of the use of deception, instigation,
auto-suggestion and a leading question in order to extract Solomon's
designation as royal successor from the senile king.

Nevertheless, it is true that the narrative gives us the impression that Adonijah did ascend the throne at En Rogel without
David's consent. This impression comes, in addition to the allega-
tions of Nathan and Bathsheba, from suggestive references to episodes which remind us of similar incidents during Absalom's rebellion and its aftermath: a) The counseling with Joab and Abiathar
(1 Kgs 1:7) and that with Ahithophel (2 Sam 15:12). b) The feast at En
Rogel (1 Kgs 1:9,19,25) and the sacrifices at Hebron (2 Sam 15:12).
c) The acclamation of royalty given to Adonijah (1 Kgs 1:25) and to
Absalom (2 Sam 16:16). d) Adonijah, who expected good news, was
informed of Solomon's accession (1 Kgs 1:41–48) and David, who had
waited to hear of Absalom's safety, was told instead of his death (2
Sam 18:24–32).[11] e) The dispersion of Adonijah's supporters (1 Kgs
1:49) and the dispersion of Israel after Absalom's rebellion failed (2
Sam 19:9b). f) Solomon's pardon given to Adonijah (1 Kgs 1:50–53)
and David's amnesty granted to Shimei and Mephibaal (2 Sam
19:17–31).

Both the recounting of the alleged rebellion of Adonijah and
Solomon's snatching of the designation as royal successor by maneu-
vering David reflect irregular situations. The best explanation seems
to be that the ambiguity in the story stems from an apologetic
attitude toward the court intrigue on behalf of Solomon. Since the
fact that Solomon received the designation from David as his successor was of fundamental importance for the Solomonic legitimation, it was unavoidable that the historiographer should tell how it
came about. Therefore, he tried to describe the court intrigue by

---

[11] Rost (1965: 222–225; ET: 94–97) analyses all the messenger-reports in the
Succession Narrative (2 Sam 13:30ff.; 15:13ff.; 17:15ff.; 18:19ff.; 1 Kgs 1:42ff.) in
comparison with the messenger-report in the Ark Narrative (1 Sam 4:12ff.).

which Solomon received the designation in a manner that would further his aim. The historiographer had Nathan and Bathsheba tell the story of Adonijah's rebellion and bolstered the allegation by implicit references to Absalom's rebellion. Still, he avoided making up an outright fabrication to keep his narrative plausible. As a result, though some ambiguous impressions remain, he succeeds in persuading the reader to believe that Solomon and his party were compelled to resort to intrigue in order to overcome the ambitions of an unworthy contender to the throne.

The Abishag Episode (1 Kgs 1:1–4, 15b; 2:13–25)

After several years of co-regency with David, Solomon became the sole sovereign after his father's death. Judging from his passive role in the court intrigue, we may assume that Solomon was under adult age at the time of his accession. [12] Besides, in contrast to broad support from important courtiers and the general public which Adonijah enjoyed (1:7,9,19,25; 2:15,22), Solomon was helped by nobody but a few newcomers who enlisted David's mercenaries as their allies (1:8,10,26) (Ishida, 1977: 157–58; 1982; 176–78). Undoubtedly, the main purpose of the co-regency was to protect young Solomon against Adonijah and his supporters (Ishida, 1977: 170). The fact that no purge was made in the days of the co-regency shows that the foundation of Solomon's regime was shakey at the beginning, while Adonijah's party remained intact. Under these circumstances, the demise of David doubtless brought Solomon's regime to a crisis (cf. 2:22).

Against the background of this political crisis, the Abishag affair must be elucidated. The narrative begins with Adonijah visiting Bathsheba (2:13a). The names of Adonijah's mother and of Bathsheba's son are pointedly mentioned again, in order to show that this visit was made in the framework of a confrontation between the two rival parties. Indeed, Bathsheba entered into conversation with Adonijah in a tense atmosphere. She asked: "Do you come *šālôm?*" and he answered: "*šālôm*" (2:13). The identical question and answer were exchanged between the elders of Bethlehem and Samuel, when Samuel visited Bethlehem to find a future king as a substitute for Saul (1 Sam 16:4–5). The report on the elders' "trembling" *(wayyeḥerĕdû)* when coming to meet Samuel tells that they felt misgiving about the purpose of his visit. Similarly, Bathsheba's

---

[12] S. Yeivin (1976: 693) maintains that Solomon was 16 years old at his accession.

question signifies her grave suspicion about Adonijah's real intention. However, before disclosing the purpose of his visit, Adonijah skillfully relaxed her tension by telling her of his resignation of political ambition (2:15). This was done to convince her that his request for Abishag had nothing to do with a claim upon the throne. It is a well-known fact, however, that one way royal legitimacy was acquired was by the appropriation of the previous king's harem, both in Israel and in the rest of the ancient Near East (Tsevat, 1958: 237–43, de Vaux, 1958: 179, ET: 116; Ishida, 1977: 74).[13] In that case, why did Adonijah make such a request which might endanger his life? The answer is bound up with the ambiguous status of Abishag at the court.

It is by no means clear exactly what her title *sōkenet* stood for (1 Kgs 1:2,4), since she is the only bearer of the title in the Bible. Her task was "to lie in the king's bosom to make him warm" (1:2). As such she "stood before the king" (1:2) and served him (1:4,15). But the king "had no intercourse with her" (1:4b). Owing to the last remark it is on the one hand possible to regard her not as a concubine of David but as a mere nurse. However, on the other hand, we may contend that though no intercourse occurred between David and her because of his impotence, she was certainly included among David's concubines since her task was "to lie in the king's bosom."

Evidently, there were differences of opinion about the status of Abishag at Solomon's court and it appears that Adonijah attempted to take advantage of the ambiguity of the situation. First, he approached Bathsheba to use her as a backdoor to Solomon. He knew well that Solomon would hardly refuse her request (2:17a). After making her lower her guard by stating his resignation of the kingship (2:15), he induced her to believe that his request for Abishag was innocent. She was willing to intercede with Solomon for Adonijah (2:18,20–21). When hearing of Adonijah's request, however, Solomon was enraged with Adonijah and ordered the latter's execution (2:22–24). According to a common interpretation, whatever motivation Adonijah might have had, whether romantic or political, Solomon seized the request as a legal pretext to execute him, and most commentators discover some sympathetic tones for Adonijah in the

---

[13] There are several scholars who have tried to refute the thesis (see Würthwein, 1974: 37–39; Gunn, 1978: 137 n. 4), but their argument does not seem convincing enough.

narrative (Delekat, 1967: 27; Noth, 1968: 32–34; Würthwein, 1974: 11–17; Langlamet, 1976: 335; Mettinger, 1976: 27–29). We would like to suggest a different interpretation, however.

Solomon's answer to Bathsheba reveals the problem involved: "Why do you ask Abishag the Shunamite for Adonijah? Ask for him the kingdom also!" (2:22). In his view, wherein the appropriation of Abishag is regarded as the equivalent of seizing the kingship, if he had granted Adonijah's request for Abishag, Adonijah would have exploited her as a pretext for pretending again to the throne; Bathsheba had been deceived by Adonijah. Although no mention is made of Adonijah's plot, it is clear for the reader who has knowledge about Solomon's critical situation that he made the correct judgement of the problem and penetrated Adonijah's plot. Besides, the request for Abishag should remind the reader of Absalom's taking possession of David's harem (2 Sam 16:21–22). In any case, as Solomon had once warned Adonijah, when "wickedness" was found in Adonijah (1 Kgs 1:52), Solomon did not hestiate to kill him.

The opinion that the narrative of the Abishag affair was composed as an anti-Solomonic propaganda since it revealed Solomon's cruel action toward his innocent brother is a good example of the misunderstanding of a biblical passage because of the humanistic sentiment of our modern society. We must understand the original message of the narrative in light of the royal ideology of the ancient Near East, as praise of Solomon who was wise enough to prevent Adonijah's cunning plot. [14] In so doing, Solomon succeeded in establishing just kingship in the kingdom. I will deal with this last theme in the following section.

The Testament of David and Solomon's Purge (1 Kgs 2:1–12, 26–46)
The testament of David (2:5–9) provides us with additional evidence for the argument that there was no uprising against David at En Rogel. In his final words to Solomon on his death-bed, David charged Joab with the assassination of Abner and Amasa and accused Shimei of cursing David at the time of Absalom's rebellion. Some commentators are puzzled over the fact that there is no charge against Adonijah and Abiathar in the testament (Montgomery and Gehman, 1951: 83). This is not surprising, however, since the crimes

---

[14]Whitelam (1979: 152) argues that Solomon's execution of Adonijah was "a contrived judicial murder" by the monarchical authority.

with which Joab and Shimei were charged have nothing to do with Adonijah's attempt to gain the crown. In other words, David did not find any offence in Adonijah and his supporters in connection with their struggle with Solomon's party over the kingship.

I have suggested above that Adonijah was executed by Solomon as a rebel who had plotted against Solomon's regime. Likewise, Abiathar was condemned solely for taking sides with Adonijah. Indeed, his loyalty toward David is even mentioned as grounds for commuting a death sentence to banishment from Jerusalem (2:26). Admittedly, Joab was guilty of offences against David (2:5, 31–33). However, the short explanation of the reason for his execution reads: "For Joab had supported Adonijah although he had not supported Absalom" (2:28). This text reveals that Joab was actually executed not for his disobedience to David in the early days but for his conspiracy with Adonijah against Solomon (Gray, 1977: 109). Nevertheless, Solomon had a need for the authority of David's testament to execute Joab. It seems that Joab was still so influential that Solomon felt uneasy about dealing with him alone.

The testament of David was not a sufficient pretext for Shimei's execution, since David had sworn to him that he would not kill him (2 Sam 19:24). Therefore, Solomon entrapped him and succeeded in getting rid of him. Shimei was the archenemy of the House of David. It is clear that the story of Shimei's end (1 Kgs 2:36–46a) tells about Solomon's wisdom (cf. 2:9) as well as his political achievement in a matter left unfinished by David (Ishida, 1982: 186).

As I have suggested above, the relationship between David and Solomon in the Succession Narrative basically had two aspects: continuation of David's throne and criticism against David's regime. This ambivalence toward David is the characteristic feature of the Solomonic legitimation. These double aspects are also found in the narrative about the testament of David and Solomon's purge of his enemies in 1 Kings 2. The view for the continuity of the dynasty is expressed in the structure of the narrative where the following sentence is placed before the narrative of the purge: "(When) Solomon sat upon the throne of David his father, his kingdom was firmly established" (2:12). Solomon's purge is understood here as a confirmation of the eternal stability of the House of David and its throne (2:33, 45), but not as a prerequisite to the establishment of his kingdom. Evidently, this is the prevailing aspect. But the Solomonic historiographer could not finish the Succession Narrative without adding the other aspect. We find it in the very last sentence of the narrative: "So the kingdom was established *běyad šělōmōh*" (2:46b). This Hebrew phrase is generally translated as "in the hand of Solomon." But the context requires its rendering as "by the hand of Solomon."[15] Then, the sentence implies that the kingdom was established only after Solomon had solved difficult problems left unsolved by David. Solomon is contrasted here with David, whose awkward treatment of political problems had caused one rebellion and unrest after another in the kingdom.

III. Conclusions

In the foregoing analysis of the Adonijah passage in 1 Kings 1–2 I have tried to show that Adonijah and his supporters are portrayed as a rival party to the legitimate successor to the throne, after the fashion of a literary genre called "Royal Historical Writings of an Apologetic Nature." I found no doublet in support of the double redaction theories. Admittedly, the descriptions within the narrative are complicated. But this complication stems from the effort to legitimize an irregular situation, in which Solomon succeeded to the throne. If there had been no irregularity in his succession, there would have been no need for this narrative and it would never have been composed. Therefore, if we smooth over the difficulties by postulating doublets, we will never understand the intrinsic complication of the apologetic history.

In the above analysis I did not employ the literary-structural method either. I think that it is helpful for historical analysis as an auxiliary method. But the devotees of literary-structural analysis have a tendency to press their method to the end. When this analysis itself becomes their ultimate objective, it is harmful to the proper understanding of compositions, since the particular historical background of a composition is not taken into consideration. It is not surprising that, failing to find any particular motivation for composition in the Succession Narrative, scholars who use this method have given it a general title like "The Story of Kind David."

In the historical approach which I have employed, we try to understand biblical sources by making their historical settings clear. It is not sufficient for our study, therefore, to deal exclusively with biblical materials. We must get support from comparative materials

[15] For the use of *běyad* with the meaning of "by the agency or instrumentality of," see BDB, 391.

from the ancient Near East. In these comparative sources we should not expect to find direct evidence for biblical sources. From the quantitative point of view, ancient Israel was a minor phenomenon in the ancient Near East. It is rare, indeed, to discover extra-biblical material testifying to any direct contact between Israel and her neighboring peoples. Under these circumstances, I am rather skeptical about theories of direct borrowing. We must be satisfied with pertinent material which sheds light on biblical sources. For the comparative study of historical writings, therefore, compositions with similar historical situations and content are more important than those with similarities in outward appearance of style. However, the historical approach is different from typological studies. It is imperative for the historical approach that differences between biblical sources and the comparative materials are investigated meticulously while making the comparison. No two historical situations were ever identical.

With these considerations and reservations, I have suggested in one of my previous studies that the Kilamuwa inscription of the ninth century B.C. from North Syria offers a closer parallel to the Succession Narrative than do Hittite or Assyrian historical works. And with the support of this material, I have tried to show that the motivation for the composition of the narrative was the Solomonic legitimation and that the historical situation of the narrative was similar to that of the national kingdoms of Syro-Palestine at the beginning of the first millennium B.C. (Ishida, 1985). The conclusion aside, I am convinced that this comparison has offered a model for solving the problem of the dates of historical works in the Bible.

The problem of the date of biblical sources is a matter of conjecture. We may assume that documents from the ancient Near East were generally composed in the same period that they describe, since there was little possibility of altering the texts or making additions after the completion of the documents. In contrast, biblical sources are preserved not in their original forms but in the final forms after a long process of being incorporated into the Bible. From this condition there arises the problem of the boundaries of compositions and of their position in larger contexts. Needless to say, the problem is very intricate. Still it is disastrous for biblical studies that every scholar postulates his own date for the compositions, according to whatever arguments he likes, taking advantage of the inconclusive character of the problem.

In view of this, and before closing this study, I would like to make a brief remark on the date of historiographical compositions in the Bible. First of all, I recommend a serious reconsideration of the historicity of chronological information in the biblical historical writings. In other words, before resorting to hypothetical solutions, sincere attempts should be made to find explanations of the texts suitable to the historical framework which the texts set, "with a general reliance on the historical consistency of the biblical traditions" (Ishida, 1979: 490). Indeed, if we discard even the very outline of the biblical chronology, there will remain no foundation on which the history of ancient Israel can stand. Of course, there is always the possibility that later material was inserted into historical works with an earlier chronological framework. But if we examine the matter in the broad setting of the ancient Near East, comparative materials will provide us with criteria for an objective judgement. The date of biblical historical writings must be established upon a substantial foundation.

WORKS CONSULTED

Ackroyd, P. A.
1981   "The Succession Narrative (so-called)," *Int* 35, 383–96.

Ball, E.
1982   "Introduction," in L. Rost, *The Succession to the Throne of David*. tr. M.D. Rutter and D.M. Gunn. Sheffield: Almond, xv-1.

Borger, R.
1956   *Die Inschriften Asarhaddons Königs von Assyrien*. AfO Beiheft 9; Osnabrück: Biblio.

Conroy, C.
1978   *Absalom Absalom!: Narrative and Language in 2 Sam 13–20*. AnBib 81; Rome: Biblical Institute.

Crüsemann, F.
1978   *Der Widerstand gegen das Königtum: die anti-königlichen Texte des Alten Testamentes und der Kampf um den frühen israelitischen Staat*. WMANT 49; Neukirchen-Vluyn: Neukirchener Verlag.

Delekat, L.
1967   "Tendenz und Theologie der David-Salomo-Erzählung," *Das ferne und nahe Wort. Festschrift L. Rost*, ed. F. Maas. BZAW 105; Berlin: Töpelmann, 26–36.

Fokkelman, J.P.
1981   *Narrative Art and Poetry in the Books of Samuel I: King David*. Assen: Van Gorcum.

Gray, J.
1977   *I & II Kings* (3d ed.). OTL; London: SCM.

Gunn, D.M.
1978   *The Story of King David: Genre and Interpretation*. JSOTSup 6; Sheffield: JSOT.

Hoffner, H.A.
1975   "Propaganda and Political Justification in Hittite Historiography," *Unity and Diversity: Essays in the History, Literature, and Religion of the Ancient Near East*, ed. H. Goedicke and J.J.M. Roberts; Baltimore/London: The Johns Hopkins University, 49–62.

Ikeda, Y.
1982   "Solomon's Trade in Horses and Chariots in Its International Setting," *Studies in the Period of David and Solomon and Other Essays*, ed. T. Ishida, Tokyo: Yamakawa-Shuppansha, 215–38.

Ishida, T.
1973   "The Leaders of the Tribal Leagues 'Israel' in the Pre-Monarchic Period," RB 80, 514–30.
1977   *The Royal Dynasties in Ancient Israel: A Study on the Formation and Development of Royal-Dynastic Ideology*. BZAW 142; Berlin/New York: de Gruyter.
1979   "The Structure and Historical Implications of the Lists of Pre-Israelite Nations," *Bib* 60, 461–90.
1982   "Solomon's Succession to the Throne of David: a Political Analysis," *Studies in the Period of David and Solomon and Other Essays*, ed. T. Ishida; Tokyo: Yamakawa-Shuppansha, 175–87.
1985   "Solomon who is Greater than David: Solomon's Succession in 1 Kings i–ii in the Light of the Inscription of Kilamuwa, King of Y'DY-Šam'al," *Congress Volume: Salamanca, 1983*. VTSup 36; Leiden: Brill, 145–53.

Langlamet, F.
1976   "Pour ou contre Salomon? Le rédaction prosalomonienne de I Rois, I–II," *RB* 83, 321–79.
1977   "Absalom et les concubines de son père. Recherches sur II Sam., XVI, 21–22," *RB* 84, 161–209.
1978   "Ahitofel et Houshai. Rédaction prosalomonienne en 2

Sam 15–17?," *Studies in Bible and the Ancient Near East. Presented to S.E. Loewenstamm on His Seventieth Birthday*, ed. Y. Avishur and J. Blau; Jerusalem: E. Rubinstein's.

1979 "David et la maison de Saül," *RB* 86, 194–213, 385–436, 481–513.

1980 David et la maison de Saül," *RB* 87, 161–210.

1981 "Affinités sacerdotales, deutéronomiques, élohistes dans l'Histoire de la succession (2 S 9–20; 1 R 1–2)," *Mélanges bibliques et orientaux en l'honneur de M. Henri Cazelles*, ed. A. Caquot and M. Delcor; AOAT 212; Neukirchen-Vluyn: Butzon & Becker Kevelaer, Neukirchener Verlag, 233–46.

1982 "David, fils de Jessé. Une édition prédeutéronomique de l'Histoire de la succession," *RB* 89, 5–47.

McCarter, P.K.

1981 "Plots, True or False: The Succession Narrative as Court Apologetic," *Int* 35, 355–67.

Mettinger, T.N.D.

1976 *King and Messiah: The Civil and Sacral Legitimation of the Israelite Kings.* ConBOT 8; Lund: CWK Gleerup.

Meyer, E.

1907 *Die Israeliten und ihre Nachbarstämme: Alttestamentliche Untersuchungen.* Halle: Max Niemeyer, 1906; repr. Darmstadt: Wissenchaftliche Buchgesellschaft, 1967.

Montgomery, J. A. and Gehman, H. S.

1951 *The Books of Kings.* ICC; Edinburgh: T.&T. Clark.

Noth, M.

1968 *Könige 1.* BKAT 9/1; Neukirchen-Vluyn: Neukirchener Verlag.

Rost, L.

1926 *Die Überlieferung von der Thronnachfolge Davids.* BWANT 1/6; Stuttgart: Kohlhammer (repr. in *Das kleine Credo und andere Studien Zum Alten Testament.* Heidelberg: Quelle & Meyer, 1965, 119–253). [*The Succession to the Throne of David*, tr. M. D. Rutter and D. M. Gunn; Sheffield: Almond, 1982].

Sacon, K. K.

1982 "A Study of the Literary Structure of 'The Succession

Narrative,'" *Studies in the Period of David and Solomon and Other Essays*, ed. T. Ishida, Tokyo: Yamakawa-Shuppansha, 27–54.

Schulte, H.
1972   *Die Entstehung der Geschichtsschreibung im Alten Israel*. BZAW 128; Berlin/New York: de Gruyter.

Tadmor, H.
1983   "Autobiographical Apology in the Royal Assyrian Literature," *History, Historiography and Interpretation: Studies in Biblical and Cuneiform Literatures*, ed. H. Tadmor and M. Weinfeld; Jerusalem: Magnes,

Tsevat, M.
1958   "Marriage and Monarchical Legitimacy in Ugarit and Israel," *JSS* 3, 237–43.

Van Seters, J.
1981   "Histories and Historians of the Ancient Near East: The Israelites," *Or* 50, 137–85.

1983   *In Search of History: Historiography in the Ancient World and the Origins of Biblical History*. New Haven/London: Yale University.

de Vaux, R.
1958   *Les institutions de l'Ancien Testament* 1, Paris [*Ancient Israel: Its Life and Institutions*, tr. J. McHugh; London: Darton, Longman & Todd, 1961].

Veijola, T.
1975   *Die ewige Dynastie: David und die Entstehung seiner Dynastie nach der deuteronomistische Darstellung*. Helsinki: Suomalainen Tiedeakatemia.

Wellhausen, J.
1963   *Die Composition des Hexateuchs und der historischen Bücher des Alten Testaments* (3rd ed., Berlin: Georg Reines, 1899; 4th ed., Berlin: de Gruyter).

Whitelam, K. W.
1979   *The Just King: Monarchical Judicial Authority in Ancient Israel*. JSOTSup 12; Sheffield: JSOT.

1984   "The Defence of David," *JSOT* 29, 61–87.

Whybray, R. N.
1968   *The Succession Narrative: A Study of II Sam. 9–20 and I Kings 1–2*. SBT Second Series 9; London: SCM.

Würthwein, E.
1974   *Erzählung von der Thronfolge Davids: Theologische*

oder politische Geschichtsschreibung? Zürich: Theologische Verlag.

1977   Das Erste Buch der Könige: Kapitel 1–16. ATD 11/1;
          Göttingen: Vandenhoeck & Ruprecht.

Yeivin, S.
1976   "šělōmōh," Encyclopaedia Biblica 7. Jerusalem: Bialik
          (Hebrew).

Zalewski, S.
1981   Solomon's Ascension to the Throne: Studies in the
          Books of Kings and Chronicles. Jerusalem: Marcus &
          Shot (Hebrew).

Chapter 8

POST-EXILIC HISTORIOGRAPHY

H. G. M. Williamson
University of Cambridge, England

"Post-exilic historiography" ought to reflect on the methods and motives of those who wrote history in the post-exilic period, principally the authors of the books of Chronicles and of Ezra-Nehemiah.[1] There are, of course, a number of other Biblical books which relate to this period amongst both the Prophets and the Writings. However, whilst they undoubtedly contribute to our meagre knowledge of the history of the period, they are not historiographical as such, and so cannot be considered directly in the present paper. The same is true of the various extra-biblical sources of information[2] whose value for historical reconstruction can scarcely be overestimated but which again cannot be called historiographical in the strict sense of the word.

In order to allow myself space to say anything worthwhile, however, it has proved necessary to narrow even this restricted area still further. Because my views on Chronicles are already available in published form,[3] it may be of more interest here to reflect chiefly on the books of Ezra and Nehemiah. I shall therefore take my title to refer to historical works written both during *and concerning* the post-exilic period.

To those who do not specialize in this period, mention of Ezra and Nehemiah probably raises at once a number of celebrated, but

---

[1] Some would want also to include works such as Esther and Daniel 1–6. However, in addition to the problem of literary *genre* which they raise, they stand apart by reason of the fact that they do not relate to the life of the community in Palestine.

[2] Recent surveys of the relevant material include G. Widengren (1977) and W.D. Davies and L. Finkelstein (1984). On the latter, however, see my comments in *VT* 35 (1985) 231–38.

[3] See my *1 and 2 Chronicles* (1982), with bibliography of other relevant works on pp. xviii–xix.

very specific, historical questions, chronology not least amongst them. In terms of many studies which make use of these books, however, this fact has had the most doleful effect: a few specific texts are repeatedly examined without what should surely be the necessary pre-requisite of a thorough analysis and comprehension of the books as a whole and the inter-relationships of their constituent sources. (This is, I suspect, a criticism which many would wish to make within their own areas of specialization, and the general principle is illustrated by the comments of other contributors to this volume.) But such a study is a lengthy business, involving the close analysis of every part and facet of the work in order to evolve a hypothesis for their development which takes full account of all the evidence. Generalizations (Cross, 1975) which ignore significant items of relevant but contrary evidence are of little help. More useful are those who sketch out the options and so clear the ground, but are themselves hesitant to push the frontiers back with fresh suggestions.[4] Better still are detailed studies of particular parts or aspects of these books which attempt to take into account the whole range of evidence on their selected topic. As examples of this category, mention should be made of the monographs of Schaeder (1930) and of In der Smitten (1973; see also Ahlemann, 1942–43: 77–98; and Koch, 1974: 173–197) on the Ezra Narrative, Kellermann (1967) on the Nehemiah material, Pohlmann (1970) on the problems of 1 Esdras, Polzin (1976) on the language of the books, and the recent articles of Japhet (1982, 1983) on the composition of Ezra 1–6. Best of all, however, are those who have attempted a fully integrated analysis of the books, though naturally in saying this I do not imply that I agree with them in all their conclusions. Amongst commentaries, where we should expect to look first, I know of none since the magisterial work of Rudolph (1949; limiting ourselves to the present century, mention should also be made of Bertholet, 1902; and Hölscher, 1923), whilst significant monographs have been contributed by Torrey (1896, 1910), Noth (1943) and Mowinckel (1964–65; see also Talmon, 1976). It should be clear, therefore, from even this brief survey that there remains plenty of scope for the present generation of scholars.

Appropriate methods for the study of these books will naturally

---

[4] Mention might be made here, for instance, of H. Schneider (1959); J.M. Myers (1965); and a number of publications by P.R. Ackroyd, most recently his "The Jewish Community in Palestine in the Persian Period" (1984)

vary according to the kind of information which we are asking of them. Nevertheless, a fundamental key for most approaches lies in a comprehensive literary history. Source and redaction criticism are in my judgement a *sine qua non* for all further work.[5] This clearly applies to linguistic studies, since all are agreed that allowance must be made for the idiosyncracies of the different writers of the component parts of the books. It should be true too of sociological research,[6] because it is necessary to understand the social position and hence viewpoint of the writers if adequate allowance is to be made for their presuppositions in this sphere. No one, I imagine, will quarrel with its importance for historical reconstruction, nor should they, by extension, for theological and, finally, historiographical concerns as well.

Since none of this is in any sense new or even controversial, it is surprising to find that research in this area has remained virtually static for many years. With a few notable exceptions, most writers simply choose between, or slightly rearrange, the options which were already on offer in the early decades of this century. Claims of fresh light or a breaking of the impasse (whether justified or not) have generally been restricted to individual topics rather than the works as a whole.

Now, it may be, of course, that the reason for this state of affairs is that one of the established options is correct. This is a possibility which Biblical scholars are loathe to admit, however, and in the present instance they have good reason. There are several disquieting factors which suggest that the search for solutions at a quite fundamental level remains necessary. I here mention just four: (i) No one has satisfactorily resolved the problem of the *genre* of the Nehemiah Memoir. Five theories about this are currently canvassed,[7] but none does justice to all the material. Yet the Nehemiah Memoir is usually paraded as one of the most established results of source criticism in these books, if not in the whole OT. (ii) There is a substantial body of material in the later chapters of Nehemiah whose provenance and literary associations have received

---

[5]The continuing importance of these now traditional disciplines is shown with reference to other texts in the essays of Friedman and Ishida elsewhere in this volume.

[6]Note the importance attributed to these works by Kippenberg (1978).

[7]Four are summarized by Kellermann (1967: 76–84) He then adds his own fresh suggestion (pp. 84–88 *et passim*), in which he compares the NM with the "Prayer of the Accused."

little attention. It is widely agreed that not all can be attributed to either the Ezra or the Nehemiah sources, but few have penetrated beyond this negative position.

(iii) The extent, original order, *genre* and authenticity of the Ezra material continue to elicit such a plethora of contradictory views that there can be little confidence in the methods that have produced them. Whilst much of the older evidence based on literary style[8] is now seen to have been based on faulty method, nothing of potentially equal objectivity has emerged to replace it.

(iv) There has recently been a heartening response, from my point of view, to the arguments for the separation of Chronicles from Ezra-Nehemiah as regards authorship. Under the old consensus, certain perameters were established for the composition of Ezra-Nehemiah. With these removed, it is possible to look with fresh eyes at the process of our books' composition and to find quite novel results imposing themselves. I have already tried to illustrate this in a lengthy article on Ezra 1–6 (1983: 1–30), in which amongst other things I conclude that these chapters presuppose a knowledge of the combination of the material about Ezra and Nehemiah and so represent the latest phase in the books' composition. Furthermore, opinions and prejudices about the Chronicler's historiographic method have often in the past been assumed to hold true for Ezra and Nehemiah too (Torrey, 1910: 223; Cazelles, 1954: 119; Rowley, 1965: 147). In the present climate, it becomes possible to study our books afresh without such preconceived ideas.

If, then, there is reason enough to believe that fresh research is desirable, in what directions may we expect it to go? To answer this question, I shall first sketch some of the results of my own investigation. I do this in order to illustrate why I consider that a major *desideratum* is for those who will allow themselves enough time and effort to immerse themselves in these books. The kind of analysis which is necessary and which I shall just begin to illustrate will never emerge from those who are merely seeking solutions to predetermined historical or other questions. I shall then move on to outline one or two wider issues where further work seems desirable.

To start with, I find it quite extraordinary that no one has ever

---

[8] See especially the works of Torrey (1896, 1910) and Kapelrud (1944). For a preliminary response, cf. Rudolph (1949: 163–65); more recent discussions from differing points of view but all with a conscious concern for method include Williamson (1977c: 37–59); Polzin (1976); and Throntveit (1982: 201–216).

pointed out the extent to which all of Nehemiah's major achievements are paralleled in other passages not derived from his first person account. The list of participants in the wall building in Neh 3 was certainly not composed at first by Nehemiah, though I consider it probable that he incorporated it later into his own account.[9] Its standpoint is that of the work completed, with the "doors, bolts and bars" of the gates all in place. In Nehemiah's first person account, however, the work is not completed until chap. 6, and even then it is explicitly stated that "at that time I had not yet hung the doors in the gates" (v 1). Second, the account is in the third person, whereas Nehemiah's account is always in the first person, and third, the use of *>addîrîm*, "nobles," contrasts with Nehemiah's own ways of referring to the local leaders. The prominence given to Eliashib the high priest (v 1) suggests that the list was originally drawn up under priestly influence, and so is likely to have been preserved in the temple archives. It is of further interest to note the use of *>ădōnêhem*, "their lord," in probable reference to Nehemiah (v 5). The same title is used for Ezra in Ezra 10:3 on the lips of one whose family had participated in the first return many years previously (cf. Ezra 2). An origin for our present list in the same circles is not unlikely. It may be suggested as a speculation that, in view of the prominence of Eliashib, and the reference to the Meshullam who was related by marriage to Tobiah (cf. v 30 and 6:18), the list may have been drawn up originally at the instigation of those who later became antagonistic to Nehemiah in an attempt to claim from him some of the credit for the successful completion of the task.

It is generally assumed that from a chronological point of view Nehemiah's next concern was the dedication of the walls, though for separate reasons his account has been moved to 12:27–43. Commentators are agreed, however, that this paragraph cannot have been extracted as a whole from his Memoir. The first four verses include no reference to Nehemiah, the lists of the names of the priests and musicians interrupt the narrative flow and are not elsewhere the object of Nehemiah's concern, and the narrative itself is fragmentary: we are not told, for instance, where the processions started from, what happened to most of the members of the processions as they approached the temple, how the first choir reached the tem-

---

[9] I defend this conclusion and others of a similar sort throughout this paper at greater length in a forthcoming commentary on Ezra-Nehemiah for the *Word Biblical Commentary* series.

ple, and so on. It is therefore generally agreed that an extract from the Nehemiah Memoir has here been heavily reworked. For technical reasons that need not detain us now, we may ascribe vv 31–32, 37–40 and 43 to Nehemiah's account.

Unlike earlier commentators, however, I do not find it possible simply to ascribe all the remaining material to editorial expansion. There are elements of overlap between the descriptions of the processions and of the ceremony itself; there is some apparently valuable archival material in vv 28–29; and there are some slight tensions between this additional material and the surrounding narrative context, all of which makes it probable that two separate descriptions have been spliced together rather than that the final account has evolved directly out of an earlier, shorter one. The clerical and religious interests of the alternative account stand out clearly on even a superficial survey.

A third early action by Nehemiah was to arrange for the repopulation of the city of Jerusalem. He tells of his preparations for this in the opening verses of chap. 7. At this point, as is well known, his account breaks off. From a narrative point of view, the subject is resumed at the beginning of chap. 11. Most commentators assume that vv 1–2 represent an editorially reworked version of the continuation of Nehemiah's account. Closer examination shows that this cannot be the case: (i) the verses are not couched in Nehemiah's first person narrative style; indeed, he is not mentioned here at all. As they stand, therefore, these verses could contribute nothing to the purpose of his account; (ii) the style of writing differs from that of Nehemiah (Mowinckel, 1964–65: I, 48–49; Kellermann, 1967: 43). We here find *šĕʾār*, "rest, remainder," where Nehemiah uses *yeter* (2:16; 4:8, 13; 6:1, 14), *śārîm*, "leaders," where Nehemiah consistently uses words like *sĕgānîm* and *ḥōrîm*,[10] and the use of *ʿîr haqqōdeš* for Jerusalem; (iii) despite the fact of continuity with chap. 7, these verses do not supply what we have been led to expect from Nehemiah's own account. He tells how he gathered the leaders of the people in order to make a genealogical record of them, and that he then found an older record to help him (7:4–5). We thus expect

---

[10] 2:16; 4:8,13; 5:7,17; 6:17; 7:5 (a reference of particular significance since it is in the same narrative context as our present verses); 12:40; 13:11,17. *śārîm* occurs only at 12:31–32 with a comparable meaning in material possibly to be attributed to Nehemiah, but even there other considerations make it equally likely that it is due to editorial adaptation. Elsewhere in Nehemiah's writing, *śārîm* carries a more specific nuance.

him to organize the repopulation of Jerusalem with reference to family connections. What we find here instead, however, is that the people (not Nehemiah) make the arrangements on the haphazard basis of lot-casting.

It therefore appears that here too we have a fragment of an alternative account of one of Nehemiah's actions. Lot-casting at this period was a cultic, even priestly, affair.[11] If the passage describes an activity undertaken with priestly supervision, then its preservation in the temple archives is a plausible speculation. Its attachment to the following list, which we cannot deal with now, enhances this probability.

Finally, we must consider Nehemiah's various social and religious reforms recorded in chaps. 5 and 13. Some connection with Neh 10 has long been recognized (see Bertholet, 1902). Neh 10 is a first-person account by the community of a one-sided agreement into which the people entered to observe the Law of God. Quite rightly, no one has ever suggested that it was part of the Nehemiah Memoir. There have been occasional attempts to relate it to the Ezra source, but in my opinion it should be regarded as a document of independent origin.[12] Its affinities with the temple archives are suggested by (i) the conclusion of the chapter, with its summarizing note of strong support for the temple; (ii) the use of ʾaddîrêhem (v 30), which is to be compared with 3:5 and our remarks earlier about the likely origin of that chapter; and (iii) the temple as the most likely place in which, to judge from its content, some secondary material in v 40a would have been added.[13]

Now, it is remarkable to observe to what extent the individual clauses of this pledge overlap with reforms for which Nehemiah also takes credit. It is necessary only to list them to realize that the coincidence goes beyond the possibilities of chance:

---

[11] Cf. 1 Chr 24:5,7,31; 25:8,9; 26:13,14, all passages which should, in my view, be attributed to a priestly reviser of the Chronicler's original work; cf. Williamson (1979: 251–68).

[12] See especially Mowinckel (1964–65: III 142–156). In this discussion, I deal only with the account of the pledge in vv 1, 29–40. The list of those who signed the document (vv 2–28) has been added secondarily, as nearly all commentators recognize.

[13] The extent of these additions throughout the closing verses of the chapter is disputed, but clearly v 40a must be included amongst them: its switch to third person narration is out of place, and it seems to offer a summary of what is to be brought into the storerooms, which is inappropriate in the context of the pledge.

mixed marriages (10:31; 13:23–30)
Sabbath observance (10:32; 13:15–22)
abandonment of the practice of taking loans on pledge
(10:32; Neh 5)
the wood offering (10:35; 13:31)
firstfruits (10:36–37; 13:31)
Levitical tithes (10:38–39; 13:10–14)
neglect of the temple (10:40; 13:11).

Before reflecting on these observations, we must now draw in some further relevant evidence concerning the Nehemiah Memoir itself. As I have already indicated, scholars ought to have been alerted to the existence of a problem by the complete lack of agreement over the work's literary *genre*, and by the fact that most of the proposed solutions are based upon only a narrow selection of relevant evidence. Three further points also cry out for explanation:

(i) There is a long and unexplained gap between the account of the wall-building with related events and the incidents recounted in chap. 13. Taking the chronological notices of the book as they stand, we are presented with the description of less than one year's activity in considerable detail followed by several isolated topics from perhaps as much as fifteen years later. It is hardly adequate merely to reply that nothing of significance happened in the meanwhile.

(ii) Few will disagree that a solution to the problem of the Nehemiah Memoir must account adequately for the distinctive "remember" formula. Perusal of the six passages where it occurs reveals something that I have never seen even noted, namely that not one of them relates to the building of the wall. With only one possible exception (and that a negative use of the formula),[14] none even relates to the early period of Nehemiah's work at all, but can only have been written twelve years later at the earliest. It would be strange, to say the least, that if Nehemiah composed the whole Memoir as some kind of votive inscription, however defined, he

---

[14] Neh 6:14. This verse introduces a "remember" formula into an account of the first phase of Nehemiah's work. Two possible explanations suggest themselves: (i) This is the only occurrence of the formula which refers to something unmentioned in the preceding narrative, namely "Noadiah the prophetess and the rest of the prophets . . .". This may indicate that the verse was worked in at a later stage. (ii) Since this verse is a prayer against the enemy rather than a positive use of the "remember" formula, it may be intended as a prayer uttered within the historical context itself, as 3:36–37 clearly is. Either of these possibilities would remove the difficulty of 6:14 for the general view advanced above. Either seems to me easier to accept than that all the other factors referred to here are purely coincidental.

should not have specifically offered his most outstanding achievement as a major reason for God to remember him.

(iii) If we concentrate for the moment on the deeds which Nehemiah asks God to have in remembrance, we find that they are as follows:

5:19 Nehemiah has desisted from eating "the bread of the governor" throughout his first term of office because of the people's economic burdens. The earlier part of the chapter shows that much of this was due to debt slavery.

13:14 Two points are included here, care for the house of God, which may refer to the expulsion of Tobiah, and "its services," referring to the restoration of the Levitical tithes.

13:22 Sanctification of the Sabbath Day.

13:31 The foregoing paragraph treats mixed marriages, the duties of the priests and Levites, the wood offering and the first-fruits.

Perusal of this list at once reveals that every item mentioned can be directly associated with one or other of the clauses of the pledge in chap. 10, as analysed above.

This whole catalogue of observations about the Nehemiah Memoir seems to me to go beyond the possible bounds of coincidence and to demand some sort of explanation. Though such a solution may appear old-fashioned, a literary division of the material provides far and away the easiest way out. No difficulty confronts the relegation of 5:14–19; 13:4–14, 15–22 and 23–31 to a subsequent phase of composition. These few paragraphs have much in common: each concludes with a positive "remember" formula; each is a brief description without particular chronological setting; each comes long after the building of the wall, and each can be linked in some way with chap. 10. On the other hand, the rest of the Nehemiah Memoir now also takes on a degree of coherence: all is related to the task of building the wall together with its immediate sequel; nothing need come later than a year after Nehemiah's arrival in Jerusalem, if that. Furthermore, the removal of the "remember" formula leaves the narrative much more as a report on a limited project—to be expected after 2:6—than a votive or dedication text. Years later, as our earlier discussion of the alternative, priestly material has suggested, Nehemiah felt that justice was not being done to him within his own community. I suggest that he was thus moved to rework his old report, adding to it a number of short paragraphs dealing

specifically with those points for which he felt he was not being given
due credit. As an aside, therefore, we may conclude that the Nehemiah
Memoir represents a mixture of literary *genres* and that previous
discussions have been vitiated by their failure to commence with a
proper source analysis.

At this point, I should like to reemphasize that all this material
is presented by way of illustration alone. Wearisome as this survey
may have become, it is still only a beginning. What I have sketched
in itself needs refinement and extension, and even then nothing has
been said of the Ezra material, of Ezra 1–6 and more besides. Even
so, it may be hoped that sufficient indication has been given both of
the primacy of literary analysis for a correct approach to these books,
and of the sort of methods by which it should be conducted. If that
be allowed, then we may turn our attention to some consequences of
what we have noted that may also point the way forward for further
work.

First, and rather obvious, it is impressed upon us yet again to
what an extent we are dependent upon the somewhat spasmodic
light which our sources shed upon this period. Well illuminated are
the building of the second temple, the twelve months of Ezra's
work, the building of the wall under Nehemiah and its immediate
sequel (say twelve months), and an unchronological account of various reforms some twelve or fifteen years later. Limiting ourselves to
the Persian period, I have endeavoured in various articles (Williamson, 1977b: 49–66; 1979: 251–268; 1983: 1–30) to accumulate
evidence which enables us to say something about the end of that
period when, I believe, there was a major split in the Jerusalem
priesthood and many of its members left to join with other elements
at a resettled Shechem to found what we know as the Samaritan
community. To these five moments some further information can, of
course, be added from other sources of various kinds. However,
when we remember that we are dealing with a time span of over 200
years, it is quite clear that we cannot expect to write anything like
the kind of connected history with which we are familiar. As related,
each episode is virtually self-contained, and there can be no question of a cause-and-effect continuum between them. Our approach
to these materials must respect and take account of this fundamental
limitation.

Second, from even the small sample of an analysis offered above,
it emerges that the divisions of opinion within the Jerusalem community were more complicated than has been assumed hitherto.

This is not the place for me to repeat my reservations (see Williamson, 1977c: 132–140; 1977a: 115–154) about the approach to this issue by Plöger (1959) and its separate, but in many respects comparable, treatment by Hanson (1975). Rather, we should observe on the basis of the juxtaposition of material in Nehemiah that there were clearly quite sharp differences of opinion even within what are generally regarded as theocratic or hierocratic circles. It is true that the literary evidence I have adduced would not yet allow us to say that these were more than matters of style or approach, but should these be dismissed as of no consequence? Sociological examination of these texts has only just begun, but it already tempts me to feel that it has as much to teach us about the growth of sects within Judaism as do genuinely theological or religious differences. Perhaps I may amplify this with reference to Neh 9.

It is a fundamental conviction of scholars like Plöger that the books of Chronicles, Ezra and Nehemiah contain no hope of radical change in Israel's future. He summarizes and quotes with approval the following passage from Rudolph:

> We must not overlook the fact that in the second part of his presentation, the Books of Ezra and Nehemiah, he is pursuing the aim of describing the founding of the new people of God as it should be in accordance with the will of God—a community gathered around its Temple in zealous worship, protected by secure walls, in obedience to the divine Law, and inwardly separated from everything alien. This means that the actual Jewish community, especially as it is presented in Neh. xii 43–xiii 3, so fully realised the idea of theocracy for the Chronicler that there was no need of any further eschatological hope.[15]

Comparable opinions find expression in a number of studies of these works written during the last thirty years or so, especially those which regard Ezra and Nehemiah as the culmination of the Chronicler's writing.

A different viewpoint emerges, however, if we take more seriously the work of the editor who combined the accounts of the activity of Ezra and Nehemiah as an independent narrative. Neh 8–10

---

[15]Cited from W. Rudolph (1954), a translation by P.R. Ackroyd of parts of the introduction to Rudolph's *Chronikbücher* (1955), which is itself, of course, the source on which Plöger drew.

takes on central significance. For Rudolph, the present ordering was no more than the result of an accidental textual transmission. Others, like Mowinckel and Pohlmann, see the growth of these chapters as a secondary development, for they uphold the priority of 1 Esdras, where Neh 8 immediately follows Ezra 10, and they see the inclusion of the Nehemiah Memoir as coming only at a very late stage. For a number of reasons which need not detain us now, however, these chapters are better regarded as the thoughtful combination of three originally discrete literary elements into a single, focal description of a climax in the reformers' work. Presentation of the Law (Neh 8), confession (Neh 9) and a pledge by the community to keep God's Law (Neh 10) may be loosely termed a process of covenant renewal which gives coherence and direction to the other reforms which have been described (see Baltzer, 1960: 51–55 [ET, 43–47]; In der Smitten, 1973: 35–53; Kellermann, 1967: 90–92; McCarthy, 1982: 25–44).

In this, the great prayer of confession in Neh 9 is central. Here, moreover, is a text which cries out for rhetorical analysis, but which has not hitherto received such attention. Of the many insights which such an analysis affords, I single out just one for mention here.

The final stanza of the long historical retrospect is to be found in vv 22–31. It deals with entry into and life in the land, the promise of which has been prominent in the earlier sections. After treating the entry into the land in vv 22–25, the description moves on into three cycles on the pattern of rebellion, handing over to a foreign power, cry for help, and response by God in mercy and deliverance (vv 26–27; 28; 29–31). A number of phraseological parallels between these units makes the cyclical pattern stand out clearly. Naturally, we may see in this the influence of the Deuteronomic presentation of the people's history.

Within this recurring pattern, the author probably intends us to see an intensification of the severity of God's judgement. Certainly v 28b is markedly more forceful than 27a, but what of v 30c? While at first glance it seems milder, it is in fact probably to be seen as a statement about the Babylonian conquest and exile. It is difficult to see otherwise the force of lōʾ ʿăśîtām kālâ, "you did not eliminate them," in v 31, and the fact that this stands at the very end of the historical retrospect adds some support to this conclusion.

Now, it should not escape notice that this third cycle breaks off abruptly without the expected elements of a cry to God for help and his consequent deliverance. Evidently, the author considered that the restoration from that severe judgement was not yet complete; rather, he includes himself and his contemporaries as living still within a theologically exilic situation. Then, with a most powerful shift of perspective, he immediately actualizes the cry for help as in vv 32–37 he presents words of confession, petition and lament which arise from his current situation. And this is made the more poignant in the wider context of these chapters by the fact that he has already equated rebellion against God with rejection of his Law (e.g., v 29; cf. Gilbert, 1981: 307–316), whereas it is precisely a return to this law that characterizes Neh 8–10 as a whole. With the prayer breaking off at this point of bringing the congregation inside the recurrent pattern of confession and deliverance, we cannot but be left on the tiptoe of expectation as regards the future. Moreover, the substance of the lament concerning the oppressive nature of foreign domination does not allow us to interpret this expectation in any other than political terms.

Now, it may well be that Neh 9 stands somewhat isolated in this regard within Ezra-Nehemiah. Nevertheless, its centrality within the structure of the books as a whole obliges us to look again at the types of division which existed within the post-exilic community, and so reinforces the questions we have posed from other points of view as well.[16]

A third and final conclusion of our discussion, again with acknowledgement of the need for further study, is a heightened appreciation of the historiographical concern of the writers in its fullest sense. As we have seen, there was available to the editor(s) an assortment of primary sources, each giving considerable detail about some particular event or activity, but unrelated in any way to the other sources, and often at a long chronological remove from them.

As they have reached us, however, there can be no doubt that these books confront us with a single and united account of the post-exilic restoration of the people, their city and their cult. Not only is all sense of the passage of time eliminated, but isolated events have now been lifted from their strictly historical moorings to be judged instead by their theological significance. It is at this level, the level

---

[16] Of course, Plöger and Hanson are not without their critics from many other points of view as well. For a recent example, cf. R. Mason (1982: 137–154). See also a number of passages in the wide-ranging study of C.C. Rowland (1982). A noteworthy dissenting voice from a critical standpoint which in other respects is closer to that of Rudolph and Plöger is R. Mosis (1973).

of divine causality, that continuity is to be perceived; the normal laws of cause and effect are totally subordinated to this perspective. We thus have in these books a most instructive example, whose steps we can clearly trace, of the development of what in other books would be called a history of salvation.

This process is characteristic of all the major redactional layers in these books,[17] and may be summarized under three general headings.

First, a number of chronological summaries group widely diverse periods as though they were to be regarded as parts of a single whole. For instance, at Ezra 6:14 the restoration of the temple is linked with Cyrus, Darius and Artaxerxes and so covers the whole span of the books rather than the point which has been reached in the narrative. Again, at Neh 12:47 Zerubbabel and Nehemiah are noted in parallel in connection with the support of the cultic personnel, while at 12:26 the lists of priests and Levites are summarized as spanning the whole period of Joiakim, the high priest next after the initial return, Nehemiah the governor and Ezra the priest and scribe. Here the emphasis is clearly on the complementarity of function rather than on chronological separation.

Second, the even flow of dates through the books serves to give a sense of continuity to what we know otherwise was a series of disjointed acts. Thus not only are the two parts of the book of Ezra, which are historically separated by several decades, joined theologically by the astonishing phrase "After these things" at Ezra 7:1, but also, perhaps, by the dating of the events of chap. 6 to the sixth year (of Darius) and those of chaps. 7ff. to the seventh year (of Artaxerxes). Similarly, whereas historically, I believe, Ezra's reading of the Law in Neh 8 preceded Nehemiah's mission by thirteen years, it is integrated into its new setting by being dated without further qualification in the seventh month, which appears to follow smoothly after the sixth month, Elul, on which the wall was completed in Neh 6:15. Then the originally independent Neh 9 follows on "the twenty-fourth day of this month" (9:1), while Neh 10 is joined on by its introductory phrase "And yet for all this." Finally, the various reforms which close the book are also joined by their

---

[17] In my opinion, there are three such layers, (i) the combining of the narratives concerning Ezra and Nehemiah together with some of the other material from the period of Nehemiah noted earlier in this paper, (ii) the later addition of the lists in 11:21–36 and 12:1–26, and (iii) the prefixing of Ezra 1–6. It may be observed that the examples noted above draw on all three of these layers.

redactional chronological notations: "on that day" (the day of the dedication of the wall!) in Neh 12:44 and 13:1, "Now before this" in 13:4 and "in those days" in 13:15 and 23.

Third and last, the major divisions of the work are linked by having been given a parallel structure in each case which is clearly the result of editorial arrangement of source materials. Space forbids an exposition of this panel effect that runs through the books, but suffice it to say that it helpfully accounts for the two most celebrated chronological discontinuities which the books contain, namely the account of opposition that the community faced in Ezra 4 and the suspension of Ezra's reading of the Law until Neh 8. Some helpful remarks towards the elucidation of this patterning have already been offered by Gunneweg (1981: 146–161) and Childs (1979: 631–637). I have endeavoured to carry their insights forward a little in a forthcoming commentary, but it is clear that here too much remains to be done. This is an approach to Old Testament study which has attracted much attention in recent years in connection with a number of other books, and I do not doubt that the time is ripe for similar attention to Ezra and Nehemiah. Let me conclude, however, by re-emphasizing that so far as my own tentative probes in this direction are concerned, our appreciation of such patterning is likely to be heightened and so best served by an initial thorough examination of the more traditional disciplines of source and redaction analysis.

* * *

It appears at first sight ironic to conclude a volume on the future of Biblical studies with an emphatic summons to the practice of the oldest methods known to critical scholarship. Is the discipline therefore moribund, a nineteenth century dinosaur amongst contemporary academic pursuits? It is difficult to believe that anyone who has read the preceding chapters could draw such a pessimistic conclusion. How, then, should we respond to the juxtaposing of analyses and proposals which this collection displays?

Although few would doubt the value of Biblical research because of the inherent worth and historical influence of the Bible itself, it remains true of this field of study as much as any other that the health of the discipline depends upon the ability and the enthusiasm of its practitioners. Modesty demands that we leave an assessment of the former to the reader. Regarding the latter, however, participants in the San Diego Conversation will attest the good humoured but vigorous and searching discussions which followed the delivery of each of these papers. Without falling prey to pluralistic relativism, it was demonstrated again there, as, we hope, in this volume as a whole, that the future of Biblical studies is assured because of the strengths of the three major contributors to its welfare: the text itself, which remains static as a datum point; the history of its study, which shapes who we are and determines our starting point; and the present generation of practitioners, who may not agree amongst themselves but whose commitment to the text and respect for previous generations of scholars is unquestioned. Against such a rich background there is ample scope for the controlled input of each individual scholar's interests, gifts and expertise, whether aesthetic or analytical, broad or narrow, innovative or probingly conservative. This volume is thus not ultimately prophetic, for that could only be the product of a single writer revealing his fears or preferences; it is, rather, a statement that Biblical studies will continue to flourish on a wide variety of fronts and that it will do so best when it is conducted not in a state of arrogant isolation but of patient and mutual listening and response, innovation and correction.

WORKS CONSULTED

Ackroyd, P.R.
   1984   "The Jewish Community in Palestine in the Persian
            Period," in *CHJ* I, 130–61.
Ahlemann, F.
   1942–43 "Zür Esra-Quelle," ZAW 59.
Baltzer, K.
   1960   *Das Bundesformular.* WMANT 4. Neukirchen: Neu-
            kirchener Verlag [*The Covenant Formulary.* Oxford:
            Blackwell, 1971]
Bertholet, A.
   1902   *Die Bücher Esra und Nehemia.* KHAT 19. Tübingen
            and Leipzig: Mohr.
Cazelles, H.
   1954   "La Mission d'Esdras," *VT* 4, 113–140.
Childs, B.S.
   1979   *Introduction to the Old Testament as Scripture.*
            London: SCM.
Cross, F.M.
   1975   "A Reconstruction of the Judean Restoration," *JBL* 94

Davies, W.D. and L. Finkelstein (eds.)
1984   *The Cambridge History of Judaism. Volume One: Introduction; The Persian Period.* Cambridge: Cambridge University Press.

Gilbert, M.
1981   "La place de la loi dans la prière de Néhémie 9," in J. Doré, P. Grelot and M. Carrez (eds.), *De la Tôrah au Messie. Mélanges Henri Cazelles.* Paris: Desclée.

Gunneweg, A.H.J.
1981   "Zur Interpretation der Bücher Esra-Nehemia," *VTSup* 32.

Hanson, P.D.
1975   *The Dawn of Apocalyptic.* Philadelphia: Fortress.

Hölscher, G.
1923   "Die Bücher Esra und Nehemia," in E. Kautzsch and A. Bertholet (eds.), *Die heilige Schrift des Alten Testaments,* 4th ed. Tübingen: Mohr.

In der Smitten, W. Th.
1973   *Esra: Quellen, Überlieferung und Geschichte.* Studia Semitica Neerlandica 15. Assen: Van Gorcum.

Japhet, S.
1982–83   "Sheshbazzar and Zerubbabel. Against the Background of the Historical and Religious Tendencies of Ezra-Nehemiah," *ZAW* 94 and 95.

Kapelrud, A.S.
1944   *The Question of Authorship in the Ezra-Narrative: a Lexical Investigation.* SUNVAO. II Hist.-Filos. Klasse 1. Oslo: Dybwad.

Kellermann, U.
1967   *Nehemia: Quellen, Überlieferung und Geschichte.* BZAW 102. Berlin: Alfred Töpelmann.

Kippenberg, H.G.
1978   *Religion und Klassenbildung im antiken Judäa.* SUNT 14. Göttingen: Vandenhoeck & Ruprecht.

Koch, K.
1974   "Ezra and the Origins of Judaism," *JSS* 19.

Mason, R.
1982   "The Prophets of the Restoration," in R. Coggins, A. Phillips and M. Knibb (eds.), *Israel's Prophetic Tradition: Essays in Honour of Peter R. Ackroyd.* Cambridge: Cambridge University Press.

McCarthy, D. J.
1982   "Covenant and Law in Chronicles—Nehemiah," *CBQ*
         44.

Mosis, R.
1973   *Untersuchungen zur Theologie des chronistischen
         Geschichtswerkes.* Freiburger theologische Studien
         92. Freiburg/Basel/Wien: Herder.

Mowinckel, S.
1964–65 *Studien zu dem Buche Ezra-Nehemia I-III.* Skrifter
         Utgitt av Det Norske Videnskaps-Akedemi i Oslo.
         II. Hist.-Filos. Klasse. Ny serie, nos. 3, 5 and 7.
         Oslo: Universitetsforlaget.

Myers, J. M.
1965   *Ezra. Nehemiah.* AB 14. Garden City: Doubleday.

Noth, M.
1943   *Überlieferungsgeschichtliche Studien.* Halle: Max
         Niemeyer; reprinted, Tübingen: Max Niemeyer,
         1967. [Translation of first half in *The Deuteronomistic
         History.* JSOTSS 15. Sheffield: JSOT, 1981); transla-
         tion of second half in *The Chronicler's History.*
         JSOTSS 51. Sheffield: JSOT, 1987].

Plöger, O.
1959   *Theokratie und Eschatologie.* WMANT 2. Neukirchen:
         Neukirchener Verlag. [*Theocracy and Eschatology.*
         Oxford: Blackwell, 1968].

Pohlmann, K.-F.
1970   *Studien zum dritten Esra. Ein Beitrag zur Frage nach
         dem ursprünglichen Schluss des chronistischen
         Geschichtswerkes.* FRLANT 104. Göttingen: Van-
         denhoeck & Ruprecht.

Polzin, R.
1976   *Late Biblical Hebrew. Toward an Historical Typology
         of Biblical Hebrew Prose.* HSM 12. Missoula: Schol-
         ars Press.

Rowland, C. C.
1982   *The Open Heaven. A Study of Apocalyptic in Judaism
         and Early Christianity.* London: SPCK.

Rowley, H. H.
1965   "The Chronological Order of Ezra and Nehemiah," in
         The Servant of the Lord, 2nd ed. Oxford: Blackwell,
         137–68.

Rudolph, W.
1949   *Esra und Nehemia*. HAT 20. Tübingen: Mohr.
1954   "Problems of the Books of Chronicles," *VT* 4.
1955   *Chronikbücher*. HAT 21. Tübingen: Mohr.

Schaeder, H.H.
1930   *Esra der Schreiber*. Tübingen: Mohr.

Schneider, H.
1959   *Die Bücher Esra and Nehemia*. Die heilige Schrift des
          Alten Testaments iv/2. Bonn: Peter Hanstein.

Talmon, S.
1976   "Ezra and Nehemiah," *IDBS*, 317–28.

Throntveit, M.A.
1982   "Linguistic Analysis and the Question of Authorship in
          Chronicles, Ezra and Nehemiah," *VT* 32.

Torrey, C.C.
1896   *The Composition and Historical Value of Ezra-
          Nehemiah*. BZAW 2. Giessen: Ricker.
1910   *Ezra Studies*. Chicago: Chicago University Press, 1910
          (reprinted, New York: KTAV, 1970).

Widengren, G.
1977   "The Persian Period," in J.H. Hayes and J.M. Miller
          (eds.) *Israelite and Judaean History*. London: SCM.

Williamson, H.G.M.
1977a   "Eschatology in Chronicles," *TynB* 28.
1977b   "The Historical Value of Josephus' *Jewish Antiquities*
          xi. 297–301," *JTS* ns 28.
1977c   *Israel in the Books of Chronicles*. Cambridge: Cam-
          bridge University Press.
1979   "The Origins of the Twenty-four Priestly Courses: a
          Study of 1 Chronicles xxiii–xxvii," *VTSup* 30.
1982   *1 and 2 Chronicles*. Grand Rapids: Eerdmans and
          London: Marshall, Morgan and Scott.
1983   "The Composition of Ezra i–vi," *JTS* ns 34.